Reading 'Bollywood'

Reading 'Bollywood'

The Young Audience and Hindi Films

Shakuntala Banaji

First published 2006 by
PALGRAVE MACMILLAN
Houndmills, Basingstoke, Hampshire RG21 6XS and
175 Fifth Avenue, New York, N.Y. 10010
Companies and representatives throughout the world.

PALGRAVE MACMILLAN is the global academic imprint of the Palgrave Macmillan division of St. Martin's Press, LLC and of Palgrave Macmillan Ltd. Macmillan® is a registered trademark in the United States, United Kingdom and other countries. Palgrave is a registered trade mark in the European Union and other countries.

ISBN-13: 978-0-230-00172-5   hardback
ISBN-10: 0-230-00172-6   hardback

This book is printed on paper suitable for recycling and made from fully managed and sustained forest sources.

A catalogue record for this book is available from the British Library.

Library of Congress Cataloging-in-Publication Data

Banaji, Shakuntala, 1971–
    Reading 'Bollywood': the young audience and Hindi films / by Shakuntala Banaji.
        p. cm.
    Includes bibliographical references and index.
    ISBN 0-230-00172-6 (hardback)
      1. Motion pictures—India. 2. Motion pictures—Social aspects—India.
    3. Motion picture audiences. 4. Motion pictures and youth. I. Title.

PN1993.5.I8B262 2006
302.23'40954—dc22   2006042540

10 9 8 7 6 5 4 3 2 1
15 14 13 12 11 10 09 08 07 06

Printed and bound in Great Britain by
Antony Rowe Ltd, Chippenham and Eastbourne

63661020

For Ammar, Murad, Rohini and Jairus
with love;
and for Zinedine
my darling son

Contents

List of Illustrations

Acknowledgements

The research embodied here was supported by funding (R422000 34038) from the Economic and Social Research Council. For this I am enormously grateful, as it made possible both the work itself and several most enjoyable years. I thank Taylor and Francis for permission to reproduce in Chapter 6 parts of my article 'Intimate Deceptions' from their *Journal of South-Asian Popular Culture*. This book was also supported consistently by the astute interventions and encouraging critiques of David Buckingham, whom I can never thank enough and whose outlook on young people, children and the media I find unfailingly inspiring. I greatly appreciate the help of Andrew Burn, Martin Barker and Rajinder Dudrah, whose questions and insights helped to sharpen my work. I must also thank Jill Lake, my editor, for her immediate and keen interest in publishing my book and the team at Palgrave Macmillan for all their work.

I am indebted to my friends Hyeon-Seon Jeong, Liesbeth de Block, Ann Ninan, Alice Lanzon-Miller, Zoe Fowler, Vicky Armstrong, Arthur Male and Ben Fernando for kindness, conversation and moral support; to K. Leena, Rajiv Bidap, Neeta Shah and Vaishali Shirke for delightful trips to the cinema, help with proof-reading and fieldwork; to Mary McDonagh for the inestimable gift of time; and to Maria Bakaroudis and Vijayatara for encouragement and references. I could not have started this project without my family's warmth, scepticism and sustained engagement; their politics, faith and knowledge have shaped my thinking: my mother, especially, has been my most encouraging reader and kindest critic. Above all, I owe Ammar for his belief in me, the clarity and challenge of his comments on culture, media theories and my work, and for helping me to acknowledge or combat inconsistencies in my arguments. The Hindi films that I have watched with him, I can truly claim to have seen with new eyes. To the young people who participated in this research and to those who introduced some of them to me, I am deeply indebted and, although I cannot name them, their help and their voices are everywhere present in this book.

Preface

Cinema is one of the most *contested cultural sites* in India today ...
(Bharucha, 1998: 11)

This book is an enquiry into the *meanings* and *pleasures* that various aspects of Hindi commercial films come to have at various times and in various places for a sample of young British Asian and Indian viewers. It seeks to valorise neither audiences at the expense of films nor 'ordinary' viewers at the expense of critics, but to raise questions about the connections between spectatorial pleasure and ideology, as well as to contextualise and assess, critically, various claims made about the politics of Hindi films and those who watch them. Every project has a personal history that permeates its immediate concerns, and this one is no exception with its abiding interest in Hindi cinema, spectatorial pleasure, social contexts, and the politics, experiences and subjectivity of individual viewers. Growing up in 1970s Bombay, with no television but a great delight in Hindi films, I was conscious that adults around me considered popular Hindi cinema retrograde and troublesome, not as politically desirable as Art films or even Hollywood cinema. I frequently heard Hindi film narratives described as cliched or mindless, their aesthetics as vulgar or naive and, most damningly, their politics as oppressive and authoritarian. Obviously accepting this disapproval at some level, as a child I justified my undeniable enjoyment with the thought that I would escape the deleterious 'effects' of the ideologies I came to believe were purveyed by the films. This belief in what has been called 'third person effects' (Davison 1983, Schoenbach 2001) is frequently evident amongst the young viewers in this study; however, while many of them share this conviction about the vulnerability of 'others' to film influences, none of them express it in such a comprehensive manner as is sometimes implicit in the accounts of contemporary Hindi film commentators (cf. Mathur 2002: 64; Vishwanath 2002: 49–50). Indeed, in the view of many critics (Chatterji 1998; Kazmi 1999; Derné 2000; Vishwanath 2002) Hindi commercial films either ignore, utilise or sustain oppressive and unjust systems of belief and action.

More specifically, as will be seen in Chapters 1 and 2, various mediated representations – for instance of women or the nation-state – have been and still are accused of inciting, increasing and polarising as well as of policing and censoring violent debates over Indian and diasporic ethnic, sexual and gender politics (Bharucha 1995; Rao 1995). But to what extent are such accusations tenable? What are the processes by which such mediated interventions are supposed to affect the people who encounter them? Indeed, what do those who enjoy Hindi films on a regular basis think about the texts and about their own interactions with them? And what are the repercussions for one's politics and pedagogy of insisting that almost every instance of a cultural form such as Hindi commercial cinema is a vehicle for the delivery of 'messages' that seduce viewers and serve the interests of ruling elites? After a decade of discussing literature and media texts with students of various ages and ethnicities in London, I am not convinced that the answers to such questions are as accessible or as monolithic as many textual critiques might lead one to believe. Surely questions about 'culture', taken both in its inclusive sense as the values, traditions and practices of whole communities and in its more precise articulation as the musical, artistic, filmic and literary production of given sections of society, cannot lead unequivocally to answers about individual human beings and their politics, beliefs or behaviours?

Of course, in many countries, 'culture' itself is embattled terrain; and India is no exception. This is due, partly, to the sheer size of the country, the number of languages, dialects, regions, religions, beliefs and caste practices. It is also due, partly, to colonialism and the national liberation struggle, vicious and unrelenting caste, class and gender oppression, violent and xenophobic mobilisations of religious, ethnic and linguistic sentiment, the ways in which the country was partitioned and is governed, with all the ensuing material and psychic repercussions for individuals, communities and the polity. Today the conflicts going on over culture, while no less clamorous than 50 years ago, are perhaps more overt than before due to their expression across a range of media. As a recent furore over the potential for mobile phones to be used to download pornographic videos purporting to show the exploits of supposedly demure Hindi film actresses demonstrates, the ways in which religious, gender and sexual identities are articulated (or erased) by the press, by television and by commercial Hindi cinema, could be said to be in some measure a reflection of existing discourses[1] and skirmishes over the definition and control of these arenas in various sections of Indian and diasporic South-Asian society.

Initially, reviewing the best-known studies of Hindi films, I came up against a series of frustratingly simplistic binary oppositions that crystallised around notions of *audience pleasure* versus those of *textual ideology*, of *irrational emotional* responses as opposed to *rational critical* ones. To find a way out of this impasse, and with the gaps and absences of current research in mind, I formulated three key questions: First, in what ways are ethnicity, masculinity and femininity, and the relations between them, constructed and represented in contemporary Hindi commercial cinema? Second, how do audience members, especially viewers under 25, interpret the visual and verbal discourses of masculinity, femininity and ethnicity in commercial Hindi films in the light of their perceptions of their own religious, gender and sexual identities? And third, to what extent do varying class, religious, geographic, national, community, and home environments alter, influence and/or counterbalance the conceptions of ethnicity, gender and sexuality that audiences might read into Hindi films? In the course of answering these questions, both pleasures in the films and anxieties about their discursive universe are reframed and dissected in the context of meanings made from, experiences of, and things done with and to Hindi films by actual viewers in India and the United Kingdom.

Both theoretically and methodologically, the study proved challenging. During the participant observation phase of the research, which took place between August 2000 and April 2003 and encompassed over 80 film showings in Bombay and London, I chose to focus especially on the immediate verbal responses of younger film-goers – for instance, spontaneous joking comments, mimicry of speeches or expressions of satisfaction/dissatisfaction within viewing groups, and answers to my direct questions – as well as on non-verbal behaviour within cinema halls – movements, gestures, comments, shouts, whistling, clapping, standing up, crying, disapproval and laughter – which accompanied showings of films. Saliently, I found significant differences between the views expressed during in-depth interviews and the statements or behaviours of youth when in family or peer groups at film showings. The very public nature of these 'conversations' – the fact that friends and/or family members were often listening in amid the distracting noise of stall-holders, ticket touts, traffic and film music – militated against the contemplative and self-reflective responses possible in one-on-one interviews. For this reason, this book is based principally on the transcripts of extended face-to-face taped interviews with their attendant ability to clarify meaning through negotiation and thus to militate against misunderstanding rather than to render meaning fixed – as might be the case with written testimony such as letters and questionnaires.

After posting notices in local shops, clinics, schools and colleges as well as on Hindi film chat sites on the Internet, I chose around three dozen interviewees from amongst those who contacted me to reflect a broad spectrum of religion, class, gender, sexual orientation and family-background, as well as a range of ages between 16 and 25, within the

London South-Asian and Bombay communities selected. My own long-standing knowledge of, and love for, the two cities, with their culturally vibrant histories, exceptional transport networks, multiplicity of cinema halls, languages and frequent juxtaposition of different race, class and religious communities proved indispensable when selecting and carrying out in-depth interviews; if space permitted, this book would have wished to dwell at far greater length on these aspects of this audience study. In terms of the manner in which I conducted interviews, the fact that I had lived for many years in the same city space as my interviewees was also a metaphor for shared understandings of social codes and practices, possibilities and boundaries.

While the structure of the interviews was loose enough to allow subjects to pursue narratives and ideas that interested them, I provided a framework which directed attention to specific scenes, films or themes of interest to my research wherever this accorded with the topics and films already selected by interviewees. Initial questions usually aimed to establish aspects of subjects' backgrounds and sociocultural experiences, while later ones aimed to pursue, clarify, elaborate and unpick as well as occasionally to challenge the comments made by them about violence, marriage, romance, work, gender, sexuality, sex, class, religion, politics or nation in a range of contemporary Hindi blockbusters. Significantly for the types of issues with which I engage in this book, the notion of 'active interviewing' drawn from Holstein and Gubrium (1998) consistently provided me with a measure of flexibility in terms of my ability to respond to and/or comment on sensitive topics, which arose during the interviews.

This study agrees that, as Judith Mayne (1993: 172) argues: 'spectatorship needs to be treated as one of those ordinary activities, and theorizing this activity can open up spaces between seemingly opposing terms, thus leading us to attend more closely to how stubbornly our pleasures in the movies refuse any rigid dichotomies.' The analysis and theorising of the *pleasures* or, perhaps, the different kinds of pleasure on offer in commercial Hindi cinema, and a questioning of what such pleasure actually consists of and entails, was ongoing during data collection, and may be seen to inform discussions of both audience and film narratives. A need to transcend the problematic manner in which the terms 'emotion' and 'rationality' are often pitted against each other in textual accounts of cinema (Chatterji 1998; Kazmi 1998), which 'interpellate' audiences, as well as implicitly in viewer accounts, leads this book to question this entire dichotomy. My own analyses of film and interview texts seek to show the *connections* between different types of ideological discourses and social contexts, individual experiences and politics contained therein.

While analyses of data *do* question and probe the discursive perspectives from which interviewees construct their interpretations of films and the world, they do not, at any point, seek to assert that such discourses, choices and interpretations lack concrete material (social, historical) repercussions and psychic implications. As such, interviews are not simply seen as language games; and reality, off-screen, though multifaceted and plural, does not always have to be inserted into 'scare-quotes'. Furthermore, I became convinced that although my methods of gathering data were qualitative, there were meaningful ideas that could only be expressed *about the sample* by quantifying aspects of the data (cf. Murdock 1997). Analyses put forward in this book, while retaining a commitment to a broader qualitative agenda, do see even a balance of 'four to one' or 'six to 16' within sub-groups of the sample as being able to aid hypotheses about the ways in which young viewers' backgrounds and experiences might inflect their spectatorial meaning-making. This should not suggest, however, that any of the interviewees quoted in this book is seen as being *representative* of the social class, religion or other category with which they identify most closely or to which they belong.

The arguments and narratives of viewing in this book gain their validity not by giving voice to the film and life experiences and understandings of all young South-Asian viewers, but by providing a detailed picture of the concerns and meanings made by particular viewers that does, potentially, enable a better understanding of the concerns, interpretative frameworks and life-worlds of other viewers. However, lest it be assumed that the very particularity of the data limits it excessively, it should be recollected that qualitative research describes *processes* – of interpretation, identity formation, psychosocial relations as well as relations between variables such as pleasure, knowledge, experience and belief – that are not accessible with quantitative methods that might appear to guarantee representativeness. It is my belief that the analyses provided here of the processes outlined are sufficiently rigorous and persuasive to make sense beyond the boundaries of the specific cases outlined, and hence to have a more *general* relevance. The narratives and constructions of self and 'social worlds' (Miller and Glassner 1998: 105) that emerge from *subjective* accounts of media/cultural experience are analysed in the light of forms of Discourse Analysis. Potter and Wetherell's discussion of their method (1987: 168) as being about a search for *patterns* of *variability* and *consistency*, *differences* and *shared features* between accounts, as well as the forming of hypotheses about the patterns observed, proved pertinent for this study.

The chapters in this book are organised thematically around the ideas and concerns raised by critics about films and audiences, and by young audiences about the films, ideas and representations that interest them most. Both audiences' instantaneous and considered reactions to, and inflections of, film discourses leave one facing perplexing questions regarding Hindi films and one's manner of discussing them. Are these popular texts, as suggested in the accounts of some commentators, merely *escapist fantasies* which are watched to pass the time and leave no impression on the mind or the consciousness; or do the *ideologies* they contain support certain groups in society, interpellating their audiences to maintain a political *status quo*? Equally significantly, when young people dismiss or praise them, do they do so because they reject or accept the films as a whole or because they are responding to the episodic and fragmentary structure of commercial Hindi films? Could the films carry young viewers along with certain sequences and ideas while alienating them during others? Hence, how informative are studies of Hindi film texts that ignore audience responses, or studies of audiences that separate texts from historical and political contexts?

Engaging with some of the questions in the work of Hindi film commentators from the 1970s onwards, Chapter 1 discusses a range of theories of ideology as well as of culture, media and social discourse, generated by studies of Hindi commercial cinema published since the 1970s. Chapter 2 then considers the findings of the few available audience studies to date from India, the United Kingdom and North America, which involve discussions with audiences of Hindi films. Chapter 3 addresses questions about the social meanings of the act of cinema-going amongst young Hindi film viewers in Bombay and London, raising questions about the extent to which the context of viewing may alter, shape and/or reinforce individual responses to specific aspects of Hindi films. Telescoping in on representations of courtship, romance, family and marriage, Chapter 4 examines critical and 'ordinary' viewer positions on two tremendously popular films: *Hum Aapke Hain Koun ...!* (*Who Am I to You?*, 1994 Dir. Sooraj Barjatya) *and Dilwale Dulhaniya Le Jayenge* (*The One with the Heart takes the Bride*, 1995 Dir. Aditya Chopra). This leads to a consideration of the implications of the ideological discourses in these films for the psychosocial positions taken up on issues of romance and marriage by young people. Chapter 5 looks closely at the ways in which clothing and the body are regarded by young viewers, both in everyday social practices and in their spectacular metamorphoses on screen. Critical claims about male voyeurism and female prudishness are tested against discussions of young viewers' actual responses. Chapter 6, meanwhile, explores the ways in which a number of mainstream and alternative 'Hindi' films in the last 15 years have attempted to construct class-bound ideals of masculinity and femininity on screen. It also gives selective expression to young viewers' responses to these ideas, additionally aiming to give a sense of the actual context of, and attitudes towards, masculinity, femininity, sex and sexuality in the lives of young viewers in London and Bombay via existing research and testimonies gathered for this book. Via young people's comments as well as through existing critical literature, Chapter 7 articulates some of the controversies surrounding films such as *Bombay* (Mani Rathnam 1994) and *Gadar: Ek Prem Katha* (*Hurricane: A Tale of Love*, Anil Sharma 2001), which take as their subject matter cross-religious romances set against the backdrop of religious riots in India. It looks especially at the way in which issues of social class, national identity, diaspora and religious affiliation in the films resonate differently with Bombay youth and British Asians, Hindus and non-Hindus as well as those who have survived or experienced riots. Chapter 8 examines how young male viewers from contrasting backgrounds find diverse frameworks for action, self-justification or empowerment within films that present tales of anti-state terrorism. Concluding the book, Chapter 9 returns to issues of spectatorship, pleasure and ideology with an emphasis on the findings of this study.

1
Hindi Films: Theoretical Debates and Textual Studies

1.1 Introduction

Although this book is concerned primarily with the significance for and reception by young audiences of contemporary sexual and gender iconography in commercial Hindi films, both during the analyses of film texts and during the interpretation of audience self-representations and emotions, I will of necessity be drawing upon some of the theories and ideas implicit in existing accounts of Hindi film texts. Thus, in this chapter, I delineate some strands of thought that have dominated historical and theoretical scholarship on Indian 'popular' or 'commercial' cinema in the last three decades. Notably, these include debates surrounding the *effects* of Hindi cinema, the connections between *texts* and *contexts*, the *mechanisms* and *ideologies* of the medium, the significance of *realism* for spectatorship and the role of what is characterised by Fareed Kazmi (1999) as the 'tradition-modernity paradigm'.

1.2 Early accounts: from escapist fantasy to textual pleasure

'They aren't realistic!' and 'Escapist fantasy!', are frequent criticisms of Hindi films in educated/elite Indian circles or are self-deprecatingly offered by urban Indian viewers (Derné 2000; Banaji 2005) and a number of South-Asian youth in London (Gillespie 1995). These may be perfectly valid accusations if by 'realistic' one means attempting to seduce or deceive the audience into believing in the perfect correspondence between the text and the world that they inhabit. In *Sholay* (*Embers*, Ramesh Sippy 1975), one of the most widely viewed and influential Hindi blockbusters of the seventies, a virtuous woman dances on broken glass until

1

her feet bleed in order to keep her lover alive and a man with no arms kicks his enemy to death; in *Maine Pyar Kiya* (*I've Fallen in Love*, Sooraj Barjatya 1989), a spoilt, wealthy young man works in a quarry to prove his worthiness of his beloved. None of these sequences could plausibly claim to represent the material 'reality' with which most viewers might be familiar. Yet the fact that viewers respond to these sequences with apparent engagement, cheering, screaming out, groaning and referring to them repeatedly with pleasure and/or irritation during discussion might suggest that they discover in their melodramatic construction what might be called a psychological realism or realism at the level of *emotion*. Acknowledging that this might be the case, Sudhir Kakar argues that 'to limit and reduce the real to that which can be demonstrated as factual is to exclude the domain of the psychologically real – all this is felt to be, enduringly, the actuality of one's inner life.' Pertinently, writing about the viewers of the American soap opera *Dallas*, Ien Ang (1985: 44) uses the term 'emotional realism' to explain how this type of realism inheres not in the day-to-day circumstances of viewers and characters, but rather in a more symbolic or connotative realm in which domestic arguments, betrayals, joy and sorrow form bridges between on- and off-screen life.

Such understandings, based on an implicit acceptance of the dialectical relationship between emotion and rationality, as well as on a sympathy for the messiness of both viewing pleasure and mediated 'reality', although more familiar nowadays, seem to be anathema to early critics of Hindi films. Firoze Rangoonwala's pioneering text, *75 Years of Indian Cinema* (1975), and Barnouw and Krishnaswamy's thorough but somewhat eclectic institutional study *Indian Film* (1980) display the beginnings of interest in the relationship between textual structures and Indian social structures, and between generic or 'typical' features of Hindi films and the satisfaction to be derived from them by audiences. Nevertheless, Rangoonwala's final assessment of 'popular' cinema remains, like that of Chidananda Dasgupta,[1] an ultimately pessimistic one in that it insists on viewing commercial cinema in *contrast* to what is defined as 'genuine cinematic art'. 'Reality' and 'topicality', judged to be missing from commercial films, are seen as being the 'soul' of true film art. In relation to those who consume the 'bulk' of Indian films, Rangoonwala's evaluation is similarly gloomy for, in his view: '[t]he mass audience mind remains equally dormant and unresponsive to change due to the dead-weight of tradition-cum-habit as well as the extraneous socio-economic factors, like illiteracy, poverty, shortages, high prices, the black economy, social inequality and the lack of opportunity, which have all made bare reality simply unbearable on the screen' (1975: 159).

So, if life were altogether better and more bearable for India's millions, would they then abandon the Hindi film entirely and opt for 'alternative' cinema, for social realism at its grimmest? Is 'fantasy' debased and 'reality' uplifting? Having gathered information on a range of institutional contexts and processes including producers and directors from the beginning of the Indian film industry to the 1970s, distribution and exhibition policies, script-writing trends from the early studio era through to the time of publication of the study, the connections between anti-colonial struggles, nationalism and Indian film as well as the star system (including actors from vernacular cinema), Barnouw and Krishnaswamy turn, at the very end of their book, to similar thorny questions about audiences. 'What', they ask, 'do Indian films – and the popular addiction to them – suggest about the "psychic geography" of her millions?' (1980: 281) In what has now become a commonplace of popular film commentary – and in contrast to Rangoonwala's implied contention that 1970s Hindi films are utterly removed from the social context of a majority of those who view them – they then proceed to elaborate their sense of the ways in which Hindi films articulate the fears and desires of audiences around the conflicting demands of 'age-old traditions' and modernity ('industrialization', 'urbanization') via thematic references to young love and arranged marriage, the dowry system, the status of women and the primacy of the joint family. Their contention that (especially) young male audiences find in the archetypal characters and family relationships of the commercial Hindi film a reassuring sense of continuity while being at the same time able to flirt with images of modernity and 'westernisation' was not new at the time of their study, and has been reiterated since in a range of commentaries (Valicha 1988: 48–60; Derné 2000). Meanwhile, chapters by Anil Saari, Lothar Lutze and Beatrix Pfleiderer in the collection *The Hindi Film: Agent and Reagent of Cultural Change* (Pfleiderer and Lutze 1985) and articles by Rosie Thomas (1985) and Vijay Mishra (1985) in the British film journal *Screen* began to adumbrate in more precise ways a debate about the aesthetics of the commercial Hindi film. Most crucially, notions of audience pleasure were not merely relegated to the margins of such theorising, but were explored via concepts of genre and ideology.

Discovering in the deep populism of Hindi film imagery a refusal of plagiarism and a playful ability to borrow without imitating, Anil Saari notes that popular film 'reduces the "foreign" and "alien" and the inaccessible to a motley-shape, an object of parody rather than one which could make the film-goer feel inferior'. In an interesting foreshadowing of Ashis Nandy's 'slum's-eye view' metaphor,[2] Saari further argues that commercial cinema is 'the only communication media [in post-independence India] that is willing to reflect the point of view and the perspective of that dominant section of the population which is not part of the ruling elite' (in Pfleiderer and Lutz 1985: 25–6). In a field dominated by a supposedly insurmountable opposition between 'realism' and 'escapism', what might be on offer in this idea is the possibility that Hindi film texts may treat the representation of reality playfully, even apparently subversively, in order to enable the countenancing of reality; in this sense they might go beyond being merely 'escapist'[3] and, without being inherently ironic themselves, enable the taking up of ironic positions in relation to their plots and characters. This notion is not carried through by Lutze and Pfleiderer in their analyses of the talk and letters of a selection of Hindi film fans.

Pfleiderer, by her own admission more an anthropologist than a film theorist (1985: 83), sums up her findings after a range of discussions with viewers with implicitly reductive assertions:

> Younger people might ... play with film contents in the same way as with thoughts or dreams, and unconsciously test identification processes, often in a non-serious way. Older people, however, and especially women, expect educational functions from films ... Hindi films stabilize the social system by repressing new needs and, at the same time, mythologizing 'tradition': they are an instrument of cultural continuity.

> (1985: 129)

Prior to this conclusion, she had already argued that Hindi films 'serve as religious surrogates and thus turn cinema-houses into places of pilgrimage' (p. 114), that they 'may reinforce dependency patterns by producing regressive behaviour' (p. 118) and that such films act cathartically to 'discharge' viewers' own grief via the trials and tribulations of favourite screen characters. Evidently, and in a manner highly reminiscent of the Frankfurt School's critiques of 'mass culture',[4] the language in which these 'findings' are couched – 'regressive', 'dependency', 'repressing', 'pilgrimage' – implies, in a fairly crude manner, that Hindi film fans are, despite anything they might say to the contrary, the dupes of a cleverly manipulative political system and the pawns of a cynical commercial one. In either case, power and agency are located at the nexus of film Industry and State rather than in a dialogic or negotiated relationship between viewer and text. Implicit in her conclusion is a notion of direct effects which both devalues the *subjective pleasures* gained from films and ignores the possibility that the narratives of film viewing generated in her study might be open to a variety of interpretations and may, in themselves, embody a range of competing and contradictory discourses on both social and psychological phenomena.

The overemphasis of Lutze and Pfleiderer's interviews on a narrowly defined spectrum of social values mostly relating to family life has been critiqued by Ravi Vasudevan (1990), and remains a major flaw in their study of a period when Hindi films were bursting with characters raging at and fighting social injustice, state pressure, corruption and personal disillusionment. Published in the same year (1985), Rosie Thomas's explication of the generic expectations set up by Hindi films focuses on the Amitabh Bachchan cult movie *Naseeb* (*Destiny*, Manmohan Desai 1981), in which, she argues, the urge towards spectacle – song and dance, locations, costumes, fights, stunts – takes precedence over more common 'emotional drama'. After a trenchant critique of those commentators – both (implicitly racist) Western and (elite) Indian – who dismiss Hindi cinema as 'absurd', 'vulgar' and 'escapist', Thomas points out that while disempowerment may be a key theme in the fulminations of the left-wing intelligentsia against such films, the pleasures on offer for audiences of Hindi films and the modes in which these films operate have been largely ignored. This she sees, at best, as a serious short-coming and, at worst, as pure hypocrisy, for it 'neither explains [these films] in any useful way nor offers any basis for political strategy' (1985). Elaborating the link between narrative mode and spectatorial response, Thomas argues:

> Hindi films work to offer the viewer a position of coherence and mastery, both through narrative closure and by providing a focus for identification within the film ... However, spectacular and emotional excess will invariably be privileged over linear narrative development. The spectator is expected to be involved not primarily through anticipation of what will happen next, but through how it will happen and affective involvement in the happening: excitement, thrill, fear, envy, wonder, not to mention the eroticism which lies beneath the desire for spectacle itself.
>
> (1985)

Clearly, the non-normative manner in which 'affective involvement' is called upon in this extract is a far cry from the manner in which it is generally invoked, namely *in opposition to* 'intellectual engagement' or 'political understanding' (in contrast to which such emotion appears to be a debased and uncritical response). The implicit classification of 'criticism' as a rational or intellectual activity and pleasure in films as an emotional one is an issue to which attention will be drawn specifically by the contrasting comments of viewers and film theorists in Chapter 7. The categorising of emotional involvement or even emotional 'excess' as a positive feature of an audience's experience of popular media, recognisable in Thomas's commentary, is a key term of approval in *Screen* theory (for instance, in discussions of melodrama and the films of Douglas Sirk) and has now become one of the orthodoxies of writing about so-called 'women's genres' such as 'Soap Opera' or 'Melodrama' (cf. Gledhill 1987; Modleski 1990). This should not lessen the importance of Thomas's argument in a context where the elites and members of the intelligentsia were/are all too prone to make simplistic connections between the structures of sentiment in Hindi films and the poverty, illiteracy and superstition of the so-called 'masses' or the authoritarian and fascistic proclivities of the middle classes. Engaging with another prevalent criticism of Hindi cinema, namely its lack of 'realism' or 'verisimilitude', Thomas distinguishes between a mechanistic conception of verisimilitude or believability – which turns upon a highly positivistic notion of correspondence between a given physical world 'out-there' and the constructed one on screen – and what she terms the logic of a film's 'moral universe' which consists of the emotional responses of characters to each other and codes by which they are shown to relate. It is this latter feature of Hindi films, reminiscent of Ien Ang's definition of 'emotional realism' (1985: 44) and Sudhir Kakar's 'psychological realism' (1990: 30), which, if breached in the minds of an audience, can cause a film to become less pleasurable and even to 'flop' completely.

In the same issue of *Screen*, Vijay Mishra asserts that the moral codes and narratives of Hindi cinema are *ideologically* patterned via their similarity to those of the two most famous Hindu epics, the *Mahabharata* and the *Ramayana*. It is his contention that, through constant borrowing from and interpretation of these two authoritative 'meta-texts', Indian commercial films legitimise and 're-inscribe' their own values within the mythic tradition. Mishra (1985) views metonymic description as fundamental to the symbolic language of Hindi films in the same way that it is central to the signification system of the *Mahabaratha* and the *Ramayana*, and suggests that the connections between individual heroes and their star personae are transformed by the symbolic role which they come to play in the minds of their audiences. Mishra poses questions about the ways in which viewers might gain pleasure both from films which reassert the power of genealogy and the patrilineal family and from those which attempt to subvert or circumvent genealogy in mild or 'imaginary' ways via the cutting loose of orphan heroes and heroines from the kinship bonds which bind others/spectators. He locates much of the power of Hindi films to gain responses from their audiences in what he terms a 'sub-text' or 'parallel-text' which is the 'actor-text': 'Amitabh Bachchan becomes a complex 'text' in his own right, sanctioned by mythology and responding to a need for rebelliousness in the restless Indian lower middle classes' (Mishra 1985).

The Moving Image (1988), Kishore Valicha's erudite account of both Indian 'popular' and 'art' cinema, is another text which calls upon the concepts of *myth* and a *collective* or *popular unconscious* in order to explain the way in which Hindi films relate to their audiences. While introducing the notion of a coherent ideology, his account is couched in psychoanalytic terms and relies heavily on a dichotomy between the morally uplifting realism of 'serious cinema' and the (presumably) decadent and consumer-oriented 'popular' films. It is possible to see in Valicha's descriptions of 'popular' films a thinly veiled pity for their audiences who are caught up in a 'vicious cycle' of desire:

> A distinct ideological consciousness permeates the popular film. It treats its audience as an object whose hidden desires it seeks to satisfy. It vicariously offers them sex, glamour, riches: things they lack, desire, but dare not seek ... The popular film ends up as an unalterable materiality unable to rise above its mirror-like stage of communication. It is unable to invent subjects and can only present and sell the consumer to himself. Its ideological rooting can provide it only a fixed kind of structure or 'formula' ....
>
> (1988: 31)

According to Valicha, by assuming the distinction between feeling and intellect and between subjectivity and objectivity, the serious film is able to structure its reality in a more scientific and rational manner than the popular film, which deals only with *desire*. In attempting to explain the popularity of such commercial films with Indian audiences, Valicha refers repeatedly to the existence of a collective 'Indian consciousness' to which the structures of meaning in popular films speak (1988: 32). In his view, the audience is passive but covetous, acted upon by the combination of myth and narrative in a way that 'seduces' them while they are still 'unaware' of what is happening. Meanwhile, the films, tapping into the archetypal preoccupations and contradictory desires of the populace, present audience members to themselves cleansed of moral degradation and unified by an ephemeral sense of psychic coherence. Again, it is possible to see in Valicha's comments and concerns aspects of Frankfurt School theorisations of popular cultural 'consumption' as leading to mass deception and manipulation, stagnation, irrationality and ultimately the triumph of capitalist economics at the expense of human consciousness and freedom.

Shifting the ground subtly from a concept of *desires* to one of *needs*, Ashis Nandy (1995: 205) articulates the significance of commercial Hindi films as stemming from their ability to 'tap the fears, anxieties and felt pressures of deculturation and even depersonalisation which plague the Indians who do not find the normative framework of the established Indian middle-class culture adequate for their needs'. Explications such as these by Valicha and Nandy suggest that by the end of the 1980s notions of popular cultural structures of feeling and the power of the popular were beginning to be theorised in relation to Indian commercial cinema in more systematic ways than in preceding decades. Audiences *per se* were rarely approached directly, but were central to the explanatory efforts of theorists in that they were seen as being deeply implicated in the kinds of narratives, structures of feeling and preoccupations of commercial cinema. Nevertheless, both theoretically and within the media itself, countless critiques of the 'seductive' and 'escapist' tendencies of commercial cinema continued to be written; and these sparked, in refutation, textual studies of Hindi film dominated by the more apparently sophisticated and overtly political, but nonetheless functionalist theories of film based on *ideology* and *interpellation*.

1.3 Ideology, hegemony and interpellation: exploiting the form of Hindi films

Since the accounts mentioned so far, work exploring the construction of types of national or ethnic identity through popular Indian media/cinema (Chakravarty 1998; Mankekar 2000; Rajagopal 2001, M. G. Durham 2004) have brought Hindi cinema further into the academic mainstream. Sumita Chakravarty's commentary contains the propositions that, first, the '[t]rope of impersonation and masquerade is ... central to the process of movement and translation from social macrocosm to filmic microcosm' and, second, '[t]he Bombay film's prime social function may be said to be the symbolic "return" of the marginalized and the rejects of society into the body politic' (1998: 311). Watching Hindi movies, it is not difficult to comprehend why 'impersonation' and 'masquerade' become central features of Chakravarty's argument. In film after film the hero, dispossessed or exploited by the villains, returns to wealth and glory, to mete out justice and destroy the wrongdoers; evil stepmothers usurp the respect and position of their rivals to poison men against daughters and sons; rich boys turn labourers to prove their love for a beloved; men dress as women to view female-only spaces; women dress as men to avenge crimes or avoid authority. In *Chori Chori Chupke Chupke* (*By Theft, Softly, Softly*, Abbas Mastan 2001), beset by off-screen scandals due to allegations of corrupt financing and the investigation of these allegations, impersonation is carried so far that even the foetus inside a woman's womb becomes the double of another inconceivable but much believed-in child and is blessed in a ceremony of astounding, if rather surreal, seriousness. If many successful Hindi films (cf. *Trishul* (1978), *Maine Pyar Kiya* (1989) and *Lagaan*, (2001)) are about nothing else, then, they do seem to be about the construction of a dream-space which cuts across class boundaries, where aspiration and desire blend with blunt scepticism and common sense to reiterate the possibility, even the *probability* of true love, family harmony and justice for all. In this sense Chakravarty's second contention, namely that Hindi films are about the reinsertion of a sub-altern class into the 'body politic', becomes plausible, although it does not necessarily hold true for all Hindi films, particularly many of those released in the last decade.

If, as Chakravarty writes, the results of 'impersonation' are both a 'dis-avowal of fixed notions of identity' and an 'accretion', a 'piling up of identities' leading to the 'transgression of social codes and boundaries' (1998: 4), then 'masquerade' may well be central to the success of Hindi films with the impoverished populace and the lower middle classes. Is it fair to suggest as she does, then, that 'impersonation implies a form of subversion, of the illegitimate (even the monstrous) masquerading as the real thing or person, generally with the intention of displacing the legit-imate'? (1998: 5). Returning to *Chori Chori Chupke Chupke*, a film produced nearly a decade after the publication of her book, one is able to see in its whimsical borrowings – from Hollywood and older commercial Hindi films[5] – aspects of the play on identity which is so central to Chakravarty's argument. When Madhubala (Preeti Zinta), a prostitute who table-dances at a club and has no family to call her own is being blessed and cosseted in the bosom of the elite Malhotra family to whose heir she agrees to become surrogate mother, the sense of delicious transgression and danger are powerfully intertwined on screen. When the – carefully orchestrated – possibility arises that Raj Malhotra (Salman Khan) may begin to find this upstart more attractive than his own devoted and beautiful wife Priya (Rani Mukherjee), a series of 'transformations' occur during which the two women wear each other's clothes, go into dream sequences with the same man and impersonate each other both physically and emotionally. The fact that the film ends with a transformation in the 'moral' con-sciousness of the prostitute, but no real material or social alteration in her status does not necessarily mean that members of the audience would not read her as having been regenerated. She may well be perceived as *transformed and transforming* via the act of becoming 'sister' to the wife of a powerful man and mother to his child, who definitely resonates as the family's – and hence the nation's – future. In this instance not only has the notion of masquerade and impersonation been stripped, so to speak, of its negative and duplicitous connotations, but it has been legitimised as a vehicle for moral regeneration.

In terms of Chakravarty's argument, which eschews simplistic assumptions about 'identity' and 'realism', the fact that nothing 'material' has changed at the end of the film (either within its universe or off the screen) is by the by. However, for many Hindi film critics and theorists, the 'closure' offered by Indian commercial cinema to dilemmas of gender, caste and class oppression, underprivilege and corruption, is false and misleading, dangerously simplistic and disabling to political critique. While journalistic and academic commentators differ in their awareness of the importance of understanding the mechanisms by which Hindi blockbusters 'speak' to the emotions of their intended audiences, some spend considerable amounts of time analysing the processes whereby ritualised forms and conditions of production are inscribed within texts. Madhava Prasad (1998) and Fareed Kazmi (1999) offer understandings of Hindi commercial cinema which turn, respectively, on Althusserian notions of ideological 'interpellation' and Gramscian notions of 'hegemony'. In Prasad's view, while Chakravarty's reading of Hindi films correctly moves away from ahistorical and essentialist accounts of the Indian 'psyche' by placing the Hindi film within the context of the modern nation-state, her 'imperso-nation metaphor' fails to account for numerous aspects of Hindi cinema; it functions, according to Prasad (1998: 17–18) not as a theoretical framework but merely as a 'linking device' and thus neglects both audiences and generic complexities. It is to Prasad's (and later Kazmi's) studies that one can turn with the question: 'How are Hindi film audiences seen to be "interpellated" within the texts and what significance is awarded to the nature of the hegemonic discourses purveyed by Hindi films?'

Taking issue with accounts of Hindi film which see it as tailored to the 'needs' and concerns of the Indian populace, Madhava Prasad's seminal study *Ideology of the Hindi Film* seeks to locate the Hindi film within networks of politics, history and economics that are responsible for its continued production. Applying Marxist economic constructs taken from the theorisation of social relations between capital and labour, Althusserian notions of ideology and a Gramscian conceptualisation of hegemony to the realm of Hindi film, Prasad elucidates what he calls the 'ideology of formal subsumption' (1998: 6). In this analysis, the characteristic episodic and fragmentary structure of the Hindi film, with its interludes of song and dance and its polarisation between drives towards 'tradition' and those towards 'modernity', is an expression of a conflict over dominant political and economic structures which make up the nation-state. The idiosyncratic construction of Hindi films from apparently discrete parts is, in this view, tied to the mode of production of Hindi films which situates different aspects of the film in heterogeneous sectors: music, dialogue and dance are each generated independently and combined only loosely by narrative.

Viewing cultural production in India as the site of a continuing struggle over the 'form of the state', Prasad (1998: 9) notes that this struggle is manifested through the recurring allegorical dimension of the dominant textual form in the popular cinema. Narrative, subjectivity and state authority are closely linked within Hindi films, the specificity of Indian popular films being apparent in a conflict between what Prasad names 'the feudal family romance' (1998: 55) and a construction of subjectivity which is linked to the 'modernising' project of the post-independence Indian nation-state. Thus Prasad is able to explain the ban on kissing prevalent in commercial Hindi cinema not as an expression of 'prudery' or as a salient feature of some typically 'Indian' culture but as a crucial outcome of the coexistence in the realm of politics of both pre-capitalist patriarchal ruling elites and an equally patriarchal bourgeoisie who have allied themselves to the projects of the modern nation-state. He notes that '[i]n a society of castes and traditional ruling elites, the "private" cannot be represented in public (or ... images cannot be represented from a "private" point of view) because such a representation violates the ruling classes' scopic privileges' (1998: 78).

Prasad's argument highlights the fact that for the ban on kissing to function effectively on behalf of those whom it actually serves, it has to be regarded as 'meaningless', arbitrary and puritanical or else as the expression of Indian 'tradition'. For, if one looks a bit more closely at the mismatch between the continual displays of the female body on screen and the prohibition of kissing, it is possible to read in these contradictions an authoritarian proscription of representations that portray subjectivity within a 'private' sphere. Ergo, the exploration of individual (especially female) subjectivity and the depiction of what is effectively a *private* realm – in which the 'couple' exists cut off from the family and, crucially, from the authoritarian *values* of the ruling elites – might undermine the power and influence of 'an informal alliance of patriarchies' (Prasad

1998: 98) in a way that the on-screen erotic 'objectification' (see discussion in Section 5.2) of women, wholly a spectacular or 'public' event, never could. Prasad is thus able to argue that the Hindi film is never unequivocally giving the 'masses' what they want because, by its very capitalist nature, its modern technologies and dominant ideologies are first and foremost at the service of the nation-state and a powerful coalition of ruling elites. His explanation of Hindi cinema's reasons for abjuring representations of the 'private' domain while continuing to represent overtly sexualised female figures is convincing but needs to be tested against recent films as well as against the audiences' perceptions and interpretations of 'public' and 'private' realms.

Implicitly endorsing many of the ideas in Prasad's theorisation, Fareed Kazmi moves in for a closer look at a whole range of what he terms – in distinction from *popular* or *commercial* – *conventional* Hindi films (1999: 56). Initially, Kazmi's stated intention is to challenge those who continue to label Hindi conventional cinema 'kitsch' and 'escapist'. Taking the view that Hindi films are a major 'cultural and ideological force' and are nothing if not political (1999: 16), he argues that they do not *merely reflect social reality* but also *construct* it. Proposing understandings of both 'language' and 'reality' which owe much to post-structuralism and to the writings of Raymond Williams, Kazmi suggests that Hindi films are a linguistic and cultural expression of the battle over meanings and values which takes place in every society between members with different concerns and interests. Thus, after setting out a number of approaches to Hindi film such as that of media 'effects' and that of 'selective perception', Kazmi identifies his own position as being closest to that of the Cultural Studies approach utilised by the Birmingham School and Stuart Hall.

Kazmi critiques theorists such as Anil Saari, Vijay Mishra, Ashis Nandy, Lothar Lutze and Beatrix Phleiderer for what he categorises as their ahistorical and essentialist evaluations of Hindi films and their inability to move beyond the tradition–modernity binary in their thinking about both film narratives and audiences. After a trenchant interrogation of this (false) opposition, Kazmi deploys a Gramscian concept of 'hegemony' to explain the manner in which Hindi films achieve their cultural status and rally support for specific versions of reality as opposed to others. As he expresses it:

> Conventional cinema works by reflecting and expressing the 'popular element', its feelings, precepts and 'common sense'. It operates by transforming elements at large in the culture – not through inventing or imposing arbitrary materials on a stunned and passive audience

[... it] works by appropriating meaningful elements already extant in
the culture at large – as its raw materials – and transforming them in
such a way that they express a ruling class hegemonic principle.

(1999: 72)

Furthermore, he explains, 'there is always a multiplicity of interpellations
contained within the structure of almost every conventional film'
(1999: 74). According to such an analysis, the various elements of Hindi
films such as the songs, the dances, the sets and dialogues are all part of this
project of interpellation. The themes of sacrifice, loyalty, honour, religion
and joint families are intertwined with spectacular visions of hand-to-hand
combat and glamorous close-ups to cast upon the audience a kind of
'hypnotic spell' (1999: 90). In case one is tempted to ask why these
themes are successful in interpellating Indian audiences, in a twist ironically reminiscent of Barnouw and Krishnaswamy's 'psychic geography'
formulation (1980: 281), Kazmi maintains that 'a lot of pre-capitalist elements are deeply entrenched in the consciousness of the people ... they are
susceptible to, and hanker after, all these elements which are now lost to
them' and that 'Hindi conventional films exploit this psychic need very
effectively' (1999: 76).

Kazmi's wish to break what he considers to be the hegemonic strangle-
hold of Hindi conventional cinema over the minds of the Indian populace leads him to a solution which involves a redeployment of the
technologies and techniques of conventional cinema within oppositional
and revolutionary frameworks. 'Art' or 'serious' cinema with its conventional realist aesthetic he eschews as being of little use to such a subversive
project. By contrast, a cinema which used the *mechanisms* of conventional
Hindi film but focused on poverty, exploitation, oppression and mar-
ginalisation, while displaying the dignity and struggles of oppressed groups
would, in his view, be truly *popular* and could hope to affect the *status
quo* which conventional films maintain via their sanitised and conformist
treatment of the same issues. Kazmi's proposition is both respectful of
current Hindi film pleasures and attractive in its search for a transformative
consciousness.

Yet – and this is one of the crucial questions of this book – who can say
exactly what meanings conventional films do hold and 'subversive' films
will hold for their audiences or whether the solutions offered by a group
of radical film makers will of necessity be those that can alter the lives
and beliefs of the mass of Indian cinema-goers? And, more important still,
if all commercial films were *replaced by*, rather than *viewed along-side*,
politically engaged, socially radical films, what would become of the

moments of fracture and critique, the feelings of resentment and anger that, as I will suggest in Chapters 4 to 8, are generated even at present by 'hegemonic' discourses in contemporary commercial Hindi films?

With similar concerns to those of Prasad and Kazmi but a less overriding emphasis on Althusserian formulations of ideology, there is a growing body of literature broadly defined by its interest in the changing 'cultural' and 'political' paradigms with which the mechanisms of Hindi films are intertwined (John 1998; Inden 1999; Vasudevan 2000c; 2000d; 2001a; Dirks 2001; Uberoi 2001; Mishra 2002). Amongst these texts, the writings of Ravi Vasudevan (see Chapter 7), Nicholas Dirks and Patricia Uberoi (see Chapter 6) stand out for their ability to locate discursive complexity within Hindi film texts/contexts and to posit pleasure for audiences without losing sight of the political and symbolic functions of cinema. Saliently, whatever their political opinions about the films in question, none of these commentators deny the texts' multiple possibilities of pleasure and meaning for audiences. Rachel Dwyer, meanwhile, describes the depiction of romance, sex and family life in a selection of Indian cultural texts and looks at the 'struggle for succession, being fought between the old and the new middle classes ... [which] is in fact a tussle for hegemony over India's national culture ... [where] unnameable ideologies have come into conflict' (2000: 4). Without looking too closely at these 'unnameable ideologies', or giving details of the *social phenomena* of 'romance', 'sex' and 'family life', she offers some insights into metamorphoses taking place in urban Indian popular cultural consumption in the 1990s, as well as into the relationship between textual form and social context. However, given the interest of this study in issues of gender, sexuality and religious identity, it is to the burgeoning tradition of feminist analysis of Hindi cinema to which we now turn.

1.4 Cultural constructions: textual analysis and feminist critique

Ranging from analyses of the ways in which the camera 'interacts' with actors and actresses in a symbolic simulation of 'coitus interruptus' to discussions of censorship, voyeuristic pleasure during dance sequences, sado-masochistic pleasure in watching heroic suffering and female authority in the rape-revenge genre of mainstream cinema, the work of Lalitha Gopalan (1998, 2002), Jyotika Virdi (2003), Shohini Ghosh (1999, 2002), Ranjani Mazumdar (2000) and Asha Kasbekar (2001) has much to offer debates over the location of power and agency in the text–audience interaction. Mazumdar's essay takes as its point of departure the 'angry young man' of seventies cinema – for instance, Amitabh Bachchan's character in *Zanzeer* (*Chain*, Prakash Mehra 1973) and *Deewar* (*Wall*, Yash Chopra 1975) – and shows how he is displaced by a violent and 'schizo-phrenic' masculine subjectivity in films such as *Darr* (*Fear*, Yash Chopra 1994) and *Baazigar* (*Soldier*, Abbas-Mastan 1993). In these movies, psychosis becomes a justification in and of itself; the hero's violent acts no longer appear embedded within his material and psychological history. Mapped onto a physical landscape/cityscape which becomes increasingly detached from 'reality', these tales are also, to Mazumdar, about the redemption or loss of the 'utopian impulse' behind the formation and defence of urban metropolises such as Bombay. Writing in 1995 about the changing narrative strategies of Hindi commercial cinema, Rashmi Doraiswamy had already noted that the sense of logic, order and moral justice created by the tales of wronged heroes taking revenge (during the seventies and eighties) was giving way to a mode of filmic story-telling which highlighted *acts* rather than *causes*, used fewer flashbacks to con-textualise mental landscapes and favoured an anti-hero rather than the idealistic-utopian hero of old. This trend, it should be noted, has now come full circle, with the reintroduction in mainstream Hindi cinema of heroes whose qualities of kindness and bravery are reflected in their struggles on behalf of those they love or their communities (*Gadar, Lagaan, Swades, Viruddh, Veer-Zaara* and *Mangal Pandey: The Rising*, to name but a few).

Moving from masculine to feminine subjectivity, Barnouw and Krish-naswamy's proposition that Hindi films, by deploying female characters who are psychologically paradoxical in that they blend the absolute male-worshipping devotion of women from Hindu epics with the nonchalant use of costumes and tough behaviour supposedly attributable to 'liber-ated' Western women, allow male audiences to 'have their cake and eat it' (1980: 282) is echoed by Nikhat Kazmi. She writes about the appeal of the actress Madhuri Dixit as 'someone who articulates the ultimate [Indian] male fantasy by creating a female character who has miracu-lously resolved all kinds of contradictions into a homogenised whole. One that is smart and simple, sensuous and shy, aggressive and malleable, intelligent yet vulnerable' (1998: 54). Of course, such a view is posited entirely on readings of male audiences as interpellated within the texts selected for discussion rather than upon evidence garnered via discussions with 'real' male film viewers.

Similarly, expressing the frustration of many feminists with the repre-sentation of women in commercial Indian films, Maithili Rao's essay 'To Be a Woman' (1995) appears to speak both about films and for female spectators. In her words, 'women's response to popular cinema is a ceaseless love-hate thraldom because the film image ostensibly celebrates her eroticism while reducing her to a passive sex-object' (1995: 241). Increasing 'permissiveness' on the screen is seen as simply one more complicating factor in the chain of iconography which binds and degrades women, fusing within individual heroines the old dichotomies of 'vamp/prostitute/dancing girl' and 'chaste wife' and making the idea of 'woman' merely more appealing to certain men while heroines become less psychologically coherent. Male viewers who would previously have had to cheer for dancing girls and then to fall silent in respect for the loyal piety of the heroine are now, apparently, given the licence to imagine, beneath the demure sari, the sexual delights which the heroine displayed and *promised* when, as an unmarried youngster, she cavorted in 'itsy bitsy fluff' or 'disported in diaphanous saris under waterfalls' (Rao 1995: 243).

Rao's critique is not merely of the evident and overt physical characterisation of women on screen. After assessing the themes and stylistic characteristics of a number of films through the 1980s and 1990s, Rao writes of the film *Aaina* (*Mirror*, Deepak Sareen 1993), that 'the condoning of psychic violence done to women [goes] largely unnoticed. Meekness and patience are rewarded whereas the ambitious woman's attempt to exploit her sexuality for personal fame [is] condemned as morally reprehensible' (1995: 253–4). It is the way in which Hindi commercial cinema appears to reinforce certain oppressive patterns of thought and self-image for women that comes across in Rao's essay as most deeply disturbing. This impression of the 'power' of film texts forms a connection to the enjoyable writings of 'self-taught' feminist film theorist Shoma A. Chatterji. In her book *Subject Cinema: Object Woman*, Chatterji argues, among other things, that male masquerade on screen does *not* give women the identity and integrity they desire (1998: 259), upholding instead male superiority and dominance, and that contrary to performing an 'idealising' function, 'myth' in Indian popular culture has functioned to perpetuate images of women which are 'beautiful', but in which their 'inner strength' – if they have any – 'mainly derives from a man, dead or alive – father, brother, husband or son' (1998: 49). Again, Chatterji's critiques of the depiction of women – and sometimes men – in a number of contemporary commercial films may serve as a reminder of the ways in which accounts of cinema such as Chakravathy's (1998), which emphasise the democratic and disruptive potential of 'masquerade', fail to engage fully with the awkward, authoritarian or subjugated subjectivities constructed and spoken to by many Hindi films.

1.5 Beyond simplistic oppositions

Ashis Nandy insists that commercial cinema in India is highly 'protective towards traditions and towards native categories' and that mass audiences exhausted by the 'dominant principle' of Indian life, 'modernity', are only too willing to find in Hindi films a refuge from the 'oppression and exploitation in society ... inflicted in the name of modern categories such as development, science, progress and national security' (1995: 196–206). Nandy's apparently anti-modernist stance has generated controversy amongst critics on a number of occasions (Mankekar 2000: 197–8, 218–19), and, I suggest, rightly so. For, not only does such a position rest upon a misconception of what 'modernity' is and what 'tradition' may be, thus ignoring the power relations involved in constructing both categories, it also deepens the polarisation between these two categories to such an extent that coexistence becomes a paradox and people feel that they have to choose between them, thus allying themselves with views and beliefs they do not share simply for the sake of apparent consistency. If his argument were that Hindi films frequently operate around the binary of modernity and tradition, there would be no shortage of commentators to agree with him (Bahadur 1978; Dwyer 2000: 210). Indeed, what such descriptions tell us is that Hindi films, when analysed, are perceived to be structured around the *themes* of modernity and tradition which are, within each film, first of all defined in specified ways (that may or may not serve the interests of the audiences watching) and, second, critiqued, endorsed or elided in ways that appear to make the film as saleable as possible. However, this does not mean that the cynical value-laden definitions of 'modernity' and 'tradition' made by certain film makers, the invention or appropriation of certain traditions – women dancing in backless blouses, the veneration of husbands and elders – and the disavowal of others – kissing on the lips, class equality, choosing one's own life partner, women going out to work – need to be endorsed and accepted by critics as expressive of especially *Indian* values.

In fact, implicit in the identification of Hindi films with a popular longing for 'tradition' is a dangerous political trend which ignores and erases certain social, economic and cultural experiences even as it legitimises and sanctifies others: as Purnima Mankekar (2000: 218) rightly points out: 'the romantic recuperations of traditional community ... elide inequalities within communities, including so-called traditional communities.' Fareed Kazmi too argues that the danger in viewing Hindi films as expressions of a popular longing for traditional values, and as repositories of some ideal morality which functions to fulfil the needs of the 'survival sector', is the 'trap' of 'dehistoricizing and essentializing tradition' allowing almost any barbaric practice or repressive idea to be justified in its name (1999: 62). Arguing against the impulse to analyse Hindi films in isolation from their social and historical contexts, and for a reading of each film which does not reduce it to an expression of the same never-changing cohort of specifically Indian values, Kazmi (1999: 64) emphasises that 'the important thing is to understand what concept of "modernity" and what concept of "tradition" are invoked and to what objective social use they are put.' In a similar vein, and succinctly disrupting the *apparent debate* over the deployment of 'tradition' and 'modernity' in Indian cinema and the role of these concepts for the public who consume the films, Madhava Prasad writes:

> the 'traditional' is by no means identical with the interests and desires of the displaced masses .... It is true that popular films deploy this binary frequently and that thematic conflicts are structured around it. But to treat it as if it were a transparent representation of some real conflict between these two concepts is to fall into an ideological trap. For the construction of tradition is part of the work of modernity.
>
> (1998: 107)

This perspective is the one that should be borne in mind even when individual films appear to take sides in some simplistic tug-of-war between the old and the new or 'India' and 'the West'.

1.6 Conclusion

In an attempt to assess the theoretical significance of existing critiques of Hindi commercial cinema, it was noted in Section 1.2 that some commentators view Hindi films as textbook/formula productions relying on archetypal roles or stereotypes to drum up repeatedly – at one level for commercial gain, but eventually in the service of political or ideological motives – a debilitating emotional response in audiences. Such arguments, based on 'mass manipulation' models of media effects, tend to privilege classical notions of 'realism' and to label Hindi films either as 'escapism' or as uncomplicated vehicles for deleterious ideologies. However, as Bob Hodge and David Tripp suggest, 'judgements about "reality" are complex, fluid and subjective. Modality decisively affects interpretations and responses, so it cannot be ignored in any account of the media' (1986: 130). While Section 1.2 raised theoretical questions about the type of 'realism' apparently demanded of cinema before it would be regarded as more than mere 'escapism' for a population ground down by toil or made vulnerable to its 'effects' by superstition and illiteracy, I will be exploring ideas about 'escapism' and 'realism' further in relation to young women's pleasures in film narratives about the family and romantic love in Section 4.2.1 and in relation to viewers' responses to filmic riot sequences in Section 7.3.2. Implicit in early critiques of Hindi films was a notion of 'fantasy' – used in opposition to classical notions of 'reality' rather than in its psychoanalytic sense – and of *emotion as being debilitating and irrational*. This apparently clear-cut distinction between 'emotional' and 'rational' engagement, between 'fantasy' and 'critique', can be seen to be challenged from the mid-eighties onwards by critics using *Screen* theory, who wish to validate the pleasures of emotional 'excess'.

Other models of media consumption become evident in arguments about the ways in which popular 'needs' and perceptions are translated into the gross caricatures, utopian imagined communities and Manichean oppositions of commercial Hindi films. In line with such a theoretical base, other critics and theorists cited in this chapter have viewed Hindi films as the scum or froth at the surface of the boiling pot that is Indian society. They have written of its inequality, corruption and sense of injustice bubbling to the surface in a series of 'actor-texts' or roles and salient images which represent destruction, cleansing and the reorganisation of the social realm or harmony, a golden age and the dutiful interaction of individuals with their families, elders and communities. Implicitly taking issue with commentators who rely solely on the notion of ideological interpellation to delineate the meanings films may have for audiences, Bob Hodge and David Tripp argue that 'ideological effects cannot simply be read off from ideological forms analysed in isolation from the cognitive and social processes that constitute them' (1986: 99). However coherent, the readings offered to date by feminist critics of Hindi films remain primarily textual and, in order to clarify and sustain debates over the *meanings* constructed from such textual structures, *contextual* or historical, and sociological or audience research become crucial features of contemporary Hindi film scholarship.

2
Audiences and Hindi films: Contemporary Studies

2.1 Hindi films and the South-Asian Diaspora

Jatin: Pardes, Subhash Ghai again – it's this concept of Indians who live abroad being so rich, all multimillionaires – like that film with Amitabh Bachchan being filmed round here where he's the richest guy in the world. And we're not all rich, some of us are very poor. Some live in council flats in inner city areas and a lot of people just work really hard. I think that's why some British-Indian people like those movies as well because it's a bit of dream world as well.

(24 year-old, my sample, London)

A presupposition of *total unity* between subsections of any audience (whether delineated by location, ethnicity or class) appears unwarranted; the precise extent to which children, youth and their parents, or members of different religious or national groups, share the same understandings of media texts can only be gauged via research into audience perceptions of specific texts within a given, and bounded, social context. Although notions of diaspora and hybridity are not discussed extensively in this book,[1] inherent in the study of the meanings Hindi films hold for *young British-Asian audiences* is a sense of their experience as diasporic individuals.

As a teacher of Media Studies in London whose students 'read' films in quite a range of different ways, despising them and enjoying them for quite contradictory reasons, I found myself dissatisfied with the manner in which British-Asian audiences of Hindi films were somehow being lumped together into a single category, NRIs (non-resident Indians), by commentators; their hopes, desires and reasons for going to the cinema being *read* from films such as *Pardes* (*Abroad*, Subhash Ghai 2000) and

Dilwale Dulhaniya Le Jayenge (also DDLJ, *The One with the Heart Takes the Bride*, Aditya Chopra 1995[2]) in a manner which made them all appear to be obsessed with patriarchal tradition and a nostalgic desire to be embraced by and worthy of belonging to their homeland. Were these viewers so different from their Indian counterparts? Did they go to the cinema for such different reasons? Did they, any more than members of comparable social classes in Indian audiences, want to see representations of India and the diaspora consciously exorcised of poverty and social injustice? Did all British-Asian youth – including second-generation Pakistanis, Indians from the Caribbean, Africa, India and elsewhere, Bangladeshis and Nepalis – who watch Hindi films respond to them so similarly that a new category of film, the NRI romance, had to be made and repeatedly remade to satisfy their (implicitly patriarchal and materialistic) longings and tastes? Similarly, reading about theories of diaspora and notions of hybridity, I was perturbed by the simplistic views of 'cultural authenticity' or 'tradition' surreptitiously, or perhaps inadvertently, purveyed by even the most celebratory discussions of the 'mixing' of cultures that supposedly occurs, to a greater extent than 'elsewhere', in diasporic settings. In this context, a conversation I had with two young British-Asian women – Zahira (17) and Smita (18) – confirms the importance of testing and challenging assumptions about the uniqueness and/or coherence of diasporic experience.

During a casual conversation on a bus journey, Smita launched into the following anecdote about *Hum Saath Saath Hain* (*We Are All Together*, Sooraj Barjatya 1999): a family saga in which the main source of conflict is the mother's suspicion that her eldest son might not play fair with his brothers if left in sole charge of the family firm, a suspicion that is pitted against the brothers' wish to remain united under one roof. Smita had watched the film in her mother's South-London council flat and had been charmed by its colourful costumes and 'all the mucking about'. Viewing it with her British-Asian cousins she had been struck by the 'gorgeousness' of the costumes, the 'love between the brothers' and the happy songs. Somehow the film made her think that though she lived in England and though her parents had been born in Uganda, she was really 'an Indian at heart'. Zahira chimed in that she had watched the film three times and attempted to recreate some of the dresses herself when she attended her sister's wedding. *Hum Saath Saath Hain*, Zahira insisted, was 'even better than *Hum Aapke Hain Koun ...!* (*Who Am I to You?* Sooraj Barjatya 1994)', because it did not stress 'Hinduism' so much. But this celebratory enjoyment on the part of both girls was not the whole story.

A few months later, on a trip to her mother's family home in Vadodra, Gujarat, Smita again got the chance to watch *Hum Saath Saath Hain*, this time on cable television, with her mother, brother and half a dozen relatives. On that occasion, she told us, the film made her 'really depressed' – she was 'bored' by the 'lack of plot', irritated by the film mother's 'stupid and trivial concerns' and 'stressed out' by the way in which the younger women spent most of their time 'on their knees praying or serving food to men'. When I asked her what she thought might account for such a reversal of her original response, she speculated laughingly that it might have been because 'I was a year older' or had 'learnt about "Representation" on my Media A-Level course!'. On probing gently, I discovered that Smita's family had gone to Gujarat ostensibly to attend the wedding of a cousin's son but in reality to look for a suitable bride for her own brother, then 27 and working for a computer software company in London. According to Smita, the embarrassments of his predicament made her brother – who, she was aware, had a long-standing girlfriend at his place of work – more than usually harsh with her and soured the atmosphere within her normally cheerful nuclear family. Smita and Zahira's comments about *Hum Saath Saath Hain* highlight several concerns of interest for an understanding of diasporic cultural consumption.

First, Zahira's sense that some Hindi films are more 'Hindu' than others and hence, perhaps, less open to enjoyment by viewers like herself with different religious affiliations, suggests questions about the significance of differing *intersectional identities* (Brah 1996) on the *meanings* made from, or attributed to, Hindi films. Might it be plausible to see, in the increasing visibility of Hindu religious iconography and ritual in some commercial Hindi films, an effort by members of the film industry to bind some viewers to a certain vision of Indian society while at the same time excluding others? Or might that *exclusion* be a feature of the discomfort with and rejection of the vision of India as a 'Hindu nation', which many new Hindi films are apparently (Vasudevan 2000c and 2001a; Fazila-Yacoobali 2002; Vishwanath 2002) espousing? And, if either of these possibilities is correct, what then of those, in this case diasporic, viewers who actively participate in these film imaginaries of the Indian nation? If spectatorship continues in the activities and beliefs viewers hold long after a film has ceased to play before them, are they then being mobilised by the discourses of films as part of the ideological work of the Hindu Right in India?

Second, the surprise and discomfort felt by British-Asian Smita when faced with a Hindi film's discourses on youth conformity and gender subordination in the context of a 'real' arranged marriage point to the disjunctions between experience that can cause a film to be read and interpreted in radically different ways by the same viewer in different contexts and at different times in their lives. Several commentators on national and cultural identity have argued, as Sunaina Maira (2002: 150) does, that diasporic youth 'do not simply become ethnic subjects' but actually become 'gendered and sexualised ethnic subjects'. The implication, that meaning is contingent on psychological situation and material environment as well as on intersections of gender, race and sexuality, and is *inflected but not fixed* by the dominant discourses of a Hindi film text, will be explored in different ways in coming chapters.

Third, the latent belief, hinted at by Smita, in the existence of 'truly Indian' values and traits, which somehow define and curtail ethnic belonging in a diasporic situation and reveal underlying notions of ethnic identity, raises questions about the types of self-recognitions and definitions cued by specific attributes of/sequences in commercial cultural products and the obscure manner in which consuming the cultural product itself becomes a marker of that 'ethnic authenticity' (Maira 2002). With regard to her sample of 'desi' youth in America, Maira maintains that 'the nostalgia felt and performed by Indian-American youth in late adolescence is, in part, a response to the childhood framing of cultural fields as discrete and incommensurable' (2002: 148). Furthermore, and supported by the testimonies of the five middle-class South-Asian American girls interviewed by Meenakshi Gigi Durham in her small-scale study of media sexuality and diaspora identity (Durham 2004), Maira warns against a sentimental acceptance of the binary that posits an everyday *praxis* that is 'contaminated', 'hybrid', 'modern' and Western and a *heart* that is 'traditional', 'pure' and 'truly' Indian. After extensive discussions of the pleasures to be found in group consumption of desi remix music, Maira correctly points to the ways in which 'these practices and structures of nostalgia [can also create] their own politics of belonging and exclude those who do not possess the requisite sub-cultural capital of ethnic authenticity' (2002: 148).

However, taking on board a conceptualisation of diasporas as being 'contested cultural and political terrains' (Brah 1996: 193) in relation to the South-Asian diaspora in Britain, it is important to ask, first, whether Hindi films, which are regarded as significant participants in mundane consciousness back 'home' (India, Pakistan, Nepal or Bangladesh), are equally significant for South Asians in Britain and, second, if they are, what kind of interventions they embody in the 'contested' terrain that constitutes this particular diaspora. Do they, for instance, represent the diaspora to itself and to those back in the homeland by harping on the 'traumas of separation and dislocation' that Brah senses to be a facet of diasporic experience? So, is there a specifically 'diasporically hybrid' subject position from which young British-Asian viewers, as opposed to their peers in Bombay, might be said to watch and interpret Hindi films? Are there cultural products in which traditions of representation have bled together to form new and exciting hybrid varieties of culture that are especially accessible to the type of sensibility hinted at above? Studies of viewers in the United Kingdom (Gillespie 1995) and North America (Bhattacharya 2004; Dudrah and Rai 2004) offer some opportunities for engagement with 'real' audiences of Hindi films.

In the best known of these studies, Gillespie sets out to chart the ways in which television (and TV-talk) mediates the transitions in cultural perspective taking place amongst Punjabi youth living in Southall at the time of her study (1989–91). In a brief discussion of Hindi film viewing, she suggests that watching Hindi films allows the youth in her study to make connections with areas of their parents' lives, to compare their own situations with those of other young people, and to learn about 'Indian' culture. The discussion circumvents engagement with the so-called 'traditions' apparently articulated in Hindi films, and focuses primarily on gendered reactions within the sample to issues of modality, and intergenerational interactions, concluding that 'while young people use Hindi films to deconstruct "traditional culture", many parents use them to foster cultural and religious traditions' (1995: 87).

Although Gillespie's study *does* acknowledge conflicts within diasporic families (between parents and daughters, for instance) and also concludes that the notion of cultural 'translation' is a better one than 'hybridity' in terms of its ability to describe processes of media consumption amongst diasporic youth, there is a sense in which the lack of political engagement with media texts and contexts can encourage precisely such conceptions of diasporic identity. Constructively, this study does not simply seek to reduce every individual response to media texts on the part of the young subjects to some clearly defined ideological viewpoint. However, an uneven acknowledgement of contemporary South-Asian history as well as an apparent anxiety about engaging with questions of politics rather than 'identity politics' or aesthetics run throughout the book and are, in some measure, responsible for the tensions which exist between the project as set out at the beginning and the outcome. Crucially, choices about which aspects of a community's cultural practice to articulate and which to dismiss, which situations to focus on and which ideologies to espouse are constantly being made by ethnographers and, if made without discussion or consciousness of their full implications, the end-product may find itself *endorsing certain aspects of a culture as 'tradition' while labelling others 'alien' or 'modern'*. In this respect, Steve Derné's study (2000) of men's talk, movie-going and popular Hindi films in a North Indian town, and Purnima Mankekar's ethnography (2000) of women's television viewing in Delhi, address some of the absences so evident in critiques of representation that 'read' audience subjectivity out of texts.

2.2 Reconciling 'tradition' and 'modernity'?
North Indian men watching movies

Derné's work (2000), based on his 1991 study of male film-goers in Dehra Dun, Northern Uttar Pradesh (UP; now Uttaranchal), draws on an earlier study of family life in a different UP city, Benares. By his own admission, most of Derné's interviewees for the former study were upper-caste, upper-middle-class Hindu males of all ages, and, as his 1991 interviews with a slightly less rigid class–caste spectrum of Dehra Dun film-goers were far less detailed and sustained than those in the earlier study, he has relied on the responses of those Benares interviewees a great deal in his analysis of the film-goers' responses. Despite the seeming narrowness of the sample, the desire to ground an analysis of the viewing of Hindi films within a distinctive sociocultural context and an emphasis on that cultural context as central to the formation and expression of interpretations of film representation as well as sentiments about films by viewers is one of the strengths of Derné's study.

Derné's examination of the ways in which 'mainstream' male viewers interpret Hindi film messages leads him to acknowledges that there certainly are aspects of his interviewees' responses which support the notion of oppositional readings of cinema messages; however, he is at pains to point out the numerous occasions on which male viewers will endorse and 'embrace' screen messages which, he argues, 'appeal directly to male interests'. As he puts it, 'men enjoy watching films that advance constructions of sexuality that bolster male power and work to reconcile many women to existing gender hierarchies' (2000: 8). Derné's insistence on the diversity of individual responses to cultural products is not unique (2000: 11): whether film-goers will be sceptical of, or adopt, cultural messages present in films cannot be taken for granted or known *a priori*. However, Derné's respondents appear to reject cinematic messages – such as those about individual romantic love, economic mobility and political change – that they might find satisfying and to endorse broader cultural analyses which denigrate Hindi films, on grounds of modality and quality, and dismiss their rebellions as unrealistic or dangerous. Reverting to a reliance on a notion of Hindi films as vehicles for ideological messages, Derné insists that one of the reasons for the disregarding of unconventional film messages by viewers as guides to their conduct in everyday life is the 'subtle conservatising tendency of cinematic messages' (2000: 16). He argues that

> While films provide a satisfying release for film-goers they do not usually generate changes in behaviour, but instead bolster existing hierarchies and world views. While young men and women enjoy the fantasy of bucking familial authority by marrying for love, few consider taking such a step. While Indians enjoy seeing corrupt authority defeated, few become politically active. In most circumstances, film-going appears to be a liminal period of fantasy wish fulfilment, a time to play with the ambiguities that Indian culture emphasises, rather than a source of revolutionary change in Indian thinking or individual behaviour.
>
> (2000: 61)

My interviews with film viewers support certain aspects of this view and challenge others. For instance, as Derné found, many Hindi films are indeed denigrated by some viewers for their lack of realism and their melodramatic tendencies; nevertheless, as I discovered, they are also viewed as sources of knowledge which can have a fairly profound impact on the life choices of young people. However, in the more pressured and public arena of cinema halls, young people whom I spoke to were less likely to take the themes of films seriously, or to engage with the possibility that their own behaviours and views were connected to the films they watched, although they were frequently willing *to impute to others* the seeming stigma of having been 'made' to do something by a film scene or narrative.

Confirming my sense of the youth audiences at Hindi film screenings in Bombay as both bound together and held apart by the narratives they encounter on screen, Derné's contention that male viewers find in Hindi films comforting signs of their own ability to negotiate between so-called 'tradition' and apparent 'modernity' brings the gender discourse/s of commercial Hindi cinema centre stage:

> [M]en cope with their ambivalences about modernity by identifying Indianness with an oppressive gender hierarchy. While films facilitate men's movement towards companionate love, they also preserve male

dominance by constructing women's adherence to oppressive gender norms as fundamental to Indian identity. In doing so, films contribute to the invention of a new ideology of male dominance that portrays men as rational and modern and women as emotional and traditional.

(2000: 114)

My own observation at the showing of the film *Yaadein* (*Memories*, Subhash Ghai 2001) points to the accuracy of the parts of Derné's observation which relate to some film *narratives*: the director unashamedly positions the female characters as the bearers of 'Indian tradition' and 'cultural value' while allowing the male characters to explore nonconformity and rebellion, albeit on a very small scale and against the clearly oppressive and 'westernised' (sic) monetarism of the Non-Resident Indian super-rich. Similarly, in *Dil Chahta Hai* (*The Heart Yearns*, Farhan Aktar 2001), when a young man wishes to enter a relationship with an older woman, the director burdens his characters with dialogues about the dangerous modernity of the young, the importance of traditional values, and the impossibility of a union between an alcoholic divorcee and a youth of 'good family'. In both films, controlled and family-orientated sexuality is posited as the ultimate defining feature of a truly 'Indian' courtship. However, as this book hopes to show, unlike most of the viewers in Derné's sample, many young people in London and Bombay choose not to take up the easiest positions that seem to be clarified for them by the final sequence of a film or by the conservative speeches within it. I will return to this idea in coming chapters; here, however, Purnima Mankekar's ethnographic study (2000) of women viewing television in Delhi provides interesting insights into this, among other issues to do with the 'power' of textual closure and the 'effects' of textual ideologies.

2.3 Beyond 'escapism' and 'reality': North Indian women watching television

As every other decade since Independence, the 1990s were a time of upheaval, conflict and change across both rural and urban India as well as the diaspora. Continuing separatist movements in the North-East and Punjab, the rise to power of an anti-Muslim, anti-Christian BJP-led coalition influenced by powerful and fascistic 'Hindu'[3] organisations like the RSS,[4] the ongoing confrontations over Kashmir that have led to the test explosion of nuclear bombs on both sides of the Indo–Pakistan border and the so-called 'economic liberalisation', with its resultant massive increase in circulation of both foreign and Indian consumer goods and media products, are processes that are central to the existence and experience of a great many Indians, just as the rise in local racism and xenophobia, the availability of transnational satellite channels such as Zee, B4U and Sony, international religious movements as well as the impact of events in the subcontinent are implicated in the everyday concerns of diasporic South Asians. Such far-reaching though temporally specific events and processes form the landscape against which any analysis of sociopsychological phenomena in modern India and the diaspora must be read. Acutely aware of the formative potential of this context, Mankekar's work (2000) suggests that different experiences and sociohistorical circumstances act both to shape relationships between politics and textual ideologies, and fundamentally to alter and/or inflect meanings made from the discourses embodied in popular cultural texts.

Methodologically, her study employs a mixture of textual criticism, ethnographic detail, audience research, historical and political commentary, and contextual interrogation (such as interviews with directors and producers of televisions serials and soaps) in order to give a sense of the sometimes labyrinthine viewing environment – or 'interdiscursive context' – inhabited by female television viewers in a lower-middle-class suburb in New Delhi. Her insight that the family is 'a politically, and hence emotionally, charged context' in which people watch television (2000: 50) is supported both practically and theoretically by her observations of the manner in which her interviewees interact with each other and with the narratives of self, other and nation on offer during prime-time viewing. Class, religion and gender are constantly isolated and called upon as categories that are both moulded by and help to fashion women's experiences of television. For instance, the 'new consumerism' evident in advertisements on national television channels is connected by Mankekar to the increasing misery and frustration of lower-middle-class daughters who are pressurised to work to provide 'luxury' items as part of dowries for their younger sisters; similarly:

> Discourses of sexuality articulated in the narratives and practices of lower-middle-class viewers converged with those found in serials … These discourses drew from and reinforced prevailing representations of the sexuality of daughters in many north Indian cultures … 'Good daughters' always deferred to the authority of the patriarchal family; in contrast those who transgressed their assigned 'place' in the patriarchal family were severely punished by exile, profound emotional anguish or suicide. The moral of these stories – that unmarried women

had to be 'protected' by their families – reinforced the patriarchal family's authority to control their sexuality.

(2000: 118)

With regard to mythological soap operas Mankekar notes that 'by conflating their construction of Woman with individual women, narratives of "Indian Womanhood" like the one contained in Draupadi's disrobing deny women a complex subjectivity ... the conjuncture in which the *Mahabharat* was produced and received was marked by the "hijacking" of mainstream Indian nationalism by Hindu nationalism'. In *Doordarshan's* version of both the *Ramayan* and the *Mahabharat*, '[t]he humiliation of women is avenged by men who interpret it as an assault on their masculinity' (Mankekar 2000: 252, 217).

Several of Mankekar's interviewees relate anecdotes indicating the ways in which televisual narratives of female 'confinement', 'rebellion' or 'punishment' are echoed in their own experiences with strangers, mothers, fathers, husbands and in-laws. They sometimes express appreciation for the manner in which they are being 'protected' from possible molestation outside the home and sometimes evince scorn for the notion that remaining within the family space guarantees one's sexual safety.[5] These findings are interestingly similar to those described in relation to textual accounts of Hindi film viewing presented in Chapters 4 to 8.

Of even more relevance to discussions of gender, Hindu nationalism and popular culture in Chapter 7 is Mankekar's treatise on the ways in which the explicitly racist, casteist, patriarchal and authoritarian representations of human relations in the televised version of the epic *Ramayana* are understood and discussed by lower-middle-class women in her sample. Both contextual and textual, the discussion focuses on the ways in which the televised serial constructs an 'imagined community' of Hindu viewers based on patriarchal authority, violence and the exclusion of 'Others' who are coded as being intellectually inferior, sexually predatory and morally evil. Noting that 'gender and sexuality are central to the construction of militant Hindu identities' (2000: 166), Mankekar quotes right-wing ideologues who maintain that the serial has energised Hindus by reminding them of their 'heritage' and of what they owe to themselves and to the 'God' Ram. As far as the viewers in Mankekar's sample are concerned, while most are drawn to multimodal aspects of the programme such as music and choreography that are reminiscent of Hindi films, almost all the Hindu viewers appear to be encouraged by the serial's ideological call and use it to 'consolidate their Hindu identity' and to naturalise the slippage between 'Hindu' culture and 'Indian' culture.

Tellingly, Mankekar notes that unlike Hindu viewers, the non-Hindu viewers never use the words 'culture' or 'history' in relation to the serial and, where they choose to view it, do so simply as a 'story' (2000: 183). Mankekar draws the conclusion that while the serial has a limited range of discourses, the responses to it are heterogeneous as '[v]iewers' interpretations of what they watched were mediated by their class, gender, generation and ethnicity'. She continues: '[t]hese modes of engagement contradict representations of mass culture as totalising or intrinsically manipulative, and that of consumers of mass culture as homogeneous or passive' (2000: 223). These conclusions, while based specifically on television viewing in India, are reiterated to a certain extent in Nandini Bhattacharya's survey-based study of South-Asian diaspora women watching 'Bollywood' in their American basements (2004: 175), where responses about mothering, nation, gender and Hindi films all confirm that while many viewers do concede that both for themselves and their children they read 'moral messages' and 'life lessons' into the films, these 'messages' are not seen as straightforward or monolithic and may serve as precursors for discussion, challenge, humour, irony or disavowal.

In relation to critical theory notions of ideological interpellation, Mankekar's discussions of programmes about gender, patriotism and nationalism break down individual viewers' affective investments in narratives about war, honour and the nation to show that balanced against supposedly eulogising attitudes towards the nation are more simple fears about being left alone (because of some national crisis); about being a woman in a society that *demands sacrifice*; and about having to look and behave as if one is strong, regardless of the external circumstances. Thus, she suggests, nationalist narratives that try to play on viewers' sense of pride in a certain type of national subjectivity are not always successful in smoothing out contradictory feelings on the part of *female* viewers who might see themselves as marginal to, or even threatened by, the events in these narratives (2000: 287–8). Mankekar's constant unpicking of national, political and community rhetoric about Indian and/or Hindu 'tradition' initiates repeated assessments of the forces actually shaping India's national identity (which includes the nation's relationship to tropes of 'modernity' such as 'luxury' consumer goods) whether via, in collusion with, or entirely unrelated to, television programmes.

2.4 Conclusion

One of the advantages of a study which invokes the perspectives of audiences, or sections of an audience, as well as examining films directly is the facility with which hypotheses about the feelings and desires of the 'masses' and about the deployment and effects of discourses on gender, sexuality or religion/ethnicity/nation, can be tested and challenged. Similarly, the need to view concepts like tradition and modernity within the framework of a variety of political and aesthetic ideas utilised by spectators should alert us to the possibility that films may work at different times in the interests of differing sections of an audience and, indeed, that the actual meanings and pleasures which spectators make from the filmic discourses, though frequently predictable, are never entirely transparent. Indeed, efforts have been made by studies in the media ethnography and post-structualist Cultural Studies traditions to distance audience research from simplistic assumptions about the connection between fictive 'images' and 'real' readers' psychic responses (Cf. Clover 1992; Buckingham 1993 and 1996; Barker and Brooks 1998; Mankekar 2000).

An acknowlegement of potential ambiguities in the interpretative process is, I suggest, highly relevant to an analysis of audience responses to gender, sexual and ethnic representation in twenty-first-century Hindi commercial cinema. Asha Kasbekar (2001: 289, 305) notes correctly that the complex role of the female spectator of Hindi films has yet to be explored fully, especially in relation to the pleasures of erotic spectacle. In the recent collection *South Asian Women in the Diaspora* (2003) frequent reference is made to Butlerian notions of subversive 'performance' of identity. In 'Undressing the Diaspora' Bakirathi Mani examines 'clothing as a vehicle for the performance of ethnic identity' (2003: 117), discussing the types of 'mixed' clothing (Indian scarves with jeans, shorts with kurtas, etcetera) popular with diasporic youth in North America and the transgressive status of these clothing choices, in the light of discussions about drag queens and the subversive potential of 'staging' dress. Correctly, Mani cautions that clothing also essentialises by effectively 'creating' gendered and sexual ethnic subjectivities. Seemingly, however, despite this warning, while the individual or group performances of ethnicity available to *diasporic* youth are proffered for consideration as 'an epistemological confrontation with the narrative paradigms of multicultural states' (2003: 130), little attempt is made to unpick the problematic manner in which *diaspora* itself is often deliberately *constructed* as *more open to the potentials* of 'performative' identity and hybridity, than anywhere 'back home'. Even in audience studies 'female viewers' are still being discussed *en masse* and in others we appear to be returned to a dualist framework in which the 'hybrid' (diaspora) is opposed to some 'authentic essence'. So where does this leave other understandings of media reception, other projects for social change, other sites of cultural struggle, other 'collective' audience identities such as class and religion, for instance?

Derné (2000), to a certain extent, and Mankekar (2000), entirely, move towards an understanding of cultural consumption in India as comprising interwoven processes of *negotiation* between individuals and texts, producers and texts, individuals and sociocultural groupings as well as between individuals and their own prior experiences. In their view, the *immediate* context of viewing – namely the companions with whom one attends a film showing or watches a programme, the location and type of theatre or the position of the television in the type of living room – is central to the experience of Hindi film or television texts and might influence, alter or even shape entirely an interpretation of a textual message or representation. In an attempt to historicise and relate current hypotheses around the function of cinema-halls, Chapter 3 offers a brief review of literature regarding the social function of cinema-going in Britain, India and the United States of America, assesses the types of cinema and home viewing experience open to youth in London and Bombay and, via extracts from field notes and from in-depth interviews, explores the physical and psychological contexts in which Hindi films are encountered. Refusing to see Hindi films either as inconsequential or as 'vehicles for ideology', it is concerned to articulate the Hindi film viewing event in its totality, where the film can become part of a larger set of experiences and criteria for choosing or refusing the choice of similar future experiences. Among the issues raised are, first, the extent to which young audiences in both cities use the cinema as a semi-private space; second, the question of whether viewing in the context of a living-room/family environment becomes a marker of social inclusion or exclusion and, third, the manner in which the social context of viewing may alter, shape and/or reinforce personal responses to specific aspects of Hindi films.

3
Contemporary Hindi Film-Going and the Viewing Context in Two Countries

3.1 Why watch audiences?

At a commonsense or superficial level, people everywhere have beliefs and opinions about the reasons why others go to the movies and the things they do there. Take, for instance, these statements by middle-aged middle-class men and women I spoke to in Bombay[1]: 'Lower-class men whistle at the screen when a heroine walks on, they cause all the disturbance, education will change that'; 'College students go to the cinema to watch rubbish – they have no taste these days!'; 'Television is a more comfortable way of watching films than going to the cinema'; 'No decent woman wants to see nudity in Hindi films'; 'Lower-class people are only attracted to the cinema halls because of the sex-rape scenes and all the fighting, nowadays films are cleaner so these types don't attend so much.' Some of the assumptions made here are so evidently prejudiced along lines of class or gender that we might discount them. Others contain more subtle misapprehensions and may well enter cultural studies literature around Hindi films without much debate.

Supposedly at a more analytical level, many major strands of film theory have focused on textual representations and claims about spectators have been 'derived' from the encounters between critics or theorists and texts. Noting this, Christine Geraghty (2000: 1) argues that 'studying how we watch films – in multiplexes, on video, in theme parks, on television – is an important part of understanding what films mean within a culture' and, according to Henry Jenkins (2000: 166) 'the difference between audience research and other film theory is not whether or not we discuss spectatorship, but how we access and talk about audience responses.' In the light of such beliefs, in this chapter, after reviewing the books and articles currently in circulation about the cinema hall experience of film-goers in Britain, the United States and India during the last century, I present some of the reasons that young Hindi film-goers in Bombay and in London give for going to the cinema. In addition, I describe, albeit in a partial and episodic manner, the behaviours they evince while visiting cinema halls.

Throughout my analyses, I attempt to retain a sense of having been and continuing to be an individual viewer, a member of sundry Hindi film audiences past, present and future. Also, and equally importantly, it is crucial that the data and findings I delineate be read in the context of theories of identity such as those outlined by Wendy Hollway (1989). Such an awareness, of the ways in which subjects' accounts of themselves and their environment contribute – albeit in a tortuous manner – to knowledge of the social domain, informs all discussions and descriptions of cinema-going in this chapter. Linked to such a concern should be a recognition both of the 'roles' that people frequently perform within families and of the ways in which these roles can alter narratives of film viewing produced in response to specific interview questions (cf. Buckingham and Bragg 2004). As such, this chapter's concern, throughout, remains *the social meanings of the act of cinema-going*. Pertinently, in a recent study, Rajinder Dudrah reflects on how Hindi film-going and narratives about viewing Hindi films may be construed in the lives of some diasporic South Asians. Noting that 'Bollywood films ... transcend national sensibilities both in their production and distribution' (2002: 20), Dudrah takes a look at the ways in which diasporic Hindi cinema-going in the United Kingdom, both pre- and post-video boom, is used both as an end in itself and for a number of other social purposes such as family get-togethers, meetings with influential members of the community, relaxation and socialising. A section on the history of Birmingham's main Hindi film venues argues forcefully that these histories are deeply implicated in the changing of patterns of differential racial access to urban space and to the 'making visible' of Black British people as citizens who, 'on the way to becoming spectators', 'move through the city' (2002: 27). This metaphor for claiming a space for oneself in a city via movement through it on the way to cinema halls has a specially poignant resonance for many of the young people in my study.

In Bombay, especially, the dual desire to remain invisible from 'adults' who would reject or punish their cinema-going (especially in mixed-gender groups) but also to enjoy the treats of being visible in more affluent and unfamiliar parts of the city appear repeatedly in accounts of viewing; in London, the 'inability' to enjoy public space beyond the marginal or ghetto areas by going to mainstream theatres in 'town' was clearly linked both to age and class as well as family ethos, and many I spoke to were unwilling to admit that they had never been alone to Central London let alone to a cinema there. Thus identities, of various sorts, are performed and rehearsed during film viewing and the interview process. Of course, the extent to which young people use the cinema halls as physical spaces of escape or seclusion from their families, as opposed to venues for meeting with friends and sharing family outings, will be a key issue in coming sections. Throughout this chapter, however, Janet Staiger's warnings that watching a film is certainly *not a bounded event*, and that *talk in the movie theatre* does not necessarily entail engagement, critique or an impulse towards democracy (2000: 44–54), should be borne in mind.

3.2 Cinema halls and audiences in historical and geographic perspective

As Jenkins (2000: 172) notes: 'film theory's abstract generalisations about spectatorship often depend upon essentialised assumptions about "archetypal" exhibition practises.' However, the contexts within which films are consumed worldwide and have been consumed historically are tremendously disparate and varied. Three book-length studies (Docherty, Morrison and Tracey 1987; Gomery 1992; Stempel 2001) as well as a handful of articles (Geraghty 2000; Jenkins 2000; Williams 2000) provide insights into the British and American cinema hall experience at various stages during the twentieth century.[2] Indian cinema halls, too, have often been the subject of heated debate. S. V. Srinivas (2000) informs us about the viewing conditions in Andhra Pradesh viewing spaces in the 1940s and 1950s as well as about the debates over viewing conditions that raged in the Telegu film journal, *Roopvani*, during these decades, while Sara Dickey (1993) and Steve Derné (2000) in their respective ethnographies of sections of South (Tamil film) and North (Hindi film) Indian audiences provide sporadic insights into the contemporary urban cinemagoing experience.

According to Steve Derné (2000: 61): '[i]n most circumstances, filmgoing appears to be a liminal period of fantasy wish fulfilment, a time to play with the ambiguities that Indian culture emphasises, rather than a source of revolutionary change in Indian thinking or individual behaviour.' While the notion that in order to be socially significant or psychologically meaningful films must encourage, or be responsible for, overt displays of 'revolutionary' or 'pathological' behaviour is at best highly questionable, if the *act* of film-going is crucial to understanding

Indian viewers' relationships to the cultural products they consume, then it is reasonable to assume that some description of this context is called for in a study of Hindi film audiences.

From the cockroach and rat-infested, spit-stained and sweaty cinema halls of the Bombay suburbs in the 1970s to the plush air-conditioned spaces of newly constructed viewing spaces in contemporary Bombay and Delhi,[3] from the modern seats, screens and auditoria in Kuala Lumpur mall theatres to the cosy, old-fashioned ambience at an 'Asian' cinema hall such as the *Himalaya Palace* in London, Hindi films have been viewed in a range of 'public' contexts. Srinivas, noting that there were in fact 'protracted struggles across [India] asserting the right of lower castes to be physically present' (2000) at film showings, goes on to describe how, in India, during the 1940s and 1950s:

> cinema halls had up to five different classes, ranging from the floor class – the cheapest in which audience sat on the floor – to 'Reserved' or 'Box' which had chairs or even sofas ('Bhalaki', 1951: 37). All classes had separate seats for women, which were sometimes partitioned by bamboo, wooden or tin screens ... whenever new films were released, cinema halls were packed beyond capacity in all classes ... theatres were poorly ventilated and fans were too few or didn't work at all ... dogs roamed freely around the auditorium; there were no toilets in some halls and in others they were dirty ... Adding to the general discomfort, women brought infants who wailed at crucial points in the film.
>
> (Srinivas 2000)

Notwithstanding this depressing plethora of sensory discomforts – Srinivas differentiates between those caused by management contempt and negligence and those to be laid at the door of 'uncivilised' and inconsiderate cinema patrons – viewers attended cinema halls by the hundred and filled performances to overflowing, as they continue to do today in many parts of India. Nor have the conditions in certain cinema halls improved all that much since the 1930s. Fire safety in Indian cinema halls is a concern to many and tragedies such as the one at the New Delhi *Uphaar* theatre[4] continue to occur due to poor conditions, negligent construction and/or dubious management practices such as keeping fire doors chained shut or turning a blind eye to smoking in the foyer. Overcrowding and pressure on toilets during the intervals lead audience members to further abuse the facilities: on three occasions in six months, I noticed mothers allowing small children to urinate either in the hand-basins of Bombay cinemas or actually along the side aisles. And, while one might be tempted to think of such unsavoury viewing

conditions as a 'Third World' phenomenon, there is testimony to suggest that in London, too, the contemporary Hindi film viewing experience may be plagued by off-screen difficulties. In an article entitled
'The State of Our Cinema Halls!', the editor of the online 'asiagigs' mag-
azine laments the disrepair and lack of punctuality at Hindi film showings in London. I include this account in order to temper the tendency
towards a romanticising of the sensory aspects of a trip to the cinema
to watch a Hindi film that may be a feature of the next section of this
chapter:

> You are greeted with a miserable looking building in desperate need of
> a facelift ... rude (maybe unintentional and typical Asian customer
> service) staff, smelly halls (old seats, which they forgot to change when
> the buildings were purchased!) ... Majority of these places have poor
> sound systems ... stale popcorn [or] extortionately priced samosas ...
> During the film, the experience is like being at home. Whistling ...
> loud comments from the audience, constantly ringing mobile phones,
> people walking in and out of their seats during the performance ...
> Toilets are usually ill-equipped.

Although this account clearly covers management issues such as time-
keeping and cleanliness, Srinivas's analysis of *Roopvani* readers' letters
leads me to note that complaints such as those about noisy behaviour by
audience members represent one strand in a long-running battle for
control of the cinema hall space. This conflict is also, and perhaps more
importantly, one which contests the definition of a genuine 'film viewer'
and raises questions about who *may* and who *may not* call themselves a
member of an audience.

As Srinivas (2000) has pointed out, the configuration of such a thing
as an 'audience' consciousness amongst those who visit cinema halls is
a complex affair, which far outstrips mere sociological portraits of those
who attend the spaces demarcated as cinema halls. The democratising
influence of cinema within the public sphere cannot be taken for granted,
nor can any particular spectator's sense of empathy with the rest of the
'public' in the shared space be presupposed. As may be seen when working-
class Neetu remarks that her family try not to sit with the rowdies in the
lower stalls, but are forced to do so due to financial pressures; and in
Kalpesh's remark that in India audiences really know how to 'enjoy themselves', young spectators from different genders, religions, castes, classes
and cities prove repeatedly during their responses and comments that
those who attend cinema halls are not a homogeneous mass, but frequently enjoy and dislike, return for and critique entirely different and

often unexpected aspects of films and film-going. Moreover, while the attendance at cinema halls – even those which provide unsavoury conditions – might suggest devotion to the medium on the part of those who attend, the other aspects of cinema-going, such as its propensity to be utilised as a place where families and friends can socialise or couples can gain privacy, must be taken into account when assessing the role of Hindi film viewing in the lives of young people.

3.3   Going to the cinema in Bombay: reality, refuge or romance?

On numerous occasions during my observations, I attended the movies that happened to be showing at the time. These ranged across genres: *Aks* (*Reflection*, Rakesh Omprakash Mehra 2001) a thriller, *Lagaan* (*Tax*, Ashutosh Gowarikar 2001) and *Lajja* (*Shame*, Raj Kumar Santoshi 2001) broadly classifiable as social films; *Gadar: Ek Prem Katha* (*Hurricane: A Tale of Love*, Anil Sharma 2001) an 'Action romance'; *Yaadein* (*Memories*, Subhash Ghai 2001) a 'family' romance; while *Love Ke Liye Kuch Bhi Karega* (*I'll do Anything for Love*, Fardeen Aktar and E. Niwas, 2001) and *Dil Chahta Hai* (*The Heart Yearns*, Farhan Aktar 2001) were urban romantic comedies. *Yaadein* and *Lagaan* made it onto the UK top-ten lists, while *Dil Chahta Hai* and *Lajja* were screened at theatres across London. *Gadar: Ek Prem Katha* (set against the backdrop of vicious Sikh–Muslim/Hindu–Muslim partition riots and replete with anti-Pakistani sentiments) was a hit across the North of India, but not as popular with diasporic audiences.

At one run-down theatre in Bombay, a young Muslim taxi-driver told me that he found the entire film and what he characterised as its 'pro-Hindu tone' unsettling because, to him, it was mixing politics with entertainment in a way that stirred up communal tensions. Its love story he viewed as a mere 'pretext' (*bahana*) for inciting religious intolerance. I will return to such feelings about films in Chapter 7.

During a visit to a suburban cinema hall called *Shaan* in Bombay (Figure 3.1) where *Gadar* was showing, I encountered young people from poorer backgrounds. Because of this theatre's less well-heeled image (it is almost 25 years old and the upholstery shows it), its clientele is different from that found in Central Bombay cinemas and the newer suburban theatres. Despite heavy rain, almost 60 people were waiting from 3 until 6 because they had failed to get tickets for the 3 o'clock showing:

Shaan, August 2001. 4.30 p.m.   I speak first to three young women construction workers originally from Kolhapur in central Maharashtra.

Figure 3.1 Entrance hall at Shaan theatre, Bombay

Each carries a baby ... They see Hindi films twice a month, on off-days from construction work while, they tell me enviously, their 'men' (*mardlog*) go to the pictures at least twice a week. I ask about why they like the films. They tell me 'storyline' and 'narrative' (*kahani*), and the young men with them – whom they say are their brothers (they prefer to see films with their 'brothers' rather than with their husbands, but when I ask why they start to giggle) – come forward and tell me they like to watch 'romance' (said in English) and 'love stories' (said in Hindi). The last films the women saw were *Rahul* (the story of a little boy) and *Chori Chori Chupke Chupke* (CCCC; about a rich family's search for an heir and the use of a surrogate mother to produce one). I ask what they liked about CCCC and why they are seeing *Gadar*. They tell me first that they like the stories, but then ... it appears that the stories are often perceived to be remote from their lives; they say that they cannot understand why people do the things they do in the films ('why do they hide [significant bits of information] from each other? ... rich folk are strange' (*Chupathe kyon hai, amir log ajeeb hote hai*)). When I repeat, 'what is it you like?', they reply 'setting', 'the beautiful landscapes', 'the buildings'; they are in awe of a church they saw in CCCC. One woman says, 'we work making all these [buildings], sometimes we want to see what they look like inside' (*apni mehnat se banthi hai, yeh sab ...*) and the others nod. I ask if they consider Sunny Deol, the star of *Gadar*, a good actor, and they shake their heads. 'He's an old man now!' (*Budda ho gaya*), says one of the 'brothers' and the women laugh. When I repeat my question about why they are prepared to wait three hours in the rain and pay so much money to see a film in which they don't even like the star, they tell me that it is 'the whole experience': buying the tickets with their own money, eating 'wada pao' (bun stuffed with fried potato), sitting with their little kids in air conditioning. Primarily, they dwell on how 'beautiful' (*sundar*) and clean (*saaf*) everything is and how tasty the food is outside that you 'just have to buy it'.

The public context of the conversation with these young female construction workers militated against any personal revelations about individual lives and attitudes to films. Nevertheless, it was possible to see that they genuinely felt excitement and pleasure in the experience of going to the cinema (Figure 3.2). Their derogatory comments about the storyline and behaviour of characters in CCCC suggest a viewing position that remains aloof from much of the melodramatic tension on screen. Their strong sense of themselves as belonging to a particular class, and as being different from the middle and upper classes depicted in films, remains with them even in the cinema hall environment and interacts with other aspects of their lives to shape their interpretations of the

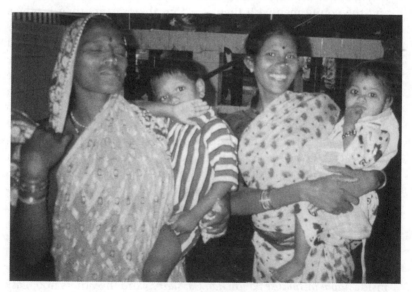

Figure 3.2   Young construction workers waiting for the next show

films. Their experience of films was, of course, also one that included the *act* of 'going to the cinema' as a pleasurably sociable leisure activity.

Describing movie going in America from the 1920s onwards, Gomery emphasises the sensory allure of theatre attendance; 'bathed in cool air, going to the double feature and having a coke and a bag of popcorn had become a part of the fabric of American life' (1992: 81). A few years on and 'Drive-in theatre owners sold not only an assortment of candy and soft drinks and fresh popcorn, but also hotdogs, coffee, milkshakes, ice-cream, toffee apples, steak sandwiches, hamburgers, pizza and potato chips' (1992: 81). Like many of Gomery's American viewers, several youth I interviewed associate cinema-going with the consumption of food, the presence of friends, and a chance to relax away from the heat. An amusing table, included in Vasudevan (2001b) contrasts the hot buttered popcorn and passing perfume smell of Delhi's PVR Anupam with the fresh food, fresh tea and fresh piss smell of Swarn Talkies.

Clearly, class differences are discernible in the food sold inside cinema halls as well as in the upkeep of halls. Indeed, the cold air and hot popcorn of the *PVR Anupam* correspond to the atmosphere to be experienced at a new theatre like *Movietime* in Malad, Bombay, which charges significantly higher prices for tickets than theatres like *Pinky* or *Shaan*, and also operates a telephone booking and advanced ticket delivery service clearly aimed at an up-market audience. In Figure 3.3, the bottles of

Figure 3.3   Inside the Gaiety-Galaxy complex, Bombay: middle-class refreshments

mineral water and coca-cola being sold alongside hot dosas, omelettes, samosas and tea at the stall are all comforting on a rainy evening.

This sense of the cinema being a 'liminal' space in which viewers can elude, for a while at least, the material conditions of their social status in the 'outside world' while partaking in the utopia created both on- and off-screen, is not confined to viewers in locations such as Bombay. Christine Geraghty (2000: 3) argues that in Britain between the 1940s and 1960s, '[c]inema remained a place of refuge from privations outside', and both white and Afro-Caribbean A-Level students in South-East London told me that they liked nothing better than to 'lose' themselves in a 'warm' cinema hall, with wide seats, plenty of coke, popcorn and a good sound system. Coextensive with such a conceptualisation of the cinema-going experience as 'escape' in a very physical sense from the material conditions of the audiences' lives, the 'escape' offered by cinema halls can be a psychological and social one.

According to less well-off male viewers, significant numbers of young married men, too, spend as much time as possible with their friends hanging around movie theatres, waiting in queues to buy tickets or viewing films. This suggestion was echoed by the younger women manual labourers (quoted above), whose husbands attended Hindi movies twice a week and almost never took them along. In all cases it was both the ambience of the whole experience – eating food at roadside stalls (Figure 3.4), relative privacy, sitting down in the dark with friends or relatives, the colours and songs – that was referred to as the reason for such regular attendance along with the presence of particular actors and the narratives of specific popular films. Summing up this finding in relation to his own research in the Madhya Pradesh city of Bhopal, Amit Rai (2002) writes that experiences of Hindi cinema viewing challenge us 'to understand contemporary film culture as a complex negotiation of history, pleasure, and commodity culture – as a sometimes raucous, comedic, but always differential bodily experience of social and cultural power'.

My findings diverge from Derné's (2000: 33, 36) in so far as in Bombay there appear to be significantly more groups of young women and girls attending films without male companions (Figure 3.5) than there appear to be in Dehra Dun, and also larger numbers of women – housewives, labourers, domestic servants, schoolgirls and college students – sitting in the cheaper front seats. Interestingly, while none of the female viewers in Bombay stressed, or felt safe commenting on, their use of cinema halls as venues for romantic trysts with boys/young men, several young men insisted that their girlfriends were the ones who initiated trips to

Figure 3.4   Food outside the cinema hall – part of the cinema experience

Figure 3.5   Three young women, unchaperoned, attend a 6–9 p.m. showing of *Devdas* in Bombay

the cinema by 'insisting' that they should be taken to see specific – usually highly romantic – films.

In addition, in Bombay, younger women too participate in film viewing rituals such as singing along, shouting out, clapping for dialogues they approve of, whistling at sexy heroes or passing sardonic comments, though to a lesser extent than men and often when in the cover of a group and/or as an act of self-conscious and quasi-parodic bravado when encouraged by friends. During a showing of *Lagaan*, when the character Gauri was shouting 'Bhuvan!', the name of her beloved, on screen, a young woman in the audience called out in a fake masculine voice, 'I'm here Gauri! How long I've been waiting for you!', eliciting screams of applause from her friends and rude comments from men around them. Interestingly, at another showing of *Lagaan*, it was a male youth who responded to Gauri's call with, 'I'm down here, come and get me!' On several occasions, as during showings of *Astitva* (*Existence*, Mahesh Manjrekar 2000) and *Lajja* (*Shame*, Raj Kumar Santoshi 2001) young women broke into spontaneous and prolonged applause during 'feminist' speeches by screen characters.

An issue which requires further exploration is the notion that the 'liminal' space of the movie theatre, or even the living-room when a film is being screened on television, separates not only the actual act of viewing but also the content of the films from the actions, attitudes and beliefs of everyday life. One of my most fascinating observations occurred at a showing of *Lajja* in the 'Cinemax' in Goregaon, a fairly recent and nicely decorated Bombay cinema hall:

> **September 2001:**   Well before the show starts [6.15], the theatre is 'housefull' … By the time the doors open, there are several (I count ten) groups of young women, crossing class and religion, as well as a fair number of family groups. There are more men visible now, although they are mainly with college or family groups. The woman across the aisle from me has a toddler. As the titles come up, this viewer, who looks in her early twenties and is dressed in a salwar khameez, puts her little daughter in the aisle and gives the child the end of her dupatta [scarf] to hold on to. It seems like a practised gesture and she exhibits no anxiety about her toddler thereafter. Throughout the film, I hear the noise of tongues clicking in irritation when unjust things happen, and hisses of anger or disapproval when there is violence against women. Young women, some in jeans, others in salwar khameez, stand up and cheer for Madhuri Dixit, [the pregnant dancer, betrayed by her boss and deserted by her lover]

when she makes a rousing speech criticising the actions of Sita in the *Ramayana*. There is applause from men as well as women when a bride-to-be stands up and denounces her marriage ceremony as a sham because the in-laws keep asking for more dowry. The loudest approval and applause from men and younger women, however, is elicited by Ajay Devgan, in his role as the old-fashioned aveng-ing angel/bandit, when he thunders on-screen with his strong UP accented Hindi and his bright sword. People scream at him and clap-ping covers his first speech. There is clapping from many of the women and a few men in the audience during Manisha's didactic femi-nist speech and people stay till the end credits roll, in contrast to the showings of *Yaadein* I attended where they began to exit the hall before the end of the film. The film also elicits plenty of laughter, and I see no adults crying when the lights come on. The toddler next to me giggles and dances through the songs in the first half and doesn't join the other little girls and boys hurtling up and down the aisle all through the show. She holds the scarf her mother gave her tightly and chews on it at points. When she sees a woman on screen covering her head with a saree, this little kid tries to pull the scarf over her own head. During the scene when 50-year-old village mother, Rekha, is being beaten and raped by the upper-caste men because her son has dared to love a high-caste girl, in the audience, the little girl's mother allows the end of her scarf to drift out of her grasp; her toddler moves off at first then scuttles back and stands in the aisle next to her engrossed mother, screaming away when Rekha screams on screen, and then crying for several minutes unnoticed despite the change in narrative mood. Outside and after the film, I hear comments like: 'Must get so and so to see it' and 'I really liked Madhuri's character' from college girls, and also one Maharastrian man saying to his female compan-ions, 'I really liked it but how many men will that appeal to?'

My observations suggest that many of those attending the showing were aware in advance of entering the cinema hall of the nature of the film's storyline. There were notable gestures of horror and disgust – ears were covered, heads turned aside – during the gang-rape scene, and cheering later when a slipper is thrown at the leader of the rapists. While horror is not a popular genre in India, the gestures I observed were reminiscent of those displayed by the women in trade-press photographs of audi-ences watching Hitchcock's *Psycho*. Analysing these photographic records of audience response, Linda Williams (2000: 367) notes that '[w]hereas the men look intently, most women cringe, refusing to look at the screen ... or they cover their eyes.' Interestingly, I noted that during Rekha's screams for help on screen, some men sitting with families and younger men in mixed-gender groups did not look at the screen or at their female companions, but looked instead at the ground until the altered tempo of the music alerted them to the arrival of the heroic man. Possibly the film's implication of masculinity in the torture of women, which broke men's direct gaze at the screen, was offset by its seemingly naive positing of bad men (who rape women to punish them) versus good men (who kill men to avenge the honour of women), which allowed male viewers to resume looking at the screen. One thing that must not be forgotten, in this context, is that the portrayal of rape on the Hindi film screen, which has a long and unsavoury history over the past four decades, has not and does not always elicit such a clear response of dis-identification from watching male members of the audience (cf. *Father, Son and Holy War*, Patwardhan 1994; Derné 2000).[5] Similar to but surpassing Williams's men in the *Psycho* audience photographs, other men in other audiences where rape has been depicted on screen have asserted 'their masculinity' not only by looking but also by whistling and, in certain almost all-male audiences, by making gestures and calling out encouragement to the rapists on screen. Thus all observations of audience behaviour may be, by their very nature, fluid and misleading: the very presence of a certain type or composition of audience – in terms of genders, classes and religions – may provoke or suppress, encourage or alter individual responses. These responses, which in one sense can be seen as interactions with the texts being viewed, are in another, perhaps more important sense, interactions *between* audience members and have practical – and political – ramifications both during and beyond the moment of viewing in the cinema hall.

Alone in their homes, viewers who had been cheering in the cinema hall (as they told me) or had wept watching *Lajja* together with their relatives on DVD, told me that they did not feel either the confidence or the certainty that they had felt when watching the film in a group. Often young viewers came across as overwhelmed by a sense that others who watched the film, especially community and family elders, were 'hypocritical' in their support for down-trodden heroines as well as their overt abhorrence for customs like dowry on screen and their steady refusal of young people's rights off-screen. Nevertheless, when watching the film surrounded by supportive and appreciative others in the audience, young people testified to having felt a sense both of collective pleasure at the resistance to injustice and of justified outrage at the perpetrators of such injustice.

In Bombay cinema halls, if the theatres are not full to capacity, it is not uncommon for young men and women to arrive in groups, wait for the films to begin and then to move off in couples to seats which are empty at the back or sides of the theatre, away from their friends. Nikhil, a 25-year-old working-class Gujarati in Bombay explains how, 'if you think about it, the joy and pleasure, that kind of fun that you have seeing a film in a theatre, you can't have that seeing it on TV at home' and asserts that 'It is the feeling of going out to the theatre that adds to the fun.' Married and with a 9-month-old baby as well as two younger brothers and a sick mother living with him in a two room shanty-town house on the far outskirts of the city, Nikhil's anecdote about taking his first girl-friend to the cinema reveals one aspect of the role cinema halls have played in his life:

> I used to wait for her outside her school ... Actually, she wanted to see a movie, so I said yes. I had to impress her, didn't I? So I took her away from that area where we stayed. I took her to townside [proud voice] to the Metro theatre. We went when we were supposed to be at school. It was our last year. And there we were, sitting and watching, and I was just lost in some dream about her, my girl. I was holding her hand and it was cool in the theatre. There were so much crowds there also and everything and I was working late in the nights with my father ... so I was tired and I just rested my head on her shoulder, like this [bends his neck sideways] and then she suddenly got up and pushed me off and hissed in my ear, 'What is this rubbish picture we are seeing?' And I was somewhat stunned ... I had not even looked to see what was the film. I just wanted to impress her so I had bought the tickets without looking, thinking 'it's the *Metro* theatre' ... I tried to tell her, 'let's just stay there and watch', but she wouldn't let me touch her hand any more and then there was a girl dancing on the screen nearly [laughs] without clothes. Like she was dancing [pause] and my girl got up and annoyed everyone; she started to move out of the seats. She went to the foyer and I had to follow her.
>
> (NKL.1/*Hindi*)

The almost farcical nature of his encounter with the reality of his girl-friend's avowed taste in Hindi films, suggests that Nikhil's use of the cin-ema hall as a place in which to relax, impress her and be physically close to her were quite different from her use of the hall as a place of escape from her family and from school but also as a place of entertainment. Her genuine interest in the film and her anger at its vulgarity perplex

Nikhil not because he liked the movie and she didn't, but because he had not expected her to be so interested in the narrative or spectacle of the particular film they were watching. To him, the viewing of a film, during a workday, in an up-market theatre, was a partly symbolic gesture rather than an act of dedicated spectatorship (cf. Barker and Brookes 1998: 148). Another young man I interviewed explained how, on one occasion, he and his girlfriend had no sooner taken their seats in a cinema hall in order to be alone together undisturbed than they were spotted by an elderly male relative of hers ahead of them in the stalls and 'all hell broke loose'.

Not unexpectedly, most young people I spoke to in Bombay preferred to watch films with their friends and peers rather than with their parents. Problematising charges by some academic commentators that *all* Hindi films play to reactionary audiences who both publicly and privately accept and even identify with their (retrograde) ideological stances, the audiences I observed in Bombay responded very differently to the two supposedly 'youth' films *Yaadein* and *Dil Chahta Hai*. *Yaadein*'s unsophisticated and ideologically crass dialogues were met with humorous scepticism or scorn by some of the 18 to 24 age group, eliciting wisecracks during melodramatic scenes. In the course of a particularly emotionally charged sequence, when the hero, Hrithik Roshan, is to be married off to an heiress from another rich family and cries out, 'I am selling myself! I am for sale!', a young female member of the audience responded at the top of her voice, 'How much for? I'll buy you!', eliciting storms of laughter and clapping. Such laughter and clapping at ludicrous points in the narrative, and finally straightforward boredom, expressed by the number of youth talking almost continuously in the last hour, were the norm at other showings of *Yaadein*. Thus, I suggest, *while it is important to understand the mechanisms by which Hindi films attempt to mould and consolidate various collective identities amongst viewers, the strategies adopted to carry out this task vary from film to film and affect sections of audiences very differently*, pushing men into groups at times and at others uniting young people in nebulous or temporary ways which are central to an understanding of commercial Hindi cinema reception.

3.4 Hindi films in London: ethnic nostalgia or empowered viewing?

Diasporas have been and continue to be linked, *by definition*, to ideas of change and struggle as well as to ideas of nostalgia and stasis. Rather than discovering a single, coherent 'diasporic response' to the act of Hindi film viewing, I found major differences between the film viewing contexts and experiences of young British-Asian people from different communities in London. While many of the young people of Indian or Pakistani origin whom I interviewed (and who happened to come from lower-middle-class and middle-class homes) were fairly frequent visitors to Hindi cinema halls (at least once a fortnight), understood Hindi at least minimally, and also felt that their parents might be classified as greater film fans than they themselves; the teenage viewers from Bangladeshi homes, where the income was minimal and the language spoken quite different (meaning that parents were less likely to be ardent fans of Hindi films), described a totally different viewing experience. Unlike those of the young viewers from more affluent homes/communities, the narratives of spectatorship gathered from British Bangladeshi high-school and college students centred on the viewing of satellite television and videos in their homes or in the homes of friends or relatives, and very occasional trips with family, older brothers or sisters to view films in cinema halls.

Having observed audiences going to see the film *Lajja* in Bombay during its opening weeks and ascertained from interviewees in London that they had seen it with their families in London at suburban theatres over the same period, I visited a central London cinema hall to find out if young people would attend to 'escape' from the family crowds in Southall, and whether it was true that the Hindi film 'craze' started by *Lagaan* was really 'crossing over' to the white population. In Leicester Square, *Lajja* was showing with subtitles. The manager's comment that even when *Lagaan* was showing, there were rarely more than one or two non-Asians in the audience did surprise me. However, the fact that there were only 17 people at this weekday showing was not surprising in the light of the fact that tickets are priced at £9.50 or concessions £7.50, and are relatively expensive compared to those at some of the suburban halls showing Hindi films. Willesden Bellevue, having a 'cheap' day on Wednesdays, would have cost only £3.00 for the same film. A weekday showing of another new release, *Haan Maine Bhi Pyaar Kiya* (*Yes I too am in Love*, Dharmesh Darshan 2002) in February 2002 at this 'community' theatre yielded very different results:

> **Willesden Green 'Bellevue':** This is a matinee performance, yet there are over 100 people in a theatre whose seating capacity is 190. *Haan Maine Bhi Pyaar Kiya*, released at the weekend, has been moderately attended (35–50 persons) for all of its weekday showings, whereas *Kabhi Kushie Kabhi Gham* (aka *K3G*, *Sometimes Happiness, Sometimes*

Sorrow, Karan Johar 2001) was advance booked for six weeks after release and still draws crowds.

The Audience: Consists primarily of women aged 30 plus as well as little children, some in prams, some of primary-school age. There is not a single non-white face. Twelve teenage-looking girls, all but three dressed in salwar khameez. Six men, all clearly 30plus and accompanying families. The younger women have come with kids and prams rather than with other youth. This is a 'family' audience. In terms of religion and region there appear to be a few Nepalis, Hindu Gujaratis, Muslims (from India and Pakistan) speaking Hindi or Urdu as well as a few Punjabis. Hindi is the lingua franca. Some sit together before the show to exchange news, although they move to sit with families when previews begin. There is absolutely no flirting, no holding hands, no young people sit together ...

During the film: Little boys wander around and talk to their parents, climb over seats and ask for food. Other little children are fed and put to sleep. Several of the older women chat softly during songs and some even get up to walk around or change seats to get a different view ... The older women are at pains to ensure that some of the young women are enjoying the film. It appears that the choice of outing was theirs and several times I hear the question, 'Well, what do you think?', and replies like, 'It was quite boring but it's looking up now', 'The acting isn't that good, but Karishma's sarees are good', or 'The songs aren't that good' from jeans-wearing teenage girls to their aunts/mothers.

The notable absence of young men at this showing was repeated throughout my observations at daytime showings in Feltham, Wood Green and Southall. Similarly, the preponderance of 30plus women in the audience was also a feature of other observations. The manner in which younger children walked around during the showing and moved seats was another feature common to most daytime showings. Rather than being places where young people can go to escape from routine surveillance and gossip, as cinema halls in Bombay frequently appear to be, or where men of all ages go to 'watch' women on- and off-screen, during weekdays Hindi film showings in cinema halls in London appear to be places of social confluence and/or refuge for groups of 30 to 60-year-old South-Asian women. The character of the audience totally changes the character of the film viewing experience. When I asked young people outside evening showings of Hindi films why they don't go during the daytime, responses varied from, 'Why would I go anywhere where I can bump into my relatives?' and 'I've got school/college', to 'I'm not so interested in Hindi films – if I bunked college I'd go shopping and/or out with my boyfriend/girlfriend and/or to see the latest Hollywood release.' These feelings were echoed during in-depth interviews.

Other viewers, however, watched Hindi films from early childhood. A low achiever at school and with difficulties in English and comprehension in other subjects, Hamidul saw Hindi films as exciting and exotic entertainment rather than as purveyors of moral values. From a tremendously poor family on a council estate, he never went to the cinema to watch Hindi films but watched them with his mum and sisters at home. I was not surprised by how many recent Hindi films he had seen when he told me that he knows people who distribute pirated copies of VCDs and DVDs. Padma, a 22-year-old, British-Nepali student, recounted in a playful manner both the experiences of her mother and aunt, as well as her own experiences, watching Hindi films in different contexts:

Padma: [When I was a kid] back in the early eighties we didn't used to go to the cinema we had a secondhand VCR and my dad would come back from the restaurant, 'cause he'd live in the restaurant 'cause he didn't have the cash to travel there every day, and then he'd bring us five tapes and he'd go, 'you've got to watch 'em all today 'cause I've got to take them back tomorrow.' [laughter] And my mum and my aunt – we lived in a joint family – would be really confused and they'd put this film in and they'd go, '*Right* there's Amitabh Bachchan [pause] and Jaya Bahaduri [pause] and she dies in that movie', and the next film they'd put in and she's alive again and they'd be like, 'What on earth happened? She died!' [laughter] I started off watching pretty early, I was like glued to the TV. I think mum still gets confused now when we go to the cinema … Then, my uncle took my aunt to the cinema when they first got married and she was only 16, yeah, and like she told me, 'it was all dark and scary and it was really horrible', she had to shuffle past people in the dark and then 'this thing played and I didn't even know the language' … Now we go to the cinema at Harrow-on-the-Hill and [pause] there's one in East Ham where I used to go and [pause] Wood Green cinema, that's nice. I watched *Kabhie Kushie Kabhi Gham* at the Warner Brothers Cinema in Leicester Square with my mum – me, my aunt, my cousin and like a whole group of Asian Bengali women friends of theirs … We were all crying right from the beginning and when Shah Rukh Khan comes out with his sequinned shirt, a friend of my mum's comes over to us, like leans over to us, and says, 'He bought his shirts in Green street!' [laughter]. We were all sitting there going, 'is it good, is it good?', 'Yeah it's good', 'Are we crying yet?', 'Yeah, we are!' ... [laughter]

(PAD.1/*English*)

Padma's mixture of wry humour and sympathy regarding the 'mistakes' that her 'uninitiated' mother and aunt made watching films in their youth and her hilarity when recounting her own tearful appreciation of *Kabhi Kushie Kabhi Gham* signal her confidence and experience in the world of Hindi film viewing. Padma's viewing of Hindi films was, at different times, social and personal, a link to her community roots and an enjoyable pastime. However, her assessments of the films' ideologies moved, like those of many of the young viewers I interviewed, between critical scepticism and acceptance, depending on the extent of her cultural, political and life experience in relevant areas. As I will discuss in Chapters 4 to 8, the ability to move from sharp irony and critique to laughter and empathy with film narratives was a recurrent characteristic of discussions about Hindi films with young viewers.

Attending an evening showing of the film *Haan Maine Bhi Pyaar Kiya* at the Croydon Safari, I noted a wider age range, a more equal gender balance amongst South-Asian viewers and a larger proportion of young couples, both married and unmarried. The fact that both Hindi and Hollywood films show at the Croydon Safari ensures a diverse group of viewers. However, while three of the Asian couples I spoke to were going to see *Monsters Inc* or *Ocean's Eleven*, not a single non-Asian bought a ticket for the subtitled *Haan Maine Bhi Pyaar Kiya*, reminding me of Gary Younge's lament about the new Star City cinema complex just outside Birmingham:

> In this thirty-screen multiplex cinema ... globalised culture has been carved into celluloid slots and sold with popcorn. *Bichoo*, *Boys Don't Cry* and *High Fidelity* are just a few of the films showing within a few hundred metres of each other, but those who are watching exist alongside each other as in a parallel universe. This is where Hollywood meets Bollywood (to which six screens have been dedicated) and where different ethnicities congregate but rarely coalesce – a segregated experience within an integrated space.[6]

3.5 Conclusion

With regard to attendance at film theatres, a pattern emerges suggesting that viewing differentiates along lines of gender, country, class and life cycle. Married women in Bombay, girls from strict (highly religious and/or highly male-dominated) families in both London and Bombay and British-Asian boys from deprived communities/families were far more dependent on television and video as means for watching films than unmarried women in Bombay, those earning their own wage and young people from middle-class homes in London. Of those who visited the cinema most regularly amongst the youth I spoke with, college students appeared to have the greatest degree of leeway in terms of choice of companions and of films. However, in Britain, the picture is further complicated by the accessibility of Western films to youth, the importance of television viewing as a means of social integration at school (on this topic, see also Gillespie 1995) and the popularity of Hindi films in some South-Asian communities amongst women aged 30 or above.

In contrast to the data gathered in Bombay, my observations and interviews in London suggest that young British-Asians have different and sometimes more ambivalent experiences watching Hindi films. In the home and around the television set Hindi films can either be viewed as dull and/or harmless parental nostalgia, as 'normal' entertainment on a par with a soap opera such as *Eastenders*, or as exciting and educative links to an 'alternative' cultural frame; in the cinema, Hindi films can be viewed either: (1) with families, (a) with willing participation in such a cultural bonding ritual and form of sociable entertainment, or (b) as reluctant adjuncts to parents, 'dragged' along but preferring Hollywood films, or (c) as passive members of families willing to participate but not particularly interested in the films; or (2) with friends, (a) for pleasure because all are Hindi film fans, or (b) because there is a need to show allegiance/loyalty to distinctively 'Asian' as opposed to 'Western' cultural forms, or (c) a mixture of both these attitudes. Cinema halls showing Hindi films in London are rarely 'used' by viewers in the same way as cinema halls in Bombay. While almost all of those whom I interviewed were self-declared fans of Hindi cinema, there were scores of others whom I approached in London, but who politely refused as they had little interest in Hindi films and did not speak Hindi. By contrast, in Bombay I rarely found young unmarried people in the 16 to 26-year-old age group who did not watch Hindi films. In Bombay, even middle-class or highly educated young people, who said that they preferred the 'realism' of Hollywood and Arthouse cinema, had watched some of the latest blockbusters and knew older films such as *Padosan* (*The Neighbour*, Kesto Mukherjee and Jyoti Swaroop 1968), *Sholay* and *Pyaasa* (*Thirsty*, Guru Dutt 1957) as well.

Just as the ways in which young people respond to questions about their spectatorship may be altered by the context/s in which the social act of interviewing takes place, the social act of viewing films in a group along with members of an audience in a quasi-public space such as a cinema hall can have a profound impact on the nature of spectatorship encouraging certain types of meaning-making and suppressing or pathologising others. The laughter or tears of others, the ways in which their presence inhibits or confirms certain individual emotional impulses, the sardonic commentaries which introduce alternative ways of reading a text or confirm one's own scepticism (Staiger 2000: 52) can make the experience an entirely different one from that which might take place in the privacy or claustrophobic ambience of a living-room. Collective 'audience' anger and critique, experienced albeit briefly, or amusement, pity, disgust, desire, patriotism, irony and hatred, shared for however short a time and in whatever illusory manner, do indeed reaffirm loosely held beliefs, relieve loneliness and increase particular configurations of group identity for many young people. Similarly, the sense that one is a minority within a crowd of spectators – thinking and feeling unconventionally or subversively – and the knowledge that one must suppress these responses for fear of rejection or disapprobation, are also provoked in young people by cinema hall viewing. Thus it becomes apparent during observations at cinema halls as well as during in-depth interviews, that the consumption of Hindi films generally takes place in part via an interaction between individual and collective consciousness of filmic, narrative and cultural norms and expectations. In Chapter 4, I explore these norms and expectations in relation to family, romance, courtship and marriage by presenting case studies of responses to some of the most-watched Hindi films of the 1990s, primarily *Hum Aapke Hain Koun ...!* and *Dilwale Dulhaniya Le Jayenge*.

4

'A man who smokes should never marry a village girl': Comments on Courtship and Marriage 'Hindi Film-Style'

First in *Dilwale Dulhaniya Le Jayenge* (DDLJ) there was the carefree boy. And then this girl comes into his life, Kajol, she alters him incredibly ... it was the whole experience of being in love that changed him. When a man is in love, he is willing to go to different places. I just liked that part so much ... when he leaves London, and goes to Punjab following her. Finding any little excuse, he catches her. Even in my life, trying to meet with my girl is an enormous tension; it was so difficult, I had to watch everything and people watched me too, and her, and it was very hard to get time alone together. In DDLJ the way it is, it is so in my life too. There is so much similarity between my life and that in the movies, I can't even explain to you. Then there's the time when Shah Rukh talks to Kajol's mummy, it happened the same with me: I too had a talk with her mother. Her mother also advised us, she understood us. But her father doesn't know. He may suspect. Her father is exactly like Amrish Puri, strict, jealous, his face is always angry. I try so hard to make Uncle talk to me ... but he is always frowning and strict like the father in DDLJ.

(Rahul, 21-year-old viewer interviewed by author,
Bombay, 2002)

[I]n *Pardes* when Shah Rukh is with Mahima and they are talking about the cigarettes I didn't like that because [her fiancé] was lying to her and he should not have lied to the woman he was going to marry. It gives a bad image. *A man who smokes should never marry a village girl.*

(Meeta, 17-year-old viewer interviewed by author,
Bombay, 2000)

4.1 First, the texts

Here, both texts and audiences take centre stage. They do so not merely by means of the diverse narratives of viewing generated during the research around which this book is shaped but also via an analysis of both specific film sequences and critical commentaries on these films. This chapter is devoted to a case study of two of the movies which were discussed most fiercely by young interviewees in relation to romance and marriage – *Dilwale Dulhaniya Le Jayenge* (*The One with the Heart Takes the Bride*, henceforward DDLJ) and *Hum Aapke Hain Koun ...!* (*Who Am I to You?*, henceforward HAHK); concurrantly this chapter is committed to exploring the ways in which specific filmic embodiments of concepts such as 'romance', 'family' and 'tradition' interact with wider cultural conceptions of such ideas to become meaningful within young viewers' social and psychological repertoires.

In the late 1980s, two films, *Maine Pyar Kiya* (*I've Fallen in Love*, Sooraj Bharjatya 1989) and *Qayamat se Qayamat Tak* (*From Judgement Day to Judgement Day*, Mansour Khan 1988), challenged the reign of action films, which were increasingly centred on the depiction of gang violence, rape, pillage and vengeance.[1] Both *Maine Pyar Kiya*, with its child-like romance between Suman (played by the actress Bhagyashree), a poor motherless girl, and Prem (the then little-known Salman Khan), a rich youth whose father has a childhood friendship with Suman's father; and *Qayamat Se Qayamat Tak*, with its depiction of the rivalries between two high-caste Hindu (Rajput) families and the *Romeo and Juliet*-style romance of their children, played on the audiences' empathy with young love. However, while it might appear that both these films offered audiences visions of romance and marriage on young people's terms, their very different endings – in *Maine Pyar Kiya*, after a period of struggle, Suman and Prem are united with the blessings of their respective families whereas in *Qayamat Se Qayamat Tak* the daring lovers, who elope and live alone in a rural area, are annihilated by the violence of their male relatives – emphasise the power of the 'family' as a psychic and physical force in young people's lives.

Commenting on what she labels the 'patriarchal resolution' to the plot of *Qayamat Se Qayamat Tak*, Lalitha Gopalan (1998: 132) claims that '[t]his tragic end to the love story is credible only if we accept the rationale for the feud – Rajput family honour and shame – and acknowledge that love is an unmanageable desire in this patriarchal economy.' Disregarding the moments of fracture and critique located at different points in the film, Gopalan sees the primacy of what she views as a 'patriarchal' resolution, over any previous nuances, as a measure of the film's complicity with what she maintains is its 'regressive Hindu ending' (1998: 136). Whether or not we agree to such an elision between family, patriarchy and Hinduism, in particular, as takes place in Gopalan's analysis, the extent to which any complicity with the film's perceived 'Hindu patriarchal' frame of reference is *shared by viewers* may be ascertained partially, at least, by means of audience research.

Steve Derné, writing about *Dil* (1990) and *Qayamat Se Qayamat Tak* (QSQT), argues that such films, while celebrating love marriages, also confirm the idea that 'such marriages usually have disastrous consequences' and express the dominant view of love as a 'madness that should not be allowed to jeopardise family honour' (2000: 80). Excerpts from his interviews with North Indian male viewers appear to confirm his belief that the films serve both to open up fantastic possibilities for romance and 'individualism' and to *close down on real ones* by emphasising fear, danger and social norms via violent closure or family-orientated homilies on the humiliations of 'dishonour' (2000: 82–101). Following Uberoi (1998), Derné suggests that in the 1990s romantic Hindi films moved towards a foregrounding of the importance of duty (to parents, family and clan) and sacrifice to balance against individual love and, furthermore, based themselves on the premise that the true fulfilment of love through marriage can only take place within the bounds of benign family authority. While this may be the case, here I argue that the mere assertion of a conservatising tendency at the closure of films does not entail a similar trend in the thinking of young audience members. Indeed, focus on the 'lessons' of narrative closure is an abiding characteristic of ideological analysis of film.

But why are the endings of films accorded such dramatic significance and the other moments or sequences leading up to them so little interest? Taking issue with this style of analysis, Christine Gledhill (1999: 174) notes that 'the notion that the last word of the text is also the final memory of the audience ... derives more from the exigencies of the critical essay than from the experience of films, which has no such neat boundaries.' If it is facile to hold on to the view that a film depicting the amorous delight of screen lovers as well as their contextual punishment and destruction would enthuse real lovers about the prospects in store for them after elopement, then is it not equally mechanistic to assert the purely conservative appeal of such a film? Another textual critic, Jyotika Virdi, argues that while '*Qayamat se Qayamat Tak* accepts the impossibility of the romantic notion – heterosexual romance combating feudal/patriarchal authority' – it is 'intergenerational conflict' (2003: 185) which captures the imagination of the audience. Clearly, even purely textual readings can offer widely differing, even contradictory hypotheses about the aspects of a film that hold the greatest audience appeal. What, then, should be the grounds for any critical assertions about the pull of contemporary 'romantic' Hindi films?

In my view, by recording the stances taken up by viewers in relation to the narratives of diverse Hindi films and by examining the historical, cultural and social conditions in which these films become meaningful, it becomes possible to gauge, more accurately than via even the most plausible and internally cogent textual analyses, the variety of ways in which Hindi romances operate. Thus, drawing on analyses of film viewers' comments on DDLJ and HAHK, I will argue that quite apart from the overt physical, psychological and social satisfactions afforded by the viewing context, a whole host of complicated and sometimes nebulous sensations, opinions and possibilities are uncovered in talk about these films. Intertextual engagement with the star personae of the hero or heroine, emotional linkages between film scenes and personal experience, a sense of having 'escaped' from mundane problems, a sense of gaining knowledge or wisdom, the colours and beauty of the settings, release for real frustration via anger at screen characters, a sense of satisfaction at their own proficiency in responding to the narrative cues of the film, the chance to engage with depictions of forbidden or restricted experiences such as travel or romance, and enjoyment of the lyrics, music and dance sequences are only some of the pleasures implied[2] by viewers during their discussions of DDLJ.

4.2   Everyone's favourite movie

Rahul, 21-years-old, from a strict and caste-bound lower-middle-class family in Bombay, whose lengthy exposition prefaces this chapter, insisted that DDLJ was not only his '*favourite* movie and … *evergreen* movie', but was also '*deeply* important' in his life. Kavita, a 21-year-old Christian viewer from a lower-middle-class family, was similarly smitten, telling me, 'I've seen *Dilwale Dulhaniya* 25 times … in the cinema.' Padma, of a similar age and class background, but brought up in London, also asserted that, without a doubt, this was her '*favourite*' Hindi movie. During another interview, I mentioned DDLJ to Jomir, a working-class London school student, expecting him to dismiss the film – which was released when he was only 9 years old – as dated and sentimental. Instead, he told me it was a film he would 'never forget'. Such responses were echoed by two-thirds of the young viewers I interviewed in-depth and Jomir's explanation for his judgement – 'the storyline is just so realistic, you know. [Thwarted love] really happens in so many people's lives ... It's about the lives of people in our community' – is indicative of the film's promises of 'inclusion' and 'representation' for diasporic viewers.

Patricia Uberoi (1998) attempts to elaborate the ways in which concepts of duty and desire are configured against a backdrop of 'foreign' and 'Indian' settings in DDLJ and *Pardes*. She identifies two 'dilemmas of moral choice' in these films: their concern with the nature of Indianness and the transferability of this 'quality' and their reference to what she terms 'the animating logic of South-Asian Romance', 'the conflict between individual desire and social norms and expectations in respect of marriage choice' (Uberoi 1998). The first dilemma resonates differently, perhaps, with young people in India and those of South-Asian origin living in Britain. The second, which Uberoi sees as being resolved via the 'felicitous ideal of "arranged-love marriage", that is a style of match-making where a choice already made is endorsed, *post facto*, by parental approval', is the one with which this chapter is most immediately concerned, as, according to their own testimony, this is the very quandary that faces young people I interviewed. The ambivalent views of some young people in my sample regarding types of marriage are, I maintain, familiar in communities where large and close-knit families, and/or hierarchies based on religion, are the norm.[3]

Recent sociological studies of marriage and family in India and the South-Asian diasporas (Chaudhary 1998; John 1998; Shah 1998; Ghuman 1999; Ralston 1999; and Leonard 2000) confirm that while class–caste endogamy is still the norm and domestic violence against women and young people is rife in all communities, patterns of thought and behaviour are changing amongst some groups of youth. Like several others in my sample, Harish, a 23-year-old mechanical engineer in Bombay, and Alpa, a student in London, were keen to emphasise their commitment to the form of relationship which was not quite the strict 'arranged marriage' expected by elders in their communities. Harish asserted that, '[i]f the system is changing ... then I might do that – a semi-arranged marriage.' Alpa, meanwhile, explained 'even arranged marriages aren't so much arranged these days because you have so much freedom you can get contacts and you can meet people and only if you like them you go ahead.'

Notwithstanding her optimistic presentation of the options available to those who surrender their choice of partner, at least partially, to their parents, Alpa was engaged in a clandestine relationship with a young man at her college. She also expressed deep ambivalence about her 'identity', remarking, 'I feel as if I'm *in between*. Because I've been brought up here I feel as if obviously I'm going to have different values to traditional

Indian girls. But then in other ways I've got an Indian background and I'm not going to be totally different to Indian girls.' Whether the word 'traditional', in this instance, is to be read as the defining feature of all subcontinental Indian girls or whether it defines that subset of subcontinental Indian girls who adhere to certain rigid and sanctioned behavioural codes is not really relevant. What is at issue is the way in which Alpa sees her relationships with males outside the family, and her desire for certain kinds of romantic relationships, as somehow modifying, even diluting, her 'Indianness'. Taking the comments of young people like Neha, Alpa and Harish at 'face value', it should be evident that films such as DDLJ are not 'inventing' a category of 'arranged love marriage' or 'semi-arranged marriage'[4] so much as plotting their narratives and dialogues within evolving emotional and practical frameworks.

A film full of splits and fractures, *Dilwale Dulhaniya Le Jayenge* nevertheless manages to smooth over and disavow its own anxieties. To understand the positions which young people take up *vis-à-vis* this film, it is important to recapitulate the major events of which the 'master' narrative is composed: an opening sequence in London exposing the diasporic experience of one supposedly middle-class family, the Chaudharys – mother, father and two daughters – and another, richer, father–son duo, the Malhotras; a 'tour' of Europe, taken by Simran, the elder Chaudhary daughter, and Raj, the Malhotra boy, with their respective sets of friends, during which they fall in love; the discovery of this romance and the re-migration of the Chaudharys to Punjab in preparation for the arranged marriage of Simran to Kuljeet, the son of her father's friend; the arrival of Raj, followed by his father, in Punjab and their attempts to win over the Chaudhary family; and the final confrontation, before his departure back to London, between Raj and his sweetheart's father. The following section has been split into three subsections, each dealing with aspects of the film that were singled out for comment, praise or critique by young viewers.

4.2.1   Locating the subject: 'abroad' or 'at home' in cultural practice

DDLJ establishes its initial rapport with viewers via sequences in which South-Asian characters in London think (aloud), fantasise (about belonging or romance), interact with each other (and with birds) while offering glimpses of so-called 'London' life. The music segued in with parts of the credit sequence plays to the dual themes of nostalgia for India and the promise of romantic love. Meanwhile, the film's apparent 'realism' at the beginning – Trafalgar Square with pigeons in almost monochrome subtlety, the Embankment, the Thames, corner shops, suburban back gardens, rowdy youth in cars – is deliberately juxtaposed with Baldev Chaudhary's vivid, multicoloured fantasy of peasant women and mustard fields in India. The sequences of the film set in London, however, drew little comment from my interviewees in Bombay who often began their comments about the film at the point when Raj and Simran are alone *en route* to Switzerland.

Young female viewers in Bombay discussed the scenes preceding and following the European 'tour' or 'picnic' as a period of heightened emotional involvement for themselves and one that provoked thoughts about their own lives and their wishes to leave the confines of their homes for more extended periods than was acceptable to their parents. Neha, looking back at her natal family from the equally restrictive context of her in-laws' home, opened her comments about DDLJ by linking the heroine's circumstances with her own.

Neha: [In] *Dilwale* it is like Kajol's father is *too* strict, like my father also, it is such a situation where she has to take permission *even* to go for a picnic, like I used to. Whatever things she used to do, it was like clicking with my background, ke okay, I also was scared for asking permission, so something similar. And when she cries, it was just like it is happening to me. I used to see my father's exact image in Amrish Puri. He also loved the daughter but he was *too* strict.

(NHA.1/English)

Neha singles out Simran's lack of autonomy over her own life – 'she has to take permission, *even* to go for a picnic'– as the distinguishing feature of her similarity to herself. For her, the familial and *emotional* context of the heroine in the film, whose behaviour ('whatever things she used to do') and 'background' she saw as 'clicking' with hers, was more central to her description of pleasure in the film than the sequences of romance and fantasy. Preeta, unmarried, still a student and living unhappily with her parents, is acutely aware of the possibilities depicted in the film:

Preeta: The *best* scene I liked was when Kajol and Shah Rukh they met first, when she missed the train. *That* time. That was my favourite scene.
Shaku: Go on, tell me why.
Preeta: It was like they had never seen each other before. It was something which was shown so beautifully, it was picturised so beautifully, I like it very much. It makes me think of my own life. The romance. It made me feel *like that*.

(PTA.1/Hindi and English)

Neha's refusal to linger on the romantic relationship in DDLJ as contributory to her engagement with the film and Preeta's dwelling on this relationship as central to her enjoyment can, at one level, be attributed to their relative positions in their own communities and families. As the respectable eldest daughter-in-law in a family of traders, Neha either cannot allow herself to admit, or does not trust me enough to speak about, any premarital romantic longings she might have held. As such, the discussion of any form of enjoyment centring on the developing relationship between the two young lovers in DDLJ would, perhaps, be too close to the heart of what I assume to be her self-imposed prohibition.

In contrast, Preeta – according to her, the least favoured youngest daughter in a patriarchal family – feels, perhaps, that she has nothing to lose by admitting to herself her ambitions to assert her autonomy by leaving home before marriage, and to be involved in a passionate relationship such as the one depicted in DDLJ. Such analyses reiterate not only that viewing pleasures are not uniform, stemming as they do from individual viewers' variable emphases, but also that viewers whose circumstances alter over time may come to dwell on aspects of a film differently from when they first encountered the film.

Unlike responses such as the ones outlined so far, which tended to ignore the apparent *material* realism of opening scenes in London in favour of a kind of '*emotional* realism' (Ang 1985: 44) with which they clearly identified, several British-Asian viewers were keen to discuss the presentations of British-Asian life and behaviour, as well as the behaviour of the lead pair in Switzerland. After describing her working-class Hindu Gujarati family, Nisha announced that DDLJ was a film she really loved:

Shaku: What did you think about the scene with Shah Rukh and his mates in the car outside the store?

Nisha: I think it was realistic, ain't it? Because that's what happens, ain't it? That is *so* true. [pause] And that whole issue of her dad finding out that she likes this guy, and he sends her to India. I think that shows that it's [arranged marriage] maybe bad, but I don't think that all Asian parents are like this here. Some wouldn't send their daughter to India to get married.

Shaku: You mean?

Nisha: I mean if my parents found out that I had a boyfriend, they would meet him. And they'd talk to him. And find out what he's like....

(NIS.1/*English*)

Nisha assesses the film's modality by calling on her knowledge of British-Asian (male) youth and parental behaviour. Her initial implication of my own experience – 'that's *so* true, ain't it?' – of British-Asian adolescent behaviour, based on her awareness of my teaching background, positions us both as knowledgeable viewers and residents of London, able to construe the rowdy behaviour of the hero and his mates in a particular way. Remaining within the compass of the 'realistic' generalisability she has invoked, Nisha then notes the film's depiction of Simran's father as actively separating his daughter from her lover by sending her off to India, only to find that she herself cannot accept the implications of such a reading. At a practical level, then, the fact that Nisha believes her parents would act differently from Simran's father allows her to see the film not as an exact map of 'reality' for British-Asians, but as a representation or account of a particular type of British-Asian, experience. Nisha's quick movements of thought within a few minutes of talk and her desire to unpick her own assertions were characteristic of her reflexive attitude throughout the interview. I return to her comments on sex and marriage in later chapters.

In contrast to young female viewers in both cities, who tended to locate their interest in the father–daughter relationship and salient moments of pleasure in the early playfulness of the meeting between Raj and Simran, and on the tenderness of their behaviour to each other in foreign settings, several of the young British-Asian men in my sample evinced a clear preference for the second part of the film, which is set, supposedly, in Punjab. Jomir, for instance, was adamant about his aversion for the first half of DDLJ and justified it at length:

Shaku: So tell me how you feel about the first part of the film, the part set in England.
Jomir: That's not realistic, especially the way Amrish Puri is feeding the birds. That just doesn't feel right and anything.
Shaku: Why doesn't that feel right?
Jomir: Because you just don't see that kind of thing in Asians.
Shaku: Old men don't give bread to birds?
Jomir: That's true. You know. And then when Shah Rukh Khan goes and gets beer from the shop when he's meant to close it down, that part didn't really mean anything to me, I just found it funny a little bit actually, to be honest. But then when they go to India, that's my favourite part. When the songs start. I like that the most. Not the part when they're in Switzerland so much.
Shaku: Why not? They're becoming friends there.
Jomir: Well, like Kajol she doesn't want nothing to do with him on the train station when they miss the train.
Shaku: Yeah?

Jomir: Um I don't, in real life would that happen and everything? A lady going and saying I'm going to go myself and you go. [pause] After all they're both Indian and that. I didn't like that. I just don't feel that part is interesting.

Shaku: You felt she should have agreed to spend time with him?

Jomir: Yeah. I mean you just wouldn't. She's a *lady* after all and this country she's come to [Switzerland] she's never been to before and [sceptical] she just wants to go on her own [pause] and her mates have left her and the only choice she's got left is Shah Rukh Khan, ain't it?

Shaku: You think that in a foreign country the only person you would trust would be someone from your own country?

Jomir: Exactly.

Shaku: You don't think that he might have tried something on with her?

Jomir: No. Because he's Indian.

Shaku: Oh. But don't you think –

Jomir: – She can see he's a really kind person and everything. He's just joking around and being friendly. She's Indian; he's Indian. She falls in love with him in the end, *doesn't she?*

Shaku: So you think that being *Indian* makes him trustworthy?

Jomir: Yes.

(JOM.2/*English*)

Here it is worthwhile considering Jomir's displeasure at the events he catalogues and locating this unease within the existing discourses about youth, 'Indianness' and 'foreignness', that pervade the film and many sections of the British-Asian diaspora for, in his commentary on Simran's rejection of the hero's attentions, Jomir draws on discourses from the film itself, which identify true 'Indian' masculinity with honesty, sexual restraint and moral integrity.

In my view, two very different sets of feelings and beliefs may motivate Jomir to assert his lack of interest in the scenes that present the hero in a less than transcendent state of moral supremacy. First, Jomir's empathy with Raj/Shah Rukh leads him to experience Simran's rejection of the hero as a slight to South-Asian men in general. Himself a South-Asian residing in Britain, Jomir may read Simran's rejection of the hero against the backdrop of a frequently racist discourse presenting 'South-Asian' masculinity in Britain as increasingly antisocial and 'troublesome' (Alexander 2000: 10), but also within the framework of his own community's assessment of non-Asian masculinity as threatening. As Barker and Galasiński argue: 'what is to be considered a "man" is likely to be different across different ethnic groups, while racism may take the form in which one ethnic group derides another as effeminate' (2001: 158). To the description 'effeminate', I posit, one may add the labels 'dangerous' and 'predatory' which are frequently used in the discourse of both the white and the non-white communities to characterise men from the 'other' community. Despite extensive community regulation of British-Asian women's actions and behaviour, Jomir expresses his unease with the possibility that, left to their own devices, they might cast doubt on the honour of 'men' from their own communities by rejecting their protection in favour of the de-ethnicised support of 'others' from the majority community, whom he despises. Thus, slightly reworking Barker's and Galasinski's formulation (2001: 168) – which they apply to Polish men – I wish to suggest that 'the construction of ethnicity in masculine terms' by young viewers such as Jomir, 'can be understood as being motivated by certain cultural myths and values' and 'cannot be seen in isolation from its context'.

Second, and for me quite significantly, Jomir's irritation and displeasure at even the mild autonomy accorded to Simran/Kajol by the film's narrative focuses on her gender and his perception of her as a 'lady'. Laughable as Jomir's assertion might seem that having lost her friends and being alone in a foreign place, *the only choice she's [the heroine] got left* is the hero, psychologically such a stance is not at all uncommon and is not, it must be noted, the sole preserve of Asian men. The deeply problematic belief that when away from their home country, the only people women (and even men) can/should really rely on are those from their own nation and/or ethnic group is widespread, as much rooted in a white fear of the 'native' other as in a South-Asian diasporic distrust of non-Asians.[5] However, Jomir's belief that the stranded Simran has no other options *because she is a lady* is simply a further extension of the film's supposedly amusing undermining of her agency: when she chooses to leave the company of Raj, whom she perceives to be harassing her, she quickly finds herself in trouble with the police; this is in clear contrast to the hero's resourcefulness in hiring a car and getting her out of trouble.

4.2.2 'Hero' versus 'daddy': winning a woman 'Indian-style'

4.2.2.1 *Loving daddy?*

In both London and Bombay, most of my female interviewees who chose to comment on the film, and significantly fewer young males, expressed unhappiness about the way in which Simran's stern and unbending father handled her attachment to Raj by uprooting the family and hauling her off to India to wed a man she had never encountered previously. While some were at pains to express their sympathy for Baldev Singh – and embroiled themselves in contradiction in order to do justice to the complexity of their own feelings towards fathers who were perceived to be both authoritarian and nurturing – others were forthright in their condemnation of the 'traditional' arranged marriage and, having acknowledged the source of their pleasure as being the romance, emphatic about their rejection of the film's patriarchal 'message'. Here I shall exemplify both positions in order to unfurl some of the complexity inherent in my respondents' relationship to conservative ideological constructs in Hindi films.

Implying that she had used the film to help her to come to accept her father's authority, Neha explained: '[A]fter watching [DDLJ], I tried to understand from my father's side why he won't send me [out of the house] and what things can happen after going out.' Here, because of its use in the context of DDLJ, we can surmise that Neha's phrase 'what things can happen' applies, quite poignantly, not only to the accidents or unpleasant encounters that parents may fear for their offspring, but also to the possibilities for self-realisation and emotional stimulation that may open up outside the narrow confines of the home. Such an opening up of anarchic psychological possibilities *by films*, and the potential consequences of ensuing breaches in conservative morality, were also of concern to Meeta, a much younger viewer in Bombay, from the same community as Neha.

Although at times highly enthusiastic about the romance of the two young protagonists and able to express empathy for them when they are separated, Meeta was consistent in her refusal to criticise the father in DDLJ or any other Hindi film. From an enormously restrictive lower-middle-class family, and expressing early resignation about her own impending arranged marriage, Meeta's whole demeanour would alter when she spoke about the young lovers in Hindi films such as DDLJ and *Pardes*. When I asked her how she could both express such a liking for 'love' and yet deplore the practice of 'love marriage', as she frequently did, she would smile, twist her hands in her lap and respond that she objected to the depiction of too many love marriages as they 'caused' young people to want to do such things. This position may be taken to be both a disavowal of her own tendency to dream and also an admission of her vulnerability when 'exposed' to the charms of romance on-screen. Off-screen, however, whatever Meeta's circumstances, her reluctance to critique the demands of patriarchal 'tradition' forms the basis for what can only be considered a highly authoritarian politics. That such conservative politics, while confusingly invoked by DDLJ, does not provide the only frame through which Meeta views the film is, however, of significance to this discussion.

Commenting on the way in which Simran responds to her father's controlling anger, Meeta discusses her emotions with apparent clarity and passion:

Meeta: Kajol cries when her father refuses to let her consider her dream of marrying Shah Rukh. She cries when her arranged marriage is revealed to her because her desires and dreams are broken at that point. I felt that she should get Shah Rukh and I also felt like crying watching her, because she had selected this man, she should get him.

(MTA.1/*Hindi*)

Our entire discussion took place in the kitchen belonging to one of Meeta's neighbours. This woman, who was also from Meeta's community, had closed the door so as to give us privacy. Nevertheless, Meeta frequently seemed nervous and, speaking the words quoted above, she had – apparently unintentionally – lowered her voice. Here she is in no doubt that the heroine should be allowed to continue her relationship with the man she selected for herself and that the 'desires and dreams' of a young woman are important. However, when I asked her about her feelings for film fathers who cause their daughters distress, such as the one portrayed by Amrish Puri, she was equally willing to justify authoritarian behaviour:

Meeta: ... I feel that if the youngster has done some mischief or been foolish in some way or committed a sin, then it is very necessary for the older person to make them understand the error of their ways. Sometimes they are stubborn so it is right and proper that they should be hit to make them understand what is wrong with them.

(MTA.2/*Hindi*)

In this instance, although Meeta spoke loudly and with confidence, her tone was impersonal and formal. It appeared almost as if she was 'reading' aloud from pre-prepared lecture notes or making a speech to a crowd. Initially, I was intrigued by her readiness to defend characters who were responsible for the pain and humiliation of other characters with whom she clearly empathised, surmising that there might be a great deal of masochism in the pleasure she gained from watching romance thwarted in films. Later, as her context and concerns were foregrounded during discussions of other films, Meeta's investment in discourses both of *romance* and of *patriarchy* became more apparent and I was fascinated by the interplay between her 'desires' (for romance, excitement, spontaneity) and her sense of having allied herself with the 'power' invested in patriarchal moralities.

In Chapter 2, one of the questions raised centred around the notion of a homogeneous and diasporically hybrid subjectivity. The notion that living in the West surrounded by a certain 'modern' style of life yet cocooned in a 'traditional' family structure causes British-Asian youth to feel torn in half, and thus precipitates the formation of a 'hybrid identity' as a solution, presupposes the existence of Indian youth who do *not* feel torn, who are *entirely at ease with* and have *successfully internalised* so-called 'traditional' norms and practices and rejected supposedly 'modern' ones. Yet Meeta, the most avowedly 'traditional' of the young people I interviewed in Bombay, offers, in her analysis of films, one of the most striking instantiations of 'compartmentalisation'⁶ (see also Ghuman 1999: 47), or, perhaps, of plain self-contradiction, of any viewer in my sample. Clearly believing in order and patriarchal authority at one level, at another, Meeta was forever betraying her pleasure in romance and her sympathy for disordered passions.

This contradiction between on-screen emotional investments and off-screen beliefs was one that I frequently found occurring in other combinations, or in reverse, with other viewers I spoke to. Thus, while Meeta appears to speak with two different 'voices', other interviewees, like Farsana, Kalpesh and Azhar, who were much more critical of patriarchal father–daughter relations both on- and off-screen and even, in Farsana's and Kalpesh's cases, of patriarchal gender relations *per se*, either did not recognise or recognised but did not feel their joy in the film dampened by the hero's more subtly sexist dialogues and behaviour. The sequence during which he sexually harasses the heroine in a train compartment was named by several viewers as one of their 'favourite' scenes: his choice first to tease and then to reassure her about her chastity was seen as adding virtue to his character, and his decision, in the second half of the film, to disregard the counsel of both his lover and her mother is named several times in my study – usually by young men – as being the film's *most significant message*.

4.2.2.2 Heroic pleasures?

The relationship between the lovers in *Dilwale Dulhaniya Le Jayenge* only begins on a train, in a liminal space between London and Europe. It is possible to see that narrative pleasure during the first hour of DDLJ is intimately connected with the romantic and sexual possibilities that lie before the young protagonists. The fact that their 'accidental' meeting in a locked compartment of a cross-channel train is choreographed around the heroine's body and clothing comes as no surprise. The heroine's stern attempts to distance herself physically from the hero in the confined

space are undermined by the camera shots of her breasts and the presentation of her bra, which has 'slipped' from her suitcase at a crucial moment
and become lodged beneath the hero. As Mary E. John (1998: 385) points
out, one of the ways in which unsanctioned (heterosexual) relationships
in Hindi films are normalised with audiences is via the mechanism of
'eve-teasing'.

The initial anxiety and irritation of the heroine is subdued by the way
in which the hero persuades her to trust him. Tormenting her and then
proving his decency by comforting her are only two of the many mechanisms by which her suspicion of him is turned to love and proved to be
foolish or mistaken: as Jomir rhetorically asserts about Simran's efforts
to prevent Raj from touching and harassing her on the train, '[s]he falls
in love with him in the end, doesn't she?'

Articulating a point of view that could be said to echo my own sensations on first watching DDLJ with friends in a Bombay cinema hall, Padma
expresses her feelings as being both critical and amused, hinging on the
expectations she has come to have of the signifying practices of contemporary Hindi romance:

Padma: When they first meet each other on the train, it's so cute [pause,
laughs]. It's only because he's Shah Rukh Khan that I say that. He probably is harassing her, like it's too much when he puts his head in her
lap! Any other Indian guy and I'd be going, *'Excuse me*! What're you
doing? That's harassment here!', 'Call the guard, get him kicked off the
train!' He *is* harassing her and you *only* accept it because it is a Hindi
film. You know, 'Oh it's a film!' I *mean*, if that happened in real life, you'd
be like, *'Oh my God, No!'* But that's the thing, isn't it, it takes you away
from real life. [pause]
Shaku: Does it?
Padma: I reckon that in some places that could encourage guys to try it
on, you know what I'm saying, some countries [smiling] but here guys
don't expect women to react like that [pause] ... I like the fact that
they're having a friendship. He doesn't automatically look at her and
go, 'Oh, this is the love of my life!', and she doesn't automatically look
at him and go, 'He's the love of my life.' ... Yeah, [pause] it's a bit unrealistic I think, but *so what*!

(PAD.2/*English*)

Padma's comprehension that the connection between pleasure, fiction
and reality is a complex one, elaborated in her point that a viewer's
jump between the modality of on-screen and off-screen life can work in

complicated ways to position Raj the hero as an unknown potential harasser and/or as the popular and desirable star, Shah Rukh Khan, is absolutely crucial to an understanding of the reception of the hero in these scenes. The seemingly risqué manner in which Raj displays Simran's bra – to 'tease' her but also for inspection by a (voyeuristic) audience – is offset by the long history of harasser-heroes in Hindi cinema[7] and by the audience's affinity for him because he *is* Shah Rukh Khan, the handsome and debonair star. Similarly, a knowledge of the conventions of romance in Hindi cinema suggests that because she will *ultimately* fall in love with and marry him, Simran's refusal of his advances at this stage is both a proof of her 'purity' and suitableness as a wife and also an undermining of her judgement in that she has failed to 'see' his good qualities.

Padma's ability to reconcile her beliefs in women's autonomy and rights with her enjoyment of Hindi film entertainment is a guarantee of her continued viewing and a reminder of the ways in which pleasure and ideology do not automatically follow each other off the screen in any linked sequence of meaning for viewers. As Christine Gledhill reminds us, being open to the pleasures of a mainstream text is a matter of complex *negotiation* and shifting identification rather than of simplistic submission to the ideological position of the (patriarchal) textual subject (1999: 173). Jomir, who insisted he had never, nor ever would, harass a woman but who did not view Raj/Shah Rukh's actions as harassment, experienced far less enjoyment from the scene on the train than that expressed by Padma, who was acutely aware, and critical, of the ways in which women are sexually objectified by men in the community. Padma's beliefs about gender politics – shaped by her experiences of life both in a working-class, largely South-Asian community in London and her year of study in her South-Asian 'homeland', but perhaps also called forth on the occasion of the interview by her assumptions about my beliefs – which allow her to 'name' the hero's behaviour towards the heroine as 'harassment', not once but three times, can be seen to be *both* constitutive of the meaning she makes from the behaviour of the protagonists in DDLJ *and* easily distanced from her positive experience of early parts of the film. Thus, interestingly, the only thing distinguishing the film-talk of a 'politically aware' viewer like Padma from that of a more 'conservative' viewer like Meeta might be the willingness of Padma to draw attention with playful irony to contradictions between her responses regarding situations on- and off screen. Such willingness might constitute (unemotional) reading 'against the grain' and/or might be an acknowledgement that gratification can take place during a film viewing without the endorsement of underlying ideologies (Barker and Brooks 1998: 133–50) and that one can hold beliefs at odds with the discourses unfolding on screen. This is, to my mind, a key issue for those interested both in audiences and texts. Crucially, the talk of these young women about DDLJ demonstrates that viewers are not inherently 'ironic' or 'straight'; 'irony' is one of a number of possible positions that viewers might adopt when talking about a text or sequence (cf. Thomas 2002).

4.2.2.3 The cost of honour

One of the most striking aspects of interviewees' talk about *Dilwale Dulhaniya Le Jayenge* was the way in which images of parental authority and nurturing came to signify something almost 'universal' in the minds of young people. Even more than the expressions of admiration for the hero or sympathy for the heroine, discussions about the behaviour of Baldev Singh Chaudhary (Amrish Puri) aroused the passion of young Bombay viewers. Segueing anecdote and opinion, Azhar, a lower-middle-class Muslim man married for a year to his erstwhile Hindu college sweetheart after persuading her to run away from her parental home, spoke with confidence and at length about his relationship to this film.

Shaku: Could you talk a bit more about the parts of DDLJ that interested you?

Azhar: [fast] Yes. It's wrong when the father tries to make the girl marry one man when she wants to marry another. He uses force when that is not the issue at all.

Shaku: Could you explain why you feel that?

Azhar: See, in the film, Kajol has chosen one guy, he suits her. She knows that she's going to have to spend the rest of her life with him, get on with him, correct? [*S* nods]. Or is it her father or her mother who will live with the guy? *Hah*? Tell me? So the father should recognise this and organise what she wants. With whom we are happy, with whom we feel comfortable, that's the person we should marry. Look at Shah Rukh in the film. He's a good boy. He has good capabilities. He can give her what she wants. So what's the problem? [loud] *What is the dad's problem?* ... With boys too, often there is compulsion, even if the girl is very good, [the parents] look at her and say, 'NO'. One of my friends, he married a woman he didn't even like, to please his parents. Now he completes all the formalities of having a wife, save one single one: *he does not love her*. He takes her out for meals. He brings home money. But he loves another girl ... And because of the compulsion to marry, he has been corrupted.

(AZH.1/*Hindi*)

Azhar's angry speech is intimately related to his own life narrative and the ways in which he positions himself within debates about love and marriage. Having attempted to 'win' his own in-laws' consent to marriage with their daughter and failed, he has encouraged her to elope: this is an option condemned by this film and rarely endorsed by other young viewers in my sample. And, unlike many of the interviewees in London, who believed in the possibility of reconciling their parents to a marriage of their choice (at least within caste, class and religious boundaries), Azhar's wife has had to leave both her family and her religion to enter his world. Yet Azhar expresses none of the enormity of her decision; nor does he talk about its consequences for her. He poses the problem as being similar to the one Shah Rukh faces in DDLJ: the father simply cannot see the good qualities of his potential son-in-law.

Azhar's move from explaining why it is wrong for Kajol's father to 'force' her to marry a man she does not like to the anecdote about a male friend who has been 'forced' into precisely such a sham marriage both explains and justifies the decision that he and his partner took to marry without her parents' consent. As such, his personal investment in the decision to go ahead with a marriage outside the accepted norms of his wife's community fuels his anger at the behaviour of fathers/parents both in films and reality. The barrage of rhetorical questions is aimed less at me, with whom he is talking, than at the *discourse* of arranged marriage itself, which he sees as stipulating that marriage is a collective rather than an individual contract or decision, involving parents and other relatives more than young people. As may be seen from Azhar's comments, discussions of courtship and marriage in *DDLJ*, and of the male roles therein, can be used by young viewers to springboard into serious issues about their lives and those of their friends, or about society. This feature of talk about films, that is not, it must be noted, applicable exclusively to audiences of Hindi films, is one I observed constantly with young viewers and that highlights the importance, for audience research, of an interest in the social and psychological contexts of film spectators.

In this light, Kavita's relationship with her father, whom she described as 'jolly' and having a soft heart under his stern exterior, 'not full of anger, like Amrish Puri in DDLJ', can be seen as complicated and constantly changing. Following the interview, she asserted, first, that she would be 'happy' to sacrifice her illicit relationship for her father (who has a heart condition), but then said that she would 'never' do such a thing and that he would surely never ask her to do such a thing. During the interview she moved between praising his tolerance for her sister's boyfriend to describing his intolerant behaviour and finally his insistence that her sister should marry the man of his choice.[8] In the following extract, Kavita debates her conflicting feelings about her father through chat about Baldev Singh and film parents:

Shaku: In the film, who did you support?
Kavita: Actually the daughter is only right [pause] Yah, I'm on her side. Kajol is *not* wrong, she knows her heart and she sacrifices for her parents [pause].
Shaku: And do you think Kajol should have to sacrifice for her parents?
Kavita: No! No! She should not [pause] and her father really cares for her, he knows that his daughter is sacrificing for him and he really cares. In real life also I have seen this ... That time [in DDLJ] I think that the girl is right, because always parents think only about themselves. *Our* izzat [honour], *our* khandaan [clan] ... Mostly in India I have seen the angry fathers, the ones who pay attention to their honour.
Shaku: How do you explain that?
Kavita: '*Izzat! Izzat!*' In India they think like that only!

(KAV.1/English and Hindi)

Although the shifts in this segment of talk are so rapid that being certain about what Kavita is saying is not always easy, her commentary is lent weight by the rarely publicised, but now increasingly documented torture, humiliation, persecution and horrific murder of young lovers by their own relatives across swathes of India and even, on occasion, in the diaspora.[9] Here she begins by stating what seems to be her unqualified support for the heroine of DDLJ in her desire for Raj, her lover; however, this implication is undermined when she states, 'she knows her heart and she sacrifices for her parents', suggesting that what she is endorsing is the young woman's willingness to bend to paternal authority and maternal pleading. My attempt to clarify her meaning, perhaps to elicit an unequivocal assertion of allegiance to a particular point of view on the issue of authoritarian parenting – which springs from my own background and beliefs – is in some ways at odds with the fluidity of the contradictory positions Kavita wishes to, and eventually does, take up. She is able to maintain a stance that is both practically in support of the heroine sacrificing personal desires in deference to her father (whom Kavita reads as benevolent, and appreciative of the sacrifice) and morally averse to the need for her to sacrifice. Later in the exchange, however, Azhar's angry question, '*What is the dad's problem?*', is clearly similar to the one in Kavita's mind as she gives an account of an occasion when one of her friends was forcibly married off, and asserts that clan honour is the reason for fathers' and parents' rigid control of their daughters' relationships. Her linking of 'angry fathers' to the notion of 'izzat', honour and her assertion that this is how people in India think and behave can, surely, be read as forthrightly critical in a manner consistent with Uberoi's (textual) analysis that

> Baldev Singh's honour (izzat) is ... implicated not only in fulfilling his commitment to his friend, but in ensuring that his daughter's virtue is untainted ... The discovery of Simran's European romance with Raj ... challenges his authority as a patriarch ... threatens his sacred duty as a Hindu father to *gift* his daughter in marriage ... challenges the principles of 'alliance', whereby marriage is construed as a union between two families through the exchange of women, rather than just as an arrangement between two individuals ... [and], by compromising Simran's virtue, her purity as a gift object is depreciated, and his own honour therewith.
>
> (1998: 320)

Kavita's unwillingness to commit to such precise criticism of this film father, Baldev Singh, can be seen as an extension of her ambivalent feelings for her own father. Caught between the discourse of 'the dutiful daughter' that she has learnt from her father and reads into the film, and that of the 'rights of the individual' that she is attracted to and assumes I am pursuing, Kavita's standpoint shifts, during even a limited period of interaction. Her perception of Baldev Singh is contradictory and confusing, revealing the constraints placed upon, and the insecurity of, positions taken up in talk. As noted, it is dangerous to forget that the words recorded during an interview are neither the straightforward representations of the interviewee's thoughts (Buckingham 1993: Chapter 3) nor the fixed and ultimate purveyors of their identities and opinions, but may well signal a process of self-scrutiny (Hollway 1984: 260) or, equally plausibly, reflect attempts to humour the interviewer (Seiter 1999: 18).

Yet, even via such a tentative analysis of the responses of young viewers to an assertion of paternal authority, we can begin to see that the attitudes of young people to the films they watch and the ways in which the films come to be meaningful for them are embedded in two different but overlapping networks of experience. The first one may call their own individual life histories, their unique sets of experiences from birth; the second might best be described as the culturally accepted systems of values that have surrounded them and been most frequently endorsed by those significant members of families and communities whom they trust and respect. It should therefore come as no surprise that both

Azhar and Kavita have profound emotional if not practical investments in asserting certain attitudes to films and disavowing others; or that their positions, while limited in certain respects, are neither internally consistent nor immutable. In a manner that echoes the complicated subjectivity of viewers but does not have their mutability, films themselves offer moments of critique and fracture that are sometimes but not always overwhelmed and subsumed by their closure and conclusion. I move now to a brief discussion of what Patricia Uberoi (1998: 322) has called the 'undertow of resentment and critique that lies beneath the normative culture of Indian kinship' in DDLJ.

4.2.3 'What's the point of mother?' or 'How your son-in-law always knows better': responses to female dissent in DDLJ

For me, in the opening scenes of DDLJ, several shots of Simran with her younger sister and her mother maintain a quiet but sustained counterpoint to the overt authority structure in the family. Simran and her sister, Rajeshwari, dance to Western music while their mother smilingly prances around the kitchen to its beat; Simran reads aloud to her mother from her journal about her longing for a romantic stranger; Rajeshwari lectures their mother about traditional habits, quoting homilies from her teacher, 'Miss Lucy'. As the father enters the frame, a frigid metamorphosis occurs and the house is transformed into a stereotypic version of a supposedly pure 'Indian' home. Colours appear more muted; the score alters; the young women's postures, gestures and voices change. Once set up in this manner, the wavering of the heroine's mother between a wish for her daughter to sacrifice her desires to gain her father's acceptance and a determination that her daughter should live a fulfilling life is psychologically convincing. Also, if the complexity of Kavita's response (KAV.1) is taken on board, Simran's vacillations between resistance and capitulation become plausible. During the crises provoked by the revelation of her unsanctioned love for a man, the heroine's autonomy and her agency are revoked, leaving her with little choice but to surrender to her father's wish that she should marry the son of his Indian friend. At three crucial points following Simran's physical removal from the scene of her romance, she and her mother challenge the rigid framework into which they have been inserted by suggesting that Simran should elope with her beloved. On all three occasions and in no uncertain terms, Raj/ Shah Rukh Khan, refuses to accept their plans.

In each instance, both women are silenced by his claiming of a righteous path which is superior to their 'easy' but 'deceitful' one. Baldev Singh Chaudhary is frequently depicted as domineering; Raj is never presented

Figure 4.1   Ruksana watching *Dilwale Dulhaniya Le Jayenge* as the hero placates his beloved's father

by the camera as being in the least authoritarian, angry or overbearing: nevertheless, and with a force more powerful than all the frowns of Simran's enraged father, this young man's homilies on respect and duty appear as bearers of male-identified tradition, power and control.[10]

In his insistence that he will accept Simran's hand in marriage only when it is placed there by Baldev Singh, Uberoi notes, Raj (and implicitly the director) 'identifies himself with patriarchal authority, with the "law" of the father, and distances himself from the socially subversive and sentimental complicity of mother and daughter' (1998: 325).

I was fascinated by the differing ways in which interviewees interpreted, and inflected, the discourses at play in these sequences. The moral weight of identification with the hero, Raj, although apparently felt by young people of both sexes, was more pervasive amongst the young men in my sample. Rahul and Jomir, aged respectively 21 and 16, one residing in Bombay and one in London, were keen to express their sense of Raj/Shah Rukh Khan's righteousness, thus ignoring totally the will of Simran/Kajol on the two occasions when she begs to be 'taken away' from the place where she is being forcibly betrothed to a stranger. Raj's refusal to antagonise his lover's father, and his attempts to win the patriarch's heart for his cause, were cited by both of them as instances of exemplary conduct. Neetu, 16 years old from a strict Sikh family in Bombay, involved in a relationship with a Hindu man some eight years her senior, was full of admiration for the way in which the hero behaved.

Her assertions about Raj's steadfast but respectful behaviour culminate in the statement, 'I agree they should not run away. I would never run away', and are indicative of the ways in which apparently sentimental attitudes to love and family in some Hindi films may contribute to the moral and political frameworks about courtship and marriage upon which young people call off-screen. However, and significantly, not all viewers surrender their emotional investment in characters whose moral frameworks contradict those of the films' dominant discourse. Alpa, 18 years old, agreed with Neetu's praise for the hero, but with one significant qualification: despite her endorsement of Shah Rukh Khan's refusal to elope, she viewed the mother's suggestion that the young people should run away as both practically and morally praiseworthy:

Alpa: I think it was good that they didn't run away. They stayed there, they faced up to the problem, they solved it by being there. But at the end when she advises them, what the mother did was very like it was almost honourable in a way [pause] because you just wouldn't expect that from a traditional Indian mother in a way? [pause] But at the same time when she said that they should run, you knew that it was *really* traditional because she was scared of her husband. And that's why she told her daughter.

(ALP.1/*English*)

Alpa's sense that, although the young people were right to endure suffering in order to win the girl's parents' consent, the mother too was correct to direct them to leave shows that she is not simply accepting the film's implicit rebuke to the women who wish to solve the situation by 'escaping' from it. The point that the mother's *honourable* gesture also marks the very boundaries of her power within the family by showing her terror of her husband's wrath and her conviction that he would not accept her daughter's autonomy is aptly made by Alpa. Showing a similar sensitivity to the power dynamics within 'real' families, Neha insisted that '[i]n a real situation, if the father is not listening and the guy is perfect then yes, she should listen to her mummy and run away. There is nothing wrong with that.'

The strength of the word 'honourable' and the phrase 'she should listen to her mummy' should, I maintain, remind us that films in general – and perhaps Hindi films in particular – are not read in their totality, but are dissected during the act of viewing into parts that relate more or less closely to the variable moral and political beliefs and values as well as the aspirations and fantasies of spectators (Barker and Brooks 1998;

Stempel 2001; Austin 2002). Similar issues are raised in my second case study in this chapter, which focuses on academic and 'ordinary' audience responses to aspects of the 1994 family blockbuster *Hum Aapke Hain Koun ...!* in which a young man, Prem (Salman Khan), falls in love with his sister-in-law, Nisha (Madhuri Dixit), and romances her, along with sundry aunts, cousins and in-laws, at various family functions only to discover, near the end of the film, that Nisha is to be betrothed to his suddenly bereaved elder brother.

4.3 Romancing the family: *Hum Aapke Hain Koun ...!* and its viewers

Filled from its opening scenes with an atmosphere of family harmony and the celebration of 'traditional' rites and rituals binding family members into an ever-closer unit, *Hum Aapke Hain Koun ...!* (HAHK) was mentioned by several viewers in my sample as being one of the earliest Hindi films that they really enjoyed watching with their extended families. Nisha, who watched it in London as a young teenager with her visiting cousins from India, loved the dances, especially *'Juthe do, Paise lo'* (Give the shoes, take the money), laughingly commenting: 'everyone thinks that's so dumb but they still enjoy it [and] they do the dances.' The early parts of HAHK, where the hero, Prem, and his uncle, who has brought him up, seek and find a bride for Rajesh, Prem's elder brother, are filled with sequences of family 'fun': a cricket match in which even the family pet and the servants play a part, skates, sunlit temples, paintings, a mandolin, chewing gum, chocolate, varieties of food, drink and large, bright, cheerfully decorated rooms all add to the atmosphere of informal affection and material comfort. The fact that Rajesh is betrothed to the elder daughter of his uncle's long-time college friend and one-time college sweetheart adds another layer of intensity to the proceedings: in-laws-to-be gaze at each other across rooms with looks of imploring love, drawing two different generations into the romance of marriage itself. The betrothal songs, with their throbbing emotions and naughty rhymes, as well as the mixture of antagonism and attraction between the lead pair, were, in my study, less dwelt on than the atmosphere of domestic harmony following the initial marriage.

The way in which the families coexist and never fall out was the single most popular feature of HAHK with my young interviewees' relatives, and to young viewers in London this harmony was seen as turning, in large part, upon the tolerance, good-humour and understanding of the heroine's older sister, Pooja, the 'bahu' (daughter-in-law) and 'bhabi' (elder brother's wife). Describing this character as the archetypal 'ideal Indian woman' in Hindi cinema, Nisha went on to explain:

> No one's perfect. No one. In the roads no one is. In *Hum Aapke Hain Koun ...!*, it's not Madhuri who's ideal, it's the *bhabi*. She's so sweet and so loving and she respects her family and she's so loving and she loves her husband and she's got a lovely husband and everyone's so happy about her and she's so pretty and she dresses up so nicely [pause] and her sari's perfect and her make-up is just so beautiful, she's just the happiest person in the world. [pause] Her in-laws love her, her parents love her to bits. Everyone loves her; her brother-in-law is like joking around – that relationship was so sweet. Like my dad and his bhabi.
>
> (NIS.2/*English*)

The excess that characterises this commentary – 'ideal', 'so sweet', 'so loving', 'respects', 'so loving', 'loves', 'lovely', 'so happy', 'so pretty', 'so nicely', 'perfect', 'so beautiful', 'happiest', 'love', 'love' – may, I suggest, be seen to connote an ambivalent mixture of approval, awe and scepticism in relation to the character being described. While, like Nisha, Kalpesh and Padma were also certain about their pleasure in the vivid colours, Pooja's sweetness and what they called the generally 'enjoyable' (Padma) and 'escapist' (Kalpesh) tendencies of the film, some young viewers in Bombay were especially keen to stress that when they watched HAHK for the first time, it was their aunts, mothers and family elders who were most taken with it, regarding it as a real 'family' film worthy of being viewed several times over. The absence of any evil or more than perfunctorily disruptive figures, the lack of overt or brazen sexual displays despite the burgeoning desire of the lead pair, and the general happiness amongst characters in the film, until the moment when Pooja, on a visit to her maternal home, accidentally trips on a staircase and dies of her injuries, was also seen as being crucial to the film's success at the time of its release. However, while the film's early and constant deployment of material goods – notably Prem's cars, inscribed as one of them is with slogans about loving his family – did raise some comments within my sample, from viewers who felt that 'normal middle-class families' could not dream of living in such a style, as I will show, almost all the young people in my sample who chose to comment on HAHK moved, at some point in their interviews, to a discussion of their dissatisfaction with, and anxieties about, aspects of the narrative, characterisation and plot.

The soft-focus close-ups of the lead pair which open the film are early signals of the director's almost total commitment to a version of romantic materialism purged of guilt and anxiety[11]: the heavily embroidered dresses and colourful decorations inside the palatial 'house' wherein most of the film unfolds are visual counterparts to the teasing, child-like lyrics of the songs which punctuate the 'action' approximately every seven minutes. Here I will argue that this film's departure from the conventional plot structure of even the more light-hearted romantic comedies, and its 'erasure' of all forms of active dissent via a narrative that is predicated on the jubilant celebration of marriage, courtship and birth rituals in a Hindu joint family and the elimination of all but ten minutes of narrative tension, unlike the similarly reconciliatory penultimate scenes of DDLJ, may have the odd repercussion of giving sections of the audience more rather than less cause to dwell upon their critiques of such hegemony. However, before embarking on any analysis of criticisms levelled at HAHK by viewers, some understanding of the kind of authoritative critical outrage caused by the film is necessary and appropriate.

4.3.1 Unveiling 'fascist utopia': critical accounts of HAHK

Given the amount of critical interest generated by Sooraj Barjatya's *Hum Aapke Hain Koun ...!* (Bharucha 1995; Juluri 1999; Kazmi 1999; Vitali 2000; Uberoi 2001), it is only fitting that this section should open with excerpts from a commentary by a film critic. Nikhat Kazmi's estimation of the director rests on her assessment of his films:

> In its ethical overtones ... HAHK ends up as regressive and archaic ... [upholding] a moral order that sanctifies tradition as opposed to the modern and re-entrenches a social system that is feudalistic, patriarchal and rigidly hierarchical ... There are no signs of protest, no boredom, no healthy individualism, no pursuit of personal ambitions, no clash of interests ... Here, where even the servants are treated as family members, obedience, reverence and servility are natural corollaries.
> (Kazmi 1998: 188–91)

This precarious complex of values comprising servility and sacrifice as well as worship of the upper-caste Hindu joint family and of 'modern' emblems of material wealth, Kazmi attributes squarely to the Indian political climate of the late eighties and early nineties with 'the rise of the VHP and the BJP and the emergence of the political concept of the Sangh Parivar' (1998: 191). Rustom Bharucha too insists that this is 'a film that definitely would not have been possible without a deep internalisation of the Hindu Right in popular and mass culture' (1995: 804). Echoing this point and the arguments of Vamsee Juluri (1999), Valentina

Vitali points out that the 'history' to which HAHK contributes is 'the discourse of Hinduisation' also deployed by the BJP. Furthermore, Vitali suggests, 'in the age of global capitalism HAHK consolidates the religious and upper-caste basis of the middle-class Indian subject by engaging an exclusionary project: to define the national space as Hindu and to re-enclose women in the very spaces which nationalist modernity had begun to open up' (2000). The 'upper-caste Hindu joint family' in HAHK thus becomes, according to these writers, both the most recognisable trope for 'Indianness' – the boundary beyond which incursions from lower-class, lower-caste and/or non-Hindu sensibilities can progress only by renouncing their 'otherness' – and the (prison-like) space within which female/youth autonomy and sexuality are subtly but rigidly suppressed, reshaped and controlled. As Fareed Kazmi expresses it, this film, therefore, 'colonises all people, all spaces' and 'makes invisible "other" people, "other" places, "other" lives' (1999: 143).

Meanwhile, Uberoi's audience investigation concludes that HAHK succeeded, among other reasons, because it offered a 'spectacle of unlimited consumption' (2001: 334) and because it iconised and valorised the so-called 'Indian' joint family system in a manner that purported to fill the vacuum left by a gradual erosion of illusions about the nature and role of the Indian state. Among the North Indian viewers quoted by Uberoi there seems to be a consensus that HAHK is a 'clean' and morally uplifting film, whose celebrations – betrothals, weddings, births - and values – affinity, duty, self-sacrifice – give viewers an imaginary space to which they can relate their own lives and ideals. The criticisms – of verisimilitude (2001: 336) and of ideology – are far less pronounced than the commendations. By contrast, the patterns of response emerging from my interviews half a decade after HAHK's release and Uberoi's study are considerably more equivocal.

While Nikhil, like several viewers in Uberoi's sample, spontaneously linked his liking for the film to its presentation of happy joint family life in which secrets and resentments were alien phenomena and 'brothers' lived happily alongside each other, few of the other responses I received dwelt at length on this aspect of the film. In fact, I was increasingly interested by the way in which HAHK would be introduced into interviews by young viewers, not only as an instance of a film about exemplary family relationships (Padma, Kalpesh) or containing exciting dance numbers and dazzling costumes (Nisha, Meeta) but also disapprovingly, as a film which contained images and sequences which typified, for them, the craven depths of subservience and self-abnegation to which young people are expected to fall to honour the self-serving pride of their relatives. Let me elaborate.

Neha, a talented dancer and an honours graduate, explained that she had suppressed her ambitions and talents in order to conform, first to her father's authoritarianism and then to her rather kinder in-laws' narrow-minded notions of decency and women's roles. She struggled to articulate her disquiet. When I asked a general question about the work that women are shown doing in Hindi films, she immediately mentioned HAHK:

Neha: [pause, laughing] In *Hum Aapke Hain Koun ...!* they show Madhuri cooking [pause, laughing] she is a computer programmer but *whatever you are* [pause] because of Indian tradition [pause, laughing] *whatever you are* [laughing] *you have to* go in the kitchen and cook [laughing]. *You have to* be a good cook [laughing, almost hysterical] first take care of family [breathless, long pause]

(NHA.2/*English*)

Neha's laughter, in which I did not feel able to participate, may be construed in a number of ways – as a release for the tension that talking in 'private' about difficult issues occasioned, as a way of showing her detachment from films and her ability to be critical of their stances, or as an acknowledgement of the pathos of her own predicament, which is almost identical to that of the heroine played by Madhuri. Her repeated emphasis on the phrases *whatever you are* and *you have to* may imply her awareness of the narrowness and injustice of the responsibilities imposed upon the heroine of HAHK and many other South-Asian women.

For me, watching Neha's increasing hysteria, and attempting not to 'direct' her through my questions into a deliberately critical vein, her laughter was a telling sign of dismay with the way in which so-called 'tradition' in life and films could determine the mundane level at which women are expected to function. Echoing Neha's frustration in a more articulate manner, Jatin, from a middle-class Hindu family in London, presented an analysis of his feelings that closely resonates with scholarly critiques of HAHK reviewed earlier in this section:

Shaku: So what would you say the moral values of Hindi films are?
Jatin: Well, I think in the last five years, it's become more BJP stance, more fundamentalist.
Shaku: Hm.
Jatin: 'Cause like with *Hum Aapke Hain Koun ...!*, it's like she [pause] she had a good job, she worked with computers, but as soon as she fell in love she was willing to throw it all away. And it was like even the Muslim couple in there – they're *very* Hindu in their ways. Those kinds

of movies, I don't like at all. It doesn't *sound* like it's preaching but if you just watch it, it's sort of overwhelming, even like *Dilwale Dulhaniya* is full of 'All women should *do* this, they should *be* this'.

Shaku: And your view is that [pause]?

Jatin: If women should do it, men should do it as well! ... But I don't like all this recent preaching. I just want to see a real Indian woman who is strong and who asserts themself ... the way I see it, you marry a girl for what she is, not for what she's going to be after marriage.

(JAT.1/*English*)

Fitting neatly as it does with my ideals, I find Jatin's assumption that a 'real Indian woman' is 'strong and asserts herself' comforting; however, the fact that he not only recognises but actually despises the way in which HAHK 'Hinduises' its Muslim characters and the manner in which it cynically links falling in love with a loss of woman's agency and individuality is, in the long run, more significant. Added to these sentiments, his ability to articulate his dislike as arising from the insidious nature of the discourses present in films that don't sound like they're preaching, but whose ideological stances are 'sort of overwhelming' positions Jatin amongst the most explicitly critical of the Hindi film fans I interviewed.

Deriding some of the tearful interludes in Hindi films, Jasmine too was quick to bring up the topic of HAHK, explaining: 'Madhuri cries in *Hum Aapke Hain Koun ...!* with Salman on the other end of the phone after she's decided to marry his brother instead of him – again a silly piece of supposed martyrdom on the part of the one who's crying and then the one who's comforting her saying that she's doing the right thing!' Young viewers from different classes, religions and genders located both in Bombay and in London startled me with the vehemence of their critique – based occasionally, quite ironically for the director, on misrecognitions of the characters and of the chronology of events – of this sequence. Consequently, drawing evidence from responses to HAHK, one might surmise, there are sub-plots and sequences in Hindi films which, rather than triggering sentimental pity or complicity in all sections of the audience, antagonise viewers and unintentionally provoke ideological disengagement via ironic mirth, cynical disillusionment or angry identification.

4.3.2 Deriding sacrifice: the pleasures of harsh judgement

Towards the conclusion of my interview with her, Farsana spoke once more of *Hum Aapke Hain Koun ...!* in the context of her contention that many Hindi films keep women in a subordinate social position by encouraging them to allow men to dominate:

Farsana: After Pooja dies, you know, in *Hum Aapke Hain Koun ...!*, Nisha's parents are forcing her like to get married. She is not willing to sacrifice but that guy, Salman Khan, he is *so* stupid! He is in love with Madhuri but *still* he sacrifices. He is giving up for his family and he loves his brother too much, *too* emotionally. He is *stupid*. [pause] The first time I saw *Hum Aapke Hain Koun ...!*, I liked it. But when I sat and judged the movie, like when it came on cable, I found like I was watching a video. A marriage video cassette.

Shaku: Yes?

Farsana: It was like one big fairy tale ... The professor is cooking food and chatting to the servants [sceptical], it was nothing great I found, really! [laughs. S: laughs]

(FAR.1/*English*)

Farsana's account of her changing feelings for this film might well signal the ways in which distance, in time as well as place, acts to alter viewers' responses to films and thus to disrupt both the preferred readings supposedly 'encoded' by directors and the 'interpellated' spectatorial positions assumed by much textual criticism. One of the very reasons for which the film was initially popular – its likeness to a gigantic and impossibly festive wedding video (Uberoi 2001: 334) – becomes the grounds on which young viewers like Farhana can dismiss it; its fairytale erasure of class, gender and religious conflicts, which characterised its appeal to some middle-class viewers after its initial release (and possibly into the present) is the very factor that now irritates and/or amuses young viewers in Bombay. And, in a twist that is indeed ironic given the film's attempts to deflect all sense of psychic or social conflict on to the poor manners of immodest women – Prem's paternal aunt is occasionally crass enough to refer to servants *as* 'servants' – chance, fate or destiny, Farsana cuts to the chase in her opening comments by suggesting that Nisha is being 'forced', *against her will* to make a sacrifice. In Farsana's interpretation of the film, Nisha's doting parents are transformed into the stern elders of her experience and of other Hindi film narratives, while Prem, Nisha's supremely selfless lover, is so mistaken in his obsessive love for his brother that Farsana can only express the extent of his idiocy by using the word 'stupid' twice in quick succession.

Evidently, Farsana's understanding of this sequence of events as being about Prem's 'obsessive love' for his brother differs from that of another viewer, Azhar (quoted below), for whom the sequence is the embodiment of a *principle*. Crucially, from the point of view of textual analysis, it can only be the *context* of production and consumption that refines and defines a reading of this scene, as otherwise Prem's motivations are not entirely explicit. Continuing our discussion of marriage (quoted in AZH.1), Azhar went on to exemplify his beliefs about what he saw as a ruthless pursuit of family honour by parents both on- and off-screen:

Azhar: It happens all the time, even in films ... like in *Hum Aapke Hain Koun ...!*
Shaku: Yes, do you mean the sacrifice in HAHK?
Azhar: In that film, for the family, Prem and Nisha think they are pre-pared to sacrifice their marriage, their love, everything. They think it is '*our*' family, they think about the consequences of what the family will have to hear and how people will talk about the honour of the family. So Nisha agrees to marry this older man. Prem's brother. In this day and age, the household don't care about the happiness of the young couple, they only care about their own image –
Shaku: [Breaking in] – But in HAHK the family *do* care about the happi-ness of the young couple. The film ends with a happy ending.
Azhar: [ignoring me] I tell you frankly. For their 'image' [*Eng.*], they'll do anything to their children. What nonsense! [loud, angry] They'd marry you off to a lame or blind person [*koi andhe-langde se*] just for their honour, believe me!
Shaku: Do you think that this is just in a few religions and communities?
Azhar: Absolutely not, every religion and every community does this to young people.

(AZH.2/*Hindi*)

This exchange is pertinent for several reasons, most conspicuously the fact that I take up a position in defence of (an aspect of) the film and the way in which Azhar ignores, entirely, the efforts of the director to pre-sent the young people's sacrifice as an unfortunate, accidental but morally positive choice. His claim – that the young people are prepared to sacrifice 'everything' because they think about the consequences of their actions for their family in terms of the honour of the family – is not the way in which the sacrifice is set up on-screen, where it is the *com-passion* of the young people for Prem's widowed brother and their concern for his brother's baby that are offered as incentives for the forfeiting of their own romantic bond. However, in ignoring these supposedly 'exten-uating' circumstances within the film, Azhar undermines the manner in

Figure 4.2   Ruksana and a friend debate the lovers' sacrifice in *Hum Aapke Hain Koun ...!*

which hierarchies in the film are legitimised through their apparently voluntary rather than coerced depiction (Kazmi 1999: 147).

Saliently, both DDLJ and HAHK construct the 'necessity' of sacrifice on the part of young people and then 'revoke' this 'necessity' by some alteration in the older characters' knowledge or understandings. Throughout, the imposition of patriarchal authority is never depicted as being arbitrary: in DDLJ it is provoked by the father's 'love' and his 'ignorance'; in HAHK it is precipitated by the accidental death of Pooja. It can be seen, then, that during our interview, Azhar takes up a position that dissociates his beliefs about marriage from patriarchal discourse on 'arranged marriage'. The fact that HAHK and DDLJ are not overtly advocating a 'strict' form of such a practice makes little difference to Azhar's response to them, for one aspect of his retrospective enjoyment of these films is, it is possible to see, the sense of righteous resentment engendered in him by his assessment of certain ideological stances in the films. Thus, I suggest, while Azhar's critique of HAHK (AZH.2) and DDLJ (AZH.1) has clear political implications, it may also be understood not as a *denial* of his pleasure in these films, but rather as a *manifestation* of it.

Lest it be supposed that Azhar's sensibilities as a 'Muslim' viewer make him more critical of the film than he would have been had its rituals and characters resided within an apparently Islamic utopia, I can only offer his poignant declaration that 'every religion and every community does this to young people' and direct attention to the occasions on which Hindu viewers too were critical of the sequence in question. Sonali, from a highly restrictive Maharastrian Hindu household, was mistaken about the sequence of events in which Nisha and Prem come to sacrifice their love, but scathing of the values that lead to such demands being put upon young people:

Sonali: The parents just want to be able to say that 'the kid married for us and not for themselves'. Oh god, in *Hum Aapke Hain Koun ...!* this is shown so strongly when the girl is going to be forced to marry the brother of her lover and look after his child. She agrees to it too [pause, angry] and then he also agrees.

(SON.1/Hindi)

In this extract, the anger that Sonali feels about parents in 'real life' transfers itself seamlessly on to the parents in HAHK. Sonali's mistaken assertion that the heroine agrees to her 'forced' marriage in HAHK before the hero is interesting in that it could be interpreted either as a misreading that supports her argument about parents and marriage in general or as an unconscious signal of her own deep-rooted expectation that films will represent female characters as being more pliant, malleable and supine than male ones. Whichever of these interpretations we choose, the ability of Hindi films to trigger painful as well as productive and pleasurable outpourings of anger and frustration from young people was nowhere better exemplified than by talk about marriage and family.

Especially in terms of its perception by the young people I interviewed between 2000 and 2003, marriage, in HAHK, really would seem to be between two families rather than between individuals, 'arranged', if not in name then at least in spirit. The visual spectacle, joyful family setting and romance that so captivate some viewers seem only to make the film's defence of crass chauvinism appear in cynical relief. While there is no scene in the whole film that shows anyone being 'compelled' by *external* forces to do anything more onerous than sing another song, acknowledge defeat in a game or eat another mouthful of food – a statement that is certainly not true of *Dilwale Dulhaniya Le Jayenge* – the fact that viewers persist in using the word 'forced' to describe the marriage Nisha narrowly avoids having with her lover's older brother testifies to the other 'narratives' of marriage and family in circulation within Hindi films, to the importance of memory and knowledge in responding to films, and to the discourses and experiences of courtship and marriage in existence within young viewers' communities. It is these 'real' experiences that, albeit implicitly, shape many meanings made from, and feelings about, courtship and marriage in Hindi films.

4.4 Conclusion

As can be seen from foregoing discussions, the views and attitudes to 'marriage' on- and off-screen, expressed by interviewees during their in-depth interviews, while on a broad spectrum, can be found to fall within a fairly narrow range of options.[12] Agreeing to an arranged marriage unreservedly, partly endorsing arranged marriage, partly holding out for a 'love' marriage, and opposing arranged marriage staunchly are the primary positions adopted. Furthermore, the range of discourses about marriage at play in *contemporary* Hindi blockbusters is fairly limited: duty to family generally triumphs over individual passion, which is, in turn, endorsed by the family at the conclusion of the narrative, thus validating the young people's inclination to duty and sacrifice. Other scenarios include the narrative punishment and destruction of lovers who challenge authoritarian patriarchal norms of marriage; the marriage and travails of lovers from different classes or religions; and the decision by a woman who is married off to transfer her loyalty from her erstwhile lover to the man who has become her husband. *Dilwale Dulhaniya Le Jayenge* and *Hum Aapke Hain Koun ...!* are both notable for their espousal of what have been called 'family values', the Hindu joint family system, the importance of parental sanction for marriage and the prospect that one might have to sacrifice one's own desires for the greater family good.

Interestingly, though quite predictably, views expressed about on-screen courtship and marriage were frequently at odds with opinions, beliefs and even actions regarding courtship and marriage in the context of viewers' own lives. In the case of unmarried female viewers such as Neetu, Kavita, Alpa and Ruksana, who display ambivalence about or even liking for the idea of sacrificing individual desire for the sake of a parent, and sometimes assert the correctness of such sacrifices on-screen, all were actually engaged in or had been engaged in clandestine relationships. In the case of young male viewers such as Jomir, Azhar and Kalpesh who favoured 'love' over 'arranged' marriages both in life and films, women's autonomy in families and relationships was often subordinated to a vague sense of their own family traditions and needs. Consequently, it is important to dissociate from the discourse of 'love marriage' used by young viewers any automatic assumption of an egalitarian or anti-patriarchal framework; and from the discourse of 'arranged' marriage occurring in young women's talk, a presumption of submissive acquiescence to *all* the dictates of patriarchy.

In this context, while viewers like Azhar, Jomir and Meeta were never willing to acknowledge, at least during the interviews I conducted, their inconsistent loyalties and conflicting values, several of the young viewers I spoke to *were* aware of, and commented on, such contradictions amongst their beliefs, actions and values as well as in the narratives of the films they enjoyed.

As already noted, DDLJ was named by two-thirds of my interviewees as being their favourite Hindi film of all time. Its early romanticism, the journey taken by the hero to India in pursuit of his beloved, the family atmosphere, and the refusal of the hero to elope were cited repeatedly as being pleasurable triggers for imagination as well as guides to action. Neetu and Kalpesh were both certain that running away with a lover to be married in secret is a mistaken course of action and, like Raj, they assert that they would never do it. Several North Indian viewers, in Uberoi's and Derné's samples too, appear to hold this point of view. However, in stark contrast, Rahul and Azhar were adamant that when they watched DDLJ they were suddenly aware of what they had to do in order to attain happiness – pursue their lovers against all odds and marry them, even if their parents refused to agree, even if they had to elope. Thus the film's 'closure' – a man waiting to be accepted by the bride's father before marrying her, refusing her invitations and her mother's exhortations to defiance – appears to be only as crucial to the meanings taken away from the film as any of the other salient moments in the film, perhaps *less so*, as almost all the young viewers responded with pleasure and enthusiasm to the film's romantic allure and with ambivalence or critique to its portrayal of authoritarian family relationships. In the light of the data presented in this chapter, then, critical evaluations of Hindi films, such as those offered by Lalitha Gopalan, Rustom Bharucha and Fareed Kazmi, can be seen as crucial reminders of some texts' political locations and strategic deployment of authoritarian and patriarchal ideological symbols and discourses, but inadequate if they are taken as encompassing the meanings that all or even most viewers make from the films.

In Chapter 3, I noted how the *immediate context* of Hindi film viewing was a significant factor contributing to the films' construal by young audience members. Here, I have argued that both the distinctive experiences as well as the shared social formations upon which young people call in their interpretation and evaluation of film narratives are acutely relevant to, if not inseparable from, the meanings they create from film representations and discourses. In relation to the topics of family relationships, courtship and marriage, at least, this 'wider context' of viewing, historically differentiated and permeated as it is by conflicting discourses and competing ideological values, cannot be set aside in order to 'measure' the impact of a particular film on the beliefs and actions of viewers. Collective formations alter significantly from location to location; individual life histories are contingent. Thus, films espousing conservative politics and deploying conformist endings may well contribute to and reinforce the right-wing politics of certain viewers, while giving others grounds to recoil in amusement or alarm. With regard to mainstream Hindi films such as DDLJ and HAHK, we may glimpse how excitement and irritation, acceptance and critique, ironic detachment and emotional involvement are by no means mutually exclusive binary oppositions but may coexist within viewers' accounts, appearing to surface at different points of the film, during different viewings or at different times in their lives. Pursuing Hindi film discourses further, in the realms of sexuality, masculinity and femininity, Chapter 5 discusses the common threads across, as well as the disharmonies that emerge from, young viewer's accounts of their feelings about subjects such as clothing, sex, work and violence on- and off-screen.

5
Short Skirts, Long Veils and Dancing Men: Responses to Dress and the Body

5.1 Show and sell: young viewers read clothing in Hindi films

Whether brought up in response to direct questions about attire or more tangentially, discourses around clothing were invoked at various points by each of my interviewees in conjunction with issues as diverse as sexual fantasy, financial status, religion, an apparent deterioration of moral values, and sexual harassment. One of the most common strands in discussions about dress and sexuality on-screen was an appeal to *direct effects* as grounds for censorship of film costumes. After commenting that an actress, Urmila Matondkar, 'must be hardly needing any material for her dresses', Gautham, an unmarried clerk who lives with his parents in a Bombay suburb, worries that after watching performances by Matondkar on screen young women and girls will feel pressured into wearing things that they neither enjoy not feel comfortable in. Although implicitly he is averse to the wearing of 'revealing' clothes by girls and women, he poses the issue in terms of younger women falling prey to male predations:

I've seen the younger generation of girls in schools and colleges wearing these kinds of things, netted-cloth stockings and mini skirts ... I feel that this is dangerous in the sense that the kids might be more of a target for eve-teasing and India might go the Western way with more child pregnancies; I feel that dress plays a part in this. You should wear dresses but only ones that suit you and that you are comfortable in, and a girl might wear a short skirt but keeps on pulling it down. They have no self-defence experience.

(GAU.1/*English*)

Of course, the invoking of the spectre of sexual assault as a rationale for policing the attire of women and girls is hardly novel, but it is important to recognise that, despite his conflation of the 'Western way', 'child pregnancies' and a need for 'self-defence experience', Gautham's language expresses concern about the safety of young women wearing 'filmy' or 'western' clothes and does not position him as offended by their choice of dress. Nevertheless, Gautham's avowed concern could be seen as a displaced form of disapprobation and as an expression of the commonly emphasised opinion that sexual attacks and women's clothing are directly linked to each other. And, lest this be seen as a feature only of male viewers' talk, it must be noted that several female viewers in my sample held this view. Although she 'loves' to wear jeans and T-shirts, Neha too articulates her beliefs about on and off-screen dress via notions of 'westernisation' and endangerment stating, first, that 'girls should avoid very less clothing kind of dress because it is spoiling the whole of what Indian culture is [which is] to cover yourself' and, second, that men have 'a tendency to get attracted and that is what is now leading to the crime what you see in foreign countries like because they are wearing all short skirts and that is what is leading to the rape cases'. In contrast, in an almost dialogic rebuttal of Neha's and Gautham's assumption that a woman is endangered or may be protected by the type of clothing she wears because men's thoughts are aroused or dampened by more or less revealing dress, Sonali maintains that '[e]ven if you go around totally veiled from top to toe the men will whistle and make comments.' This leads her to assert angrily: '[s]o why not show heroines in short clothes? It's female [pause] that's all the men care about [pause]. I cover up totally and still get all kinds of things said.' Echoing Sonali, Kavita too expresses her belief that 'whatever you are wearing, even if you are fully covered, boys will pass comments and worse stuff.' Thus practical experiences of sexual harassment off-screen enable a number of viewers to challenge dominant discourses about clothing, 'Indianness', safety and chastity that may appear to be shared by Hindi film directors and their audiences.

Sonali's reiteration of the idea that self-censorship in dress achieves nothing in a milieu where being female is coded as being sexual prey leads her to make connections between Hindi film dress and gender ideology. In contrast to Gautham, who only mentions the more revealing aspects of actresses' attire, Sonali is infuriated by the ways in which films show women *covering themselves up*:

Sonali: [I]n villages [pause] women are totally traditional, in sarees and veiled. They are abused if they don't and given a warning about 'shameless' behaviour.

Shaku: In your view, are the films you watch against or for … household veiling?

Sonali: Well, [angry voice] the really big blockbusters are totally in favour of veiling like that, wearing the saree over the head in front of elders and male relatives. Like *Hum Aapke Hain Koun …!*, *Hum Saath Saath Hain* [pause] these are really famous and influential.

(SON.2/*Hindi*)

In a manner that echoes critiques by Jatin, Alpa, Nisha and various other London viewers, Sonali's scorn is directed at big-budget films that, to her, assert hegemonic or dominant patriarchal discourses about the ways in which 'Indian' women should conduct themselves when in the presence of elders or strangers and, as a corollary, any spectators.

Expected 'feminine' behaviours are, as usual, inscribed in clothing, which is itself an expression of cultural practice and may be an expression of cultural control (Thapan 1997: 173). Diverging from many other respondents in her repeated emphasis on the difficulties village women face in this respect, Sonali pursues her point about the equation between certain forms of dress and certain patterns of behaviour, noting that 'in the films even educated women who wear tight T-shirts before marriage seem to change and become totally submissive after falling in love [pause] like she changes herself into a saree and she'll cover her head.' Sonali is not alone in linking a supposedly internal attribute – *submissiveness* – to an external iconic signifier – *traditional apparel*. Jatin too was keen to point out his frustration with the ways in which women's personalities appear to alter after a film wedding takes place. Sonali and Jatin are not alone in linking a view of female character to 'traditional Indian' or 'Western' apparel.

While almost every young female viewer interviewed in London questioned the representation of British-Asian girls on screen – for instance, Kareena Kapoor in bikini tops and hot-pants in *Kabhie Khushie Kabhie Gham* and Rani Mukherjee in a short orange-leather miniskirt in *Kuch Kuch Hota Hai* – Nisha was adamant that an insidious linkage between Western forms of apparel and 'promiscuity' or 'shamelessness' in the minds of many Hindi film viewers in India leaves apparently 'modern' girls like her open to censure by community elders and to harassment by men in the street. Her testimony on this issue, and her anxiety about being judged as an embodiment of a Hindi film 'idea' when out of the British context, were repeated in various ways by Hena, Alpa, Padma and Ruksana. In contrast, Preeta, in Bombay, not only admitted that she enjoyed wearing 'Western' clothing but said that she did so precisely because of what she saw as the transgressive, alluring, sexual and 'come hither' associations that they have acquired via their use in Hindi films. Her open enjoyment of male attention and her pride in her own body was, she asserted, better gratified by tight T-shirts, fitting jeans, and low-cut tops than by the salwar khameezes she routinely wore to the Gurudwara for prayers. 'It looks very sexy. That's why I'm wearing it right now', she told me, pointing to her frilly sleeveless top and tight stretch pants. Preeta's participation, without fear, in a discourse of desire, arousal, pursuit and sexuality – through an iconography of clothing in which films, unknown 'others' and her own body are actively engaged – cannot but complicate a view of 'Western' attire on the Hindi film screen as functioning in a system of erotic meaning that is entirely for the pleasure of male viewers. In fact, I suggest, whatever may apparently be said in a public context, and regardless of the film makers' dubious motives for rendering such representations for public consumption, it may be far too simplistic to think of most female viewers as offended by, or even always averse to, stereotypically 'sexualised' depictions of women's bodies in Hindi films.

Jasmine, however, clearly linked sexual harassment in a film to the clothing worn by a heroine:

[S]he seems like a useless, helpless object, waiting to be rescued. So we see huge groups in long shots. We see close-ups showing the fear in her eyes. Karishma [Kapoor] in *Raja Hindustani* when she wears 'that' red dress.

(JAS.1/*English*)

The sequence referred to by Jasmine in this extract, which depicts the negative response of a young villager when the educated and city-bred woman he loves appears in public in his small town wearing a sexy red dress instead of the obligatory salwar-kurta, is one about which I have written in greater detail elsewhere (Banaji 2002).

The fact that the heroine is then harassed by a group of local hooligans precipitates the gentle hero into an unexpected and shocking show of violence, purportedly in defence of her honour, as she looks on in horrified embarrassment. Where Jasmine's rendering of the scene has clothing being used as a triple pretext – first, for men in the film to pick on the woman; second, for the not so subtle warning to young women about what wearing such red dresses might do to them and, third, for the hero to rescue the heroine – and is imbued with feminist irritation,

Figure 5.1 Two London viewers, one head-scarfed, discuss the heroine's short red dress

another viewer, Meeta 'reads' the scene in the context of what she sees as a wider malaise in cinematic costuming:

Meeta: [A]lmost nothing at the bottom; the style of wearing them is wrong, almost like bra at the top and below only panties [pause] one should hide one's youth (javaani) a bit, everyone knows what's underneath but why show it all the time? Yes, wear sleeveless dresses, wear short skirts, but not the stuff that will make boys whistle on the streets like in *Raja Hindustani* when the girl [Karishma Kapoor] wears the red dress, and the boys hanging around shout 'higher, higher' and then [pause] boys also get spoiled like that.

(MTA.3/*Hindi and Gujarati*)

Meeta's assertion that 'boys also get spoiled like that' is both ambiguous and widely held through its basic premise that it is women who *initiate* male sexual harassment: read in one light, she is asserting that film women/real women who dress in certain ways are tempting and thus polluting boys' otherwise 'pure' minds; read in another light, she implies that after watching such a scene in a Hindi film, boys would take for granted their right to treat women in a similar manner, thus being 'spoiled' or losing their innocence. Perhaps exemplifying Meeta's sexist assumptions, several of the young male viewers interviewed in my sample were keen to differentiate between clothing appropriate to a good 'wife' and that which might be worn at other times to excite the interest of men.

In one notable instance, a viewer maintained that the hero of *Raja Hindustani* (*Indian King*, Dharmesh Darshan 1996) was 'old-fashioned' not because he disapproved of the short red dress worn by the heroine, but because he made no distinction between the types of clothing permissible before and after marriage. Enthusiastic about every type of Western/modern outfit found on a female character on screen, Azhar opened the subject by asserting that he 'really' enjoyed seeing everything, 'Jeans, dresses, minis and micros'. When I indicated that he should elaborate, he told the 'story' of his wife's altering costumes and his altered perception of her:

Azhar: [D]uring our college days, I dressed her in all those dresses, tight clothes, I told her I like it very much. In college I made her wear model dresses. While we were together. Whatever she wanted to wear. Even she felt uncomfortable wearing things sometimes and say she preferred salwar kameez and I'd tell her 'please go on, when you look so horny in it, and it's worn by actresses and models, go on'. To me I felt she should wear hipsters, sleeveless T-shirts. Even she began to like to wear those clothes.

Shaku: Does she still wear such clothes after marrying you?

Azhar: Of course not! How would she? She wears salwar khameez ... *Before* she was my girlfriend. *Now* she's my wife. There's a massive difference!

Shaku: Like in films –

Azhar: – See, in some films, like in *Raja Hindustani*, the guy doesn't like such clothes on the heroine *even before marriage*. He's old-fashioned. But I liked her to look like that and wear those things when she was my girlfriend. See, how I feel is, I wanted her to look modern [*Eng.*] when she was my girlfriend. I wouldn't let her expose [*Eng.*] much but she should wear tight jeans, which make her look modern [*Eng.*] but cover her up. It's mod. That was my attitude. Now I think she should not wear all this as it is my custom in my religion, girls should not wear masculine clothes (*mardavni kapde*), manly dresses and I am very religious, so she can't wear jeans or any non-customary wear.

Shaku: But didn't that religious principle apply before?

Azhar: See, when she was my girlfriend, I didn't think we'd get married, so it was okay. And now she's my wife. Before I didn't care if men said things about her. [laughs] But now if they say things about her, then it is an insult to me. I feel bad, you're getting my point? I don't want all that, I don't want to be insulted because of how she dresses ... I don't want her to expose her body. She never wants it either. I convinced her it was necessary for her to give up all those sorts of clothes like jeans.

(AZH.3/*Hindi*)

Azhar's multiple and casual sexist comments in this exchange – from 'I dressed her', 'I made her wear' to 'I am very religious so she can't wear jeans', '[b]efore I didn't care if men said things about her' – would be almost comic, were they not so alarmingly similar to those I heard or heard of in numerous other interviews with both young male and female viewers. Neha's husband encouraged her to wear jeans when going to the cinema with him, but bade her obey his parents and wear a sari indoors; Neetu's boyfriend asked her to wear tight jeans and T-shirts like 'Kareena Kapoor' in *Mujhe Kuch Kehna Hai* (*I Want to Say Something*, Satish Kaushik 2001), but had warned her that she would wear 'only sarees' after marriage; Alpa, in London, knew that her in-laws would not let her wear skirts or trousers and so hoped that she would be able to live separately from them; Kalpesh's older sister, according to him a 'tomboy' and a 'lawyer', had not been allowed to wear skirt-suits or trousers for 12 years after her marriage into a family in Leicester. Like Azhar, Kalpesh too wished to dissociate the idea of his 'wife' from the sexy outfits of young unmarried heroines in films. His somewhat hesitant assertion that 'obviously' he didn't want to 'marry someone who dresses like a tart', and his nervous laughter afterwards (which was supposed to cue reassurance from me, the interviewer), while perhaps indicative of his recognition of the double-standard implicit in his enjoyment of on-screen 'tart-like' outfits (*sic*) and his shunning of women who wear such outfits off-screen, are in no way critical or undermining of the social norms on women's dress.

Azhar's self-obsessed commentary on his wife's apparel and Kalpesh's confused acceptance of what he sees as visual coding for 'loose woman/ chaste woman' through dress may serve to highlight another crucial role played by dress in the landscape of gender relations for young urban viewers – where some are defined as modern and others as old-fashioned – but where the stakes are always higher for women and controlled by men. As noted in Chapter 4, Meeta was one of the young viewers most concerned to identify herself with the dominant discourses of Hindu patriarchy as evinced in Hindi films, while Azhar was one who wished most to distance himself from such traditions. Yet both Meeta's and Azhar's testimony persistently calls attention to the ways in which, when viewed without irony or resistance, the dressing of female characters in Hindi films can be experienced as a confusing narrative of temptation, punishment and repentance or enticement, followed by a timely assumption of chaste dignity. While I have tried to show that some of the ways in which young film viewers in my sample invoke issues of dress in Hindi films reflects their experiences, beliefs and allegiances off-screen, in the next section I will examine other possible interpretations of Hindi film costumes in the light of discussions about on- and off-screen attitudes to sexual desire.

5.2 Clothing, the body and the erotic promise of Hindi films

Debates around dress in Hindi films have most frequently centred round themes of nudity and/or exposure. Arguments that are either anti-Western in their gist or feminist in their intent have coincided in condemning the Indian media in general and Hindi cinema in particular for portrayals of women in tight-fitting, short, low-cut or transparent attire (Bagchi 1996; Nair 2002: 53; Gahlot 2003[1]). My intention in this section is not to deny the strength of negative feeling that on-screen female exposure calls forth within the Indian populace and the intelligentsia, nor, necessarily, to label all such feeling either as mere prudishness or anti-Western rhetoric. I simply wish to signal that, in their own talk about clothing and nudity, 'exposure' and 'covering up', young people go beyond the parameters set up by existing debates. Implicitly, by coding nudity and overt bodily exposure as 'sexual', fully clothed bodies may be relegated to an asexual realm that they, in truth, do not inhabit. Both campaigners against scantily dressed representations of women and, perhaps, some film makers themselves, may well be missing crucial aspects of audiences' enjoyment of Hindi films and of human sexuality.

Might it not be the case that, in some instances, the bodies of women and girls displayed in latex and lycra, shorts, swimming costumes, rent blouses, mini-skirts and sheer fabrics *become* or *are*, to sections of the public, *less sexual* than images of women in flowing sarees and pure white salwar khameezes with high collars and full sleeves? In relation to Jane Campion's film, *The Piano*, Stella Bruzzi argues that 'superficially restrictive clothes function as equivocal signifiers, acting both as barriers to sexual expression and as the very means of reaching sexual fulfilment.' She concludes that '[t]he power of clothes fetishism is that it exists on the cusp between display and denial, signalling as much lack as a presence of sexual desire' (Bruzzi 1997: 38). Both Jasmine and Gautham demonstrate a clear awareness of the ways in which the censorship of female nudity – the tacit Hindi film industry requirement that women remain clothed, albeit scantily, at all times and that no 'explicit' sexual acts be displayed – could be used not to dampen, but to increase the erotic potential of specific scenes and the lust of swathes of the anticipated audience. As Gautham explains:

Gautham: Actually, what Hindi films do is they entice you more than English films. Like, actually, you might find Madhuri Dixit much more sexual in the rain or a bathing scene than an English [Hollywood] actress like Jennifer [Lopez] who strips off completely. In English films they don't leave anything to the imagination, whereas in Hindi films the common man can go wild in his imagination –
Shaku: – Sorry to interrupt, does the 'common man' include you?
Gautham: Oh yes, I suppose, including me. I like Kajol mostly because her nature is lively like mine. I really like her, I might fantasise with her [pause] with her body, so it's good they don't show the whole thing. [pause]

(GAU.2/*English*)

Several issues arise from Gautham's assertions. First, in the light of Gautham's claim that he prefers the covertly eroticised heroines in Hindi films to the overt nudity of heroines in Hollywood films, accounts of Hindi film and censorship, such as that given by Lalitha Gopalan (1998) in her essay 'Coitus Interruptus and Love Story in Indian Cinema' – where she argues that directors are not as unhappy as has sometimes been made out with the various dictates of the censor board precisely because the 'public' has learnt to gain a different kind of pleasure from suggestions and allusive sexual representations – become more plausible.

Second, to view Gautham's 'use' of Hindi films merely as pornographic and hence demeaning to the female characters in films – part of the construction of a men's culture of 'dirty talk' and 'dirty thoughts' about women that makes even urban India such a difficult place to live on terms of equality with men[2] – while warranted, is, I maintain, too simplistic. Although one point of such scenes may be precisely to provoke the sexual and potentially sexist and 'objectifying'[3] response Gautham described – or a similar one – it is also possible that such interludes and representations, which invite viewers into a spectacle where clothing, suggested nudity and transferred kissing (the kissing of objects, hands, necks and abdomens instead of lips) provide much needed 'fantasy' space (Kakar 1990: 27) for segments of the audience such as, perhaps, adolescents or young women. One young lesbian viewer, Abhi, from a working-class family, told me that she uses reactions during discussions about actresses' bodies (breasts, hips and thighs) to gauge whether her friends might be open to hearing about her sexuality. Two young male viewers at the film *Yaadein* talked of their pleasure in *male* bodies on screen, their romantic identification with *heroines* and their crushes on leading actors.

Third, it is also worth recollecting that even such fantasy spaces as these are not seen as wholesome or legitimate in a social setting that denies 'common people' the right to have sexual fantasies outside of marriage and that, in addition, refuses the time and the opportunity for such fantasies to many women, even if they are married (Thapan 1997: 186). Such an awareness may lead one to understand more clearly the reasons why, even when the audiences may not deny their pleasure in a film's erotic moments, the directors cloud the issues of sex and sexuality by disavowing the sexual undercurrents in their films via the use of dance sequences, ultra-conservative dialogues and patriarchal/conformist alterations in character.

Commenting on what she sees as the chameleon ability of the commercial Hindi film to gratify desires that it appears to condemn, Asha Kasbekar argues that once it has 'established its moral credentials' and 'sworn its allegiance to the official, idealised version of Indian womanhood, the Hindi film then dedicates itself to soliciting the prurient gaze by offering ... the woman as an erotic object in the song and dance sequences' (2001: 294). She later insists that, 'by declaring it to be only make-believe, a pretence, the strategy of "performance", allows the narrative to reconcile the woman's idealized chaste Sita-image with her erotic invitations' (2001: 298). For me, some of the most problematic aspects of the most widely held critical positions on spectatorship and Hindi cinema are the implicit suggestions that female viewers' pleasures in Hindi films are: (a) monolithic; (b) likely to be compromised by the eroticisation or sexualisation (which is viewed implicitly as a form of objectification[4]) of female bodies on screen; and (c) can be safeguarded only via the stratagems of moralistic disavowal, spectacular materialism and the reassertion of authoritarian and patriarchal, but non-sexual 'roles' for women within the narrative.

With regard to such objections, at one level, data from my sample suggests that at least outside the *immediate* and *public* viewing context of a cinema hall, both male and female viewers hold a variety of psychological positions and understand images, dialogues and narratives in a range of different ways. Thus, while not necessarily particularly radical or 'politically correct', the meanings taken away from Hindi film representations of the body and the pleasures – both private and sociable – enabled by these representations are certainly not monolithic for either male or female viewers, although the publicly manifested responses may appear to be. At another level, some female viewers may well object to certain depictions of female bodies on-screen: I myself have done so on several occasions. However, surely the idea that a woman on-screen is more 'objectified' when she wiggles her hips and has her cleavage zoomed in on by the camera than when she serves a man his food or covers her head chastely in front of her in-laws is ludicrous. In at least half of my interviews – and most notably with Sonali, Jasmine, Farsana, Nisha, Jatin, Ravi, Ashok, Padma and Kavita – more fierce and forceful objections were raised to the sequences in which women were represented as being foolish (incapable of making decisions and obsessed with trivialities), servile (touching people's feet, falling in love when harassed or slapped), docile (obligingly waiting on men and elders, lowering their gaze, agreeing to get married), obedient (acting according to the wishes and whims of others and covering their heads) – all supposedly the moral window-dressing allowing women's continued engagement with these films – than to those in which women danced seductively or in which women's bodies were glimpsed through their clothes. In fact, despite frequent comments suggesting a consensus that film makers may cynically attempt to appeal to groups of male viewers by displaying actresses' bodies in flimsy garments, in a number of cases interviewees of both genders, in both locations, chose to dwell at length on their own enjoyment of dances, clothing and bodies on screen.

Clearly, one must acknowledge, the criteria for labelling a representation chauvinist is not bound up solely with the perception of that representation by the represented group. However, the complexity of debates over 'acceptable' and 'unacceptable' screen representations (cf. Buckingham and Bragg 2004) is still rarely acknowledged in most textual critiques. Even Jasmine, who comes closest to a position typical of the Indian feminist movement in the 1980s and 1990s,[5] moves from explicit condemnations of the vulgarity and sexism that she sees as inherent in screen portrayals of semi-clothed women – 'It is very patriarchal and sexist' – to a more light-hearted enthusiasm for the provocative, sexual allurement available to her and her female friends:

> I can't deny that the portrayal of a man's body often turns me on, especially when accompanied by music. I am not shy about this attraction either. I wouldn't use the word 'turn-on' in front of my parents but I have often 'oohed' and 'aahed'. I remember how Hrithik's portrayal in the dance sequences absolutely floored me in *Kaho Na Pyar Hai*. After watching this, my friends were discussing how his biceps should be transplanted to his bum!
>
> (JAS.2/*English*)

At one level, Jasmine's movement from condemnation of 'objectification' to empathy with such objectification is characteristic of a number of discussions of sexual issues by young Hindi film viewers and indicates both the shifts and reassessments taking place during an interview and the tendency of confident young viewers to condemn others for doing what they are proud of doing themselves. Jasmine's assertion that she was 'absolutely floored' suggests a palpable sexuality that is as, if not more, assertive than Gautham's. Indeed, what Jasmine's account might signal, then, is the possibility of less essentialist and moralistic descriptions of men's and women's pleasure in films.

Certainly, if the quasi-sexual pleasures inherent in the viewing of Hindi cinema as it is today are not to be labelled as perverse, and discouraged, then a reassessment of the ways in which debates around 'sexual objectification' on-screen are pursued off-screen (Ghosh 1999) may well be apposite. Indeed, for some young viewers in Bombay, talking openly about issues of the body and physical pleasure is both playful and an act of resistance:

Shaku: [smiling] Do you like it when muscles are shown?
Sonali: Absolutely! I think if they have good bodies I like to see them. My friends and I like to look and to comment on everything. I enjoy the men's bodies on screen.

(SON.3/*Hindi*)

Sonali's mischievous attitude to the portrayal of the body on-screen can be seen to undermine dominant assumptions, beliefs and claims made by some British-Asian interviewees in my sample, by community elders and in Hindi films about traditional 'Indian' girls/women and their sense of shame and honour. Nevertheless, as will be seen during discussions of the subject in Chapter 6, speaking about sex with young female viewers in Bombay is never straightforward.

5.3   Conclusion

I have tried to show in this chapter that the ways in which young viewers in my sample talk about screen representations of gender and sexuality via iconographic markers such as clothing or nudity are neither monolithic nor straightforward. Young viewers wanted to talk about much more than just the representation of nudity and/or vulgar/scanty outfits in dance scenes or on vamps. While there were a number of negative references to the exposure of women's bodies, there were as many positive references to the delights of screen clothing. The pleasures to be received from such brilliant visual displays of colours, styles and fashions, the vicarious enjoy-ment to be had from watching others wear outfits that one is not allowed to wear or prevented by lack of money from purchasing, the sexual excite-ment of watching both heroes and heroines cavort, partially disrobe and display their bodies, both in and through their screen garments, were often described *alongside* ideological critiques of the discourses evoked through other aspects of film costume. Most notably, the tendency to represent women in skimpy Western clothing before marriage and in sarees after-wards, to show them covering their heads with their sarees in front of family members or hiding their faces with veils when outside the house, was singled out by several young viewers as obnoxious and frustrating. Additionally, sometimes the class or religious connotations of certain forms of dress were referred to as being alienating and either insensitive or deliberately exclusive. *In almost all cases, young people's social back-grounds, individual upbringings and concomitant ideological frameworks con-tributed to a large extent to the meanings made from Hindi film costumes.*

Whilst I acknowledge the importance of arguments about the negative impact of the depiction of 'sexual objectification' of the female body on-screen, the significance of censorship and the connections between chastity and Indianness to understandings of popular Indian films and other media, the meanings taken away from films by young viewers are rarely unaffected by the experiences, understandings and meanings brought to these films by these same viewers. Analysing Italian director Pierre Paolo Pasolini's view of spectatorship Maurizio Viario (1993: 46) writes that for Pasolini: 'the spectator's passion is the element that allows them to re-create the message in accordance with their subjectivity.' Furthermore: 'a viewer is never free to fulfil the role of ideal spectator that the text in isolation seems to construct.' Given the ways in which our families and communities, our friends, childhood experiences and reli-gious and political beliefs may shape the way we understand and respond to the world, it seems that one cannot but acknowledge the significance of Pasolini's conceptualisation of spectatorial 'passion' as a motivating force in shaping interpretations of films. Assuredly, young viewers do sometimes express their understandings of films in ways that can easily be related to critical accounts of the ideological nexus between Hindi film texts and 'audiences'. However, they frequently go beyond these domi-nant accounts in surprising and/or disconcerting ways.

6
More or Less Spicy Kisses: Responses to Sex, Love and Sexuality

6.1 Contextualising the Indian media sex debate

In some ways *Koi Mere Dil Se Pooche* (*Someone's Asking my Heart*, Vinay Shukla 2002) epitomises the concerns of this chapter by stressing the themes of dress, sex/uality, pornography and gender relations in a supposedly 'typical' urban Indian setting. An early sequence between the hero and one of his female college friends, 'Anna', allows a glimpse of the treatment of 'other' sexualities in Hindi films. Having had her advances rejected by the hero, Anna proceeds to interrogate his sexuality, saying *in English*, 'Tell me one thing, honestly.' When Aman, the hero, asks, 'What?' She continues suggestively, 'Log kehthe hai ki tumhe ladkiyoan me koi interest nahi, *is it because you're the other type*?' ['People say that you have no interest in girls, is it because you're the other type?']. The camera lingers on both faces; his puzzled and then verging on incredulous as she insinuates, 'Kya tum ladkoan ko pasand karthe ho?' [Is it that you prefer boys?']. In Aftab Shivdasani's expression when he remonstrates, 'Anna! *Are you mad!* Obviously I'm not into boys!', the limits of most conventional Hindi films' overt discourse on non-heterosexuality are traced.[1] From that moment onwards, the hero – who works hard, studies fashion design and has a good relationship with his father – must actively woo a heterosexual love object, and defend her honour, in order to redeem himself. And, despite the film's challenge to certain myths about perfect Indian heterosexual marriage, and notwithstanding its unusual portrayal of affection between a mother-in-law and daughter-in-law, this is precisely what the script has him do.

In foregoing chapters I have stressed the importance of linking the practices of film viewing and interpretations of film to the encompassing social and historical arena. Thus, broadly speaking, I will posit that the interpretations and discourses of sex and sexual harassment, gender and the body that are foregrounded in the narratives of viewing deployed in this chapter do not exist within a hermetically sealed space exclusive to viewers and films, but circulate within communities and are inflected variously in many salient social practices. Magazines such as *Trikone*, as well as a number of academic studies in recent years, have sought to map attitudes to aspects of community practice with regard to gender and sexual relationships amongst youth in India (Abraham and Kumar 1999; Sodhi and Verma 2000; Abraham 2002) and the diaspora (see, for instance, Ghuman 1999; Ralston 1999; Leonard 2000; Maira 2002; and Kawale 2003). The Deepa Mehta film *Fire*, too, called forth a number of fascinating articles regarding Indian sexuality/ies, film representation and feminism; amongst these, Kapur (1999), Kishwar (1999), John and Niranjana (1999), Moorti (2000) and Bachmann (2002) give a flavour of the critical and *explicitly political* positions. Leena Abraham's work on the health implications of heterosexual peer networks and relationships amongst college students in Bombay offers some pertinent background for discussions of heterosexual relationships and representations in this chapter. She views sexuality as a 'cultural construct, shaped by specific historical contexts within different communities and social groups' (2002: 338) and her categorisation of students' own descriptions of their cross-gender peer relationships into three typologies – 'bhai-behen (*like* brother-sister)', 'true-love' and 'time-pass' (2002: 350) – corresponds broadly with the descriptions of and gossip about such relationships in interviews with my sample of young film viewers. Abraham's assertion that 'although true love is more romantic' and may postpone sexual intercourse until after marriage, 'time pass and true love relationships are characterized by sexual intimacy' (2002: 345) will be seen to be borne out by young film viewers' accounts of dating and romance.

Both in life and films, female 'virginity' and sexual violence remain issues of key significance for young audiences. In Bombay, the onus for remaining chaste is almost uniformly placed upon girls and women, while young men are known to engage, covertly, in a multitude of exploratory sexual practices and, sometimes, sexual violence without attracting much or any public censure. Quite apart from its social and health implications, the disparity in sexual experience between young men and women in Bombay, Abraham argues, is linked in some way to the *normative heterosexuality* prevalent in Hindi films. She then points to the prescriptive nature of the 'true love' relationship as portrayed in Hindi films, 'where it revolves around sexual desires, fantasies that are explicitly erotic at times, but stops short of transgressing the normative boundary of sexual intercourse' (2002: 347). Sodhi and Verma, meanwhile, conclude their paper on 'sexual coercion' among unmarried adolescents in a Delhi slum with the finding that '[c]inema plays a role in perpetuating gender stereotypes, by encouraging girls to idealise the notion of "true love" and encouraging boys to seek sexual gratification' (2000). So, is it the case that the depictions of romance and sexuality in Hindi films always and only contribute to conservative understandings of sex and sexuality within the viewing community? What other factors might contribute to the meanings young viewers make of film representations of sexual behaviour? And how do film representations of sexuality, masculinity and femininity become meaningful for young viewers in real contexts? These are some of the questions with which this chapter aims to grapple.

6.2 Taboo scenes: kissing, sex and the 'innocent' viewer

I was fascinated by the similarities and differences between Meeta's denial of arousal at sexual scenes, to which we will turn in a moment, and Sonali's ambivalent response:

Shaku: And other films – how do they show sex in your view?

Sonali: Oh looking into each other's eyes for ten minutes at a time [pause] what the hell are they thinking? [scornful] cheek kissing, photograph kissing, [laughs] then cut to a song! Flying clothes, gardens, mountains, I don't know [laughing]. Like in *Raja Hindustani* they're outside getting wet in the rain again [laughs] and God knows what happens to them, but suddenly she comes close to him and they 'smooch' [*Eng.*] and they are all wet and it's all seen and the men in the theatre where I saw it were so happy they were whistling, the men [laughs].

Shaku: How did you feel?

Sonali: I felt nothing. Nothing at all.

(SON.4/*Hindi*)

While the developments and withdrawals that occurs within Sonali's answer are themselves a reflection of her wish to engage with the issue, to explore her own responses and those of others, her frequent laughter acts to prevent any serious content in her discourse from becoming too threatening to customary ways of speaking about sex amongst her age group and milieu. Nevertheless, she is at pains to emphasise her non-judgemental attitude to those who were aroused by the scene of the kiss in *Raja Hindustani*. Nor is she the only viewer to express detachment from the kinds of intimacy permitted on the Hindi film screen. Padma, of a similar age in London, declared: 'I can't take [kissing] in commercial Hindi films! It's really funny! Like in *Raja Hindustani* there's a kissing scene and you go "Oh my God!" She suddenly realises she loves him *just because he kisses her*! [laughing]'.

Neither Padma nor Sonali object to the kiss at a moral level, nor do they suggest that such scenes should not be shown. However, their doubts lie at the intersection of aesthetic and modal criteria: it is the implausible *manner* of the screen kisses they have seen, and the psychological weight that these gestures are forced to bear, which give these young viewers a pretext for saying they were, or for remaining, emotionally uninvolved. Meeta, meanwhile, who does object to kiss sequences, and appears to be far more emotionally involved with the protagonists of such sequences, is equally keen to assert her lack of emotion on watching sexually charged interludes on screen:

Shaku: May I ask you a bit about sex? [she nods] ...
Meeta: Mmm. many times, many scenes. Like love marriages happen and then two people sit and ... they sink into a reverie and you know what they're thinking [pause]
Shaku: And then a song comes?
Meeta: Yes then a song and it seems that they are not showing [pause]
Shaku: Sex?
Meeta: Yes. There's a bit in *Dil to Pagal Hai* at the party, where Madhuri Dixit and Shah Rukh attend and then afterwards they [the directors] start showing it [sex?] but she runs away and stops it. A bit happens, he holds her hand [pause]
Shaku: But you feel better that they didn't show anything too explicit?
Meeta: Yes. Surely.
Shaku: But do these scenes ever make you think about these issues, sex?
Meeta: No, never. No.

(MTA.4/*Hindi*)

I prompt Meeta on two occasions during this exchange, and the possible implications of such prompting for the outcome of the interview should not be ignored; in this instance, however, I was responding to what appeared to be a division or conflict within Meeta at the point when she stopped speaking. She could not bring herself to use the word 'sex'. This did not necessarily mean, however, that she wanted to end the conversation, as her halting but fairly extended description of the sexually charged birthday night sequence in *Dil To Pagal Hai* (*The Heart is Crazy*, Yash

Chopra 1999) shows. When Meeta really cannot sustain the discussion any longer, in the context of my direct question about herself and her desires, she does not pause but is decisive and abrupt: 'No never. No.' Widely differing in their views as these two Bombay viewers are, we should be aware that Meeta and Sonali are similar and certainly not unusual, given the interview context, in their *discomfort* when asked about their own sexual arousal, expressing their interest in Hindi film sequences tentatively and withdrawing when implicated directly in the scenes they describe.

Earlier in the interview, Meeta herself brought up the theme of sexual displays in Hindi films when I had not initiated the topic. What she says here may be read as a counterpoint to Sonali's assessment of the same scene in the film *Raja Hindustani*. The sequence mentioned here by Meeta and earlier by Sonali is set in a field under a huge tree. After a child-like run across open spaces during which it becomes clear that the heroine has become emotionally attached to the hero, her chauffeur, but is unaware of her own feelings, rain forces the pair to take shelter. In the scene that follows Aamir and Karishma kiss directly on the lips, Karishma strokes Aamir's head, and the pair's lips are shown from a number of angles, prompting Nikhil, a working-class Bombay viewer to exclaim:

> That was a great scene. I liked it very much. Actually, mostly, it was the first picture in which they showed such an open kiss ... Mostly otherwise they always just show when a villain is going to rape some woman, then they show such a scene. And this is shown that they are under the experience of love and they smooch (*Pyaar ke ehsaas me*). That was what was so refreshing and new. Really unusual.
>
> (NKL.2/*Hindi*)

While Nikhil does not conceal his enthusiasm, Meeta responds to this depiction with a determined sense of shame that should alert one to the many meanings such a lingeringly portrayed screen kiss can have in different contexts. She progresses from idea to idea becoming steadily more unsettled:

Meeta: [S]ometimes I do feel that some dance steps and scenes are too forward, too [pause]
Shaku: For instance?
Meeta: Like for example, *Raja Hindustani* when they are under the tree, that five-minute scene of Karishma and Aamir Khan standing [pause] it's been made way too long and unnecessary because it didn't have to be longer than a minute and it has a really bad effect (*assar*) on girls and boys.

Shaku: In your opinion?
Meeta: Yes.
Shaku: So did it have any 'effect' on you?
Meeta: I thought they [the censors] shouldn't have shown that; I felt
   nothing was good in that scene. I didn't like it at all. I liked the film as
   a whole but if there were families there, then they would have felt
   shame (sharam) and, if a boy and a girl had come together to the cinema to watch the film, then it might give them ideas, and it has very
   bad, shameful effects.

(MTA.5/Hindi)

Elsewhere (Banaji 2002), I have discussed the salience of Meeta's perception of the length of this kiss – 'that five-minute scene' – which is actually
under a minute long. Meeta's misperception or exaggeration suggests that
the connotative impact of such a kiss, in a cinema that by and large
eschews lip-to-lip contact, may far outweigh the denotative or cinematic
significance of the moment. When pressed about the content that she
found so disturbing, Meeta escapes back to her censorious 'adult' voice,
threatening dire social consequences if a 'smooch' is allowed on to screens
across the nation:

Meeta: [she hesitates, I encourage her] A girl and a boy stand and they
   'smooch' [quickly] each other. But if any adolescent boys and girls see

Figure 6.1   Watched by two young viewers, Karishma and Aamir push boundaries
in *Raja Hindustani*

that, then they might also think 'we should also do that'. Both can get spoiled. From this the whole of India will get spoiled.

(MTA.5ctd./Hindi)

From her anxieties about family viewers and 'very bad, shameful effects' to her assertion about 'the whole of India' getting 'spoiled', it is possible to interpret Meeta's response to this kiss sequence partly as displaced shame at her own implicit arousal by a scene that her community has brought her up to believe is implicitly un-Indian: her triple denial of enjoyment – 'it's been made way too long and unnecessary', 'I felt nothing was good in that scene' and 'I didn't like it at all' – can, perhaps, be read as an indication of an intense and sustained embarrassment at the ways in which one may be *seen* being drawn into film texts when viewing them in cinema halls.[2] Were she alone, there would be no one to witness her response; were she at home, the option of leaving the room would exist, thus enabling her to distance herself from the spectacle; in the cinema hall she is 'trapped' – watching the kiss and knowing that others know she is watching it. This may account for her wish for an external censor: 'I thought they [the censors] shouldn't have shown that.' This does not mean, necessarily, that Meeta lies overtly when she claims never to feel anything during erotic scenes in Hindi films.

Inhabiting the 'traditional' sphere of a conservative and ever-vigilant community, Meeta chooses to reject – at least during our interview – the discourse of young love and erotic curiosity that is inscribed through

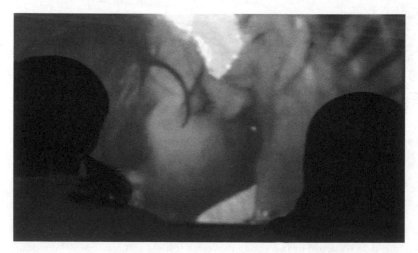

Figure 6.2   The 'smooch' viewed by South-Asian students in London

Aamir and Karishma's kiss. Instead, she initiates discourses of ethnic authenticity and moral censorship, positioning herself as a *truly Indian* moral censor – who may or may not watch, but is apparently unsullied by what she sees – and decides that kissing on screen is bad because it has bad effects on families, couples and the nation. In this context, what might surprise us, I suggest, is not that viewers such as Meeta resort to a discourse of effects in relation to screen representations of bodies and desire from which they may feel themselves to be excluded, but that some young viewers in London – who watch the same films, and may not overtly appear to face many of the restrictions faced by young viewers in Bombay – as well as many commentators should so readily accept a version of 'Indian' femininity that codes it as normative, submissive and asexual. However, in the light of all viewers' need to position themselves in relation to an 'other', neither of these discourses should be read as giving uncomplicated access to viewers' understandings of 'Indian' sexuality or femininity.

6.3 Sexuality, chastity and national honour: 'being' Indian in Switzerland and various other sexual encounters

While Meeta claims to view the entry of sexualised visual discourse into 'family films' or romantic melodramas such as *Raja Hindustani* as an invasion having negative 'effects', Sonali reads a similarly risqué scene in *Dilwale Dulhaniya Le Jayenge* in a radically different manner. Commentaries by young viewers, such as the ones mentioned in Chapter 4, about the initial meeting between Raj and Simran set up a number, but not all, of the various positions about normative middle-class gender relations and conservative heterosexual ideals of sexual 'purity' that come centre stage in DDLJ. During the sequence of interest here, dubbed by some viewers the 'Swiss hotel room' scene, in particular – at the conclusion of which, the hero and the heroine become tentatively 'aware' for the first time, of their 'true' feelings for each other – the director's beliefs about chastity and a specifically 'Indian' masculinity and femininity are show-cased.

After refusing to sleep in the same room as Raj, Simran finds herself freezing in a barn outside a Swiss chalet. Raj arrives to keep her company and, when he has fallen asleep, she drinks Cognac from a bottle and the film lunges into a sensuous and provocative sequence in which Simran dances, calls to Raj and sings a song. During this song, and supposedly under the influence of alcohol, the two young protagonists embrace, swim together in a pool and nearly kiss. Riding home together in a horse-cart as

Figure 6.3   London Bengali youth discussing the 'Swiss hotel' sequence

the alcohol wears off, they sit close together, arms around one another in the manner of acknowledged lovers or best friends of the same sex. However, awaking in the morning to find herself in bed in the hotel room dressed only in one of Raj's shirts, Simran appears distressed. When Raj shows her some lipstick marks on his chest and tells her that the previous night, 'what happened was exactly what was supposed to happen', she weeps with horror at the thought that she has inadvertently lost her virginity, prompting Raj to reassure her that he is far too 'Indian' to have even dreamt of having sex with an 'Indian' girl (presumably before marriage).

The meanings that young people may take away from this scene suggest that the ideological pressures of Hindi film sequences on sexuality may be incredibly tangled and volatile. Thus, talk-based responses to the 'Swiss hotel room' scene amongst my sample varied significantly, at times based on gender-linked ideologies and at others on more nebulous beliefs about sexuality, chastity and national character. Several of the discussions provoked by this scene, both in London and in Bombay, were indicative of young women's fears – about pregnancy, being 'taken advantage of', and being 'shamed' – and of powerful wishes to indulge sexual curiosity within a safe and non-threatening environment. Nisha, an 18-year-old Gujarati Hindu student in London who, at the time of the interview, was having a regular and consensual, although secret, sexual relationship, nevertheless read the scene as one of potential danger saying, '[i]f I was drunk and I found some guy on top of me, it'd be the scaredest thing in the world because I don't want to be pregnant before marriage, that's just the worst thing that could happen to me, 'cause I don't want to hurt my parents.'

This avowed anxiety about hurting parental feelings was one shared by other unmarried female viewers of this scene in both countries, regardless of their class or religion.[3] Meanwhile, eschewing thoughts of pregnancy, several of the young men interviewed insisted that Simran had had a 'lucky escape'. When I asked him whether he thought Simran was correct to be upset at the possibility of having had sex with Raj, 16-year-old British-Bengali Jomir responded:

Jomir: Yeah. Because after all, our Eastern culture is [pause] especially when you go to India and everything [pause] men do not go into bed with ladies and have sex, especially before marriage [pause] She's meant to be [chaste][pause] ... I think Hindi films they do actually give you some kind of taste of how good and nice our culture is actually ...

Shaku: So you don't think *any* 'Indian' man would have sex with a drunk girl in that situation? They wouldn't take advantage?

Jomir: [pause] Yeah, people would, people who lives in this country. I don't think in India, Bangladesh, Pakistan, I don't think they would. Unless they are brought up bad, like they're very poor or something like that. If they are medium [middle class] I don't think they would do something like that. They would be scared, they'd have something like that inside them telling them not to.

(JOM.2/*English*)

Working-class Jomir's singularly staunch belief in the sanctity of *middle-class South-Asian masculinity*, its ability to withstand sexual temptation, preserve female chastity, and avoid wrongdoing was unusual within my sample, but not unique. To varying degrees other male viewers – for instance, Gautham, Bhiku, Harish and Manish – believed that certain groups of men were less likely to commit rape, sexual assault or harassment than other groups of men. All those named were committed to the view that working-class or 'poor' men were more likely to sexually harass women than middle-class men. However, while Jomir, a British Bengali-Muslim, shows confidence in the traditions (or the fears) instilled by the 'culture' into young British-Asian men, regardless of their religion, *vis-à-vis* women's chastity; Manish, a British Gujarati Hindu, explicitly told me that he believed that few *Hindu* men in Britain would harass a woman or 'take advantage' of her whereas, in his view, men in India and, in particular, Muslim men were well known for doing such things.

Meanwhile, the (simplistic) assertion that Hindi films, or certain sequences in them, somehow keep young British-Asians in touch with their cultural heritage, while articulated most clearly by Jomir, was not expressed just by young male viewers, but was taken up in other contexts by female British-Asian viewers such as Alpa and Ruksana and is also to be found in critical writings about Hindi films. Nevertheless, in relation to the 'Swiss hotel sequence' in DDLJ, *the divide in terms of understandings of, and responses to, the scene was definitely more one of gender than of geography or religion.* For instance, whether, like Rahul and Azhar, they considered all male sexuality to be predatory and Shah Rukh Khan the hero to be a shining example of masculine control in a world of licence and dishonourable behaviour, or whether, like Bhiku and Jomir, they saw male sexual restraint as a specifically 'Indian' virtue, almost none of the young men I interviewed appeared much perturbed by the discourses at play in the scene. Several young female viewers, however, first tentatively and then with increasing confidence, outlined their reservations about the intentions, underlying 'ideologies' and possible 'effects' of the morning after sequence in the Swiss hotel.

Sonali remarked that in a Hindi film which wishes to be viewed as a 'family film', even when sexual intimacy or cross-gender friendship is merely *suggested* it has to be disavowed:

Sonali: [I]n *Dilwale Dulhaniya Le Jayenge* they do spend a night together but to stop assumptions about her modesty being cast they show them sleeping in different places. *Why? Why?* Why shouldn't they sleep side by side whether or not they want to have sex? [pause]

(SON.4/*Hindi*)

For Sonali, this film, like countless other Hindi films,[4] maintains its precarious balance between 'teenage' romance and (newly fashionable, middle-class) 'Indian' family 'traditions' at the expense of the woman's autonomy and control over her sexuality; she finds this disturbing and hypocritical. When I asked her what she would have done in a situation similar to Simran's, her response was cautious but prompt, '[w]ith my boyfriend? Of course I'd have sex – I'd sleep with him if … my parents were not there. If I knew him well enough and we had an understanding.' That she qualifies her statement with 'if my parents were not there' and 'if I knew him well enough and we had an understanding' does not alter the fact that, for a lower-middle-class Indian girl, talk of sexual intercourse before marriage is taboo. In a way Sonali shows the courage of her convictions and shames Aditya Chopra, DDLJ's director, by her elucidation of his film's subtext:

Sonali: [I]t seems to me that after watching things like that in films these young people here, my friends, others, they think this is how things should be, *this is the only way they should be* [emphasis hers]. If you are caught holding hands, it is seen as such a momentous thing (bahut badi baath maani jaathi hai) [pause]
Shaku: But you don't think it is?
Sonali: [laughing] Of course not! It's *nothing* [her emphasis; pause]

(SON.6b.*Hindi*)

Here it can be seen that Sonali is angered by what she sees as the director's prescriptive moralistic stance on sexual relationships. However, while Sonali may be correct in identifying the public discourse of intimacy amongst her age group and social class as being infected with a rhetoric from such sequences in films, other viewers suggest that, in practice, the films have barely any connection with the types of physical and sexual intimacies and explorations taking place in communities of young viewers. Echoing some of the comments made by Ismail about public attitudes to nudity and dress, after an extended discussion of his liking for the romantic aspects of DDLJ, Rahul, a 21-year-old metal worker in Bombay, was open about his discontent with current social practice and rhetoric on sex and sexual depictions:

Rahul: I think somehow that Hindi films indirectly do want to show sex, they do, they go almost the whole way and then pull back for fear of public opinion or censors, like the kiss in *Raja Hindustani* and other scenes. But in real life, the public is miles ahead of the movies in terms of sex. They're doing everything that the films aren't showing yet, believe me! ... Some people say in public, 'Dirt! What rubbish!', but alone they exclaim, 'Wah! Wah!' (Wow!) People never want to be *seen* thinking about sex.

(RHL.1/*Hindi*)

As Rahul indicates, various young viewers I interviewed were both aware of, and frequently participants in, a range of intimate non-platonic relationships where varying degrees of physical and sexual intimacy, and on occasion violence or coercion, were the norm. Nikhil was open about the fact that before his arranged marriage he had had a sexual relationship with an older woman whom he 'admired'. Neetu, Jasmine and Kavita, while understandably reluctant to discuss their sexual exploits on tape, were engaged in highly physical relationships with boyfriends.

Asima and Kalpana, two young lesbians whom I met at a Hindi film event in London spoke openly about their sexuality[5] and stated jokingly that their sexual relationship was 'much better than anything Preity'll get from Shah Rukh or Saif Ali [Khan]'. Asima's elderly middle-class mother was also at the event and appeared to be in the confidence of the two young women. Both young women had initially had white partners and were still in contact with their ex-girlfriends. However, they asserted, being together and especially 'being able to share things like Hindi songs, filmi club events and our total disgust about stuff like the [then impending] attack on Iraq' were Kalpana's reasons for preferring to be with 'another British-Asian'. And, as if such accounts are not enough to confirm Rahul's sense of the immensely intricate situation in real communities of viewers, right at the end of her two-hour interview, Preeta in Bombay, whose bold comments about wishing to wear sexually desirable clothes were mentioned earlier, gave a slightly sheepish but candid description of her encounters with pornographic material:

Preeta: [pause, then emphatic] *Nothing is wrong* if the boy and the girl want to do it. Nothing is wrong. But if the parents say no, then it should be [has to be] under cover again.

Shaku: So how have you found out about issues to do with sex and sexuality?

Preeta: Movies. Blue movies.

Shaku: What did you think of them?

Preeta: Wonderful. It was wonderful. It was the first time I saw it. And you've seen on the net?

Shaku: On the net? You have a computer?

Preeta: Oh no. No. We go in Cyber cafes. It's very productive out there. [laughs] I just go with one of my friends, the Muslim girl I told you about. We look at only sex sites.

Shaku: Only those sites!

Preeta: Yeah. I have got to know so many things about that [sex]. [long pause] Actually, I never knew before about how to have sexual intercourse. But watching a [blue] movie, I just came to know about all these things.

Shaku: Do your friends also use such films to learn about sexuality and sex?

Preeta: Yeah, maybe. Sometimes they laugh a lot and sometimes they feel shy too. I'm the leader of the group. We go at our friends' places, we just [rent] the cassettes ...

Shaku: What kinds of films?

Preeta: [laughing] I don't exactly remember it now but *Triple X* and things like that. At least eight of my friends have seen these movies with me. I would say ... Some of the scenes make us laugh so much, you know. But at times we just be serious, and we watch it like that [sitting forward and showing me how they stare at the screen], we watch it to see what happens.

Shaku: I'm getting the impression that for some of you sex is completely separate and romance is completely separate.

Preeta: Ya, it is. In life it comes together. But in films – no.

(PTA.2/*English and Hindi*)

After asserting her view that consensual sex before marriage is perfectly acceptable at the end of a discussion of the Swiss hotel scene in DDLJ, Preeta swiftly begins to describe her own garnering of knowledge about sex. In this trajectory that she describes, 'blue' movies and internet sex sites play an equally important role, apparently introducing not only Preeta – who is herself from a very conservative lower-middle-class family – but also her Muslim best friend, and up to eight other young friends of theirs, to various images of sexual intercourse that they, according to Preeta, have not considered before and have not encountered in Hindi films. Overall, an equal number of young men and women in my sample, springing equally from different religious and class contexts, dwelt at length, and with sustained interest, on the romantic narratives and the sexual under-currents of a range of Hindi films. In this context, Preeta's description of watching her first commercial pornographic film as 'Wonderful – it was wonderful' must serve as a caution that generalisations which categorise all male viewers of Hindi films as more focused on sex and the erotic than their female counterparts who, perhaps, are seen to await the moral sub-texts or the romance in films, do little justice to the complexities of view-ing communities or (South-Asian male and female) desire.

Returning to the Swiss hotel sequence in DDLJ via these accounts of current sexual knowledge and practices by young viewers in Bombay, it must be noted that other young female viewers were more conscious and disparaging of the scene's crude attempts to code 'Indian' feminin-ity and masculinity as, respectively, sexually *chaste* and *restrained* in com-parison with 'Western' femininity and masculinity. Having been told by

several viewers such as Alpa and Neha that they believed there were differences between 'Western' and 'Indian' views of virginity, I was interested in the annoyance evinced by other young women and by a couple
of young men when we discussed their understandings of the Swiss
hotel sequence's attitude to *ethnic* or *national* characteristics.

Farsana, a young Bombay viewer who adores DDLJ and has seen it
countless times, was passionate in her critique of what she perceived to
be the ideological subtext of the Swiss hotel sequence:

Farsana: [Emphatic, derisive] Huh! If you'll just see that no! I feel that
   nowadays there's nothing like 'Indian' girls or anything ...
Shaku: Why do you feel that?
Farsana: Because there are many females whom I know who have
   [pause] ... done *everything*. And they behave like [pause] like, 'I am just
   a virgin'. So you cannot say that this [being a virgin] makes you an
   Indian ... I don't socialise with those who think that ... [pause] that
   such a thing [virginity] makes you an Indian.

(FAR.2/*English*)

Farsana's contention is not merely that distinguishing 'Indian' girls via an
association of Indian femininity with chastity and virginity is absurd when
many of the 'Indian' girls she knows are no longer virgins; more significantly, she implies that the pressure to be viewed as a virgin leads to a social
situation in which girls in India have to pretend to be virgins in order to be
treated as *Indian* girls. Touching on a similar idea, Padma, another fan of
DDLJ, explored her varying feelings about the 'Swiss hotel' sequence via a
thoughtful analysis of the heroine's tearful response to the hero's suggestion that she had lost her virginity during the night:

Padma: And when she cries, well I think it's all to do with personal belief,
   isn't it? If it's important to you – Black people, white people it [virgin-
   ity] can be important too, it doesn't matter what colour you are, it [vir-
   ginity] can be important personally. There I know it's important to her
   culture. He reinforces it and says, 'I wouldn't do that to you. I'm a
   Hindustani.' [laughs] They're trying to reinforce that thing that
   a 'Hindustani' wouldn't do that [take a girl's virginity] ... And yeah,
   the Hindustani thing came in and I thought, 'Yeah, *right*' [pause] ...
   [The director's] trying to say that to anyone but a Hindustani [taking
   a girl's virginity] wouldn't matter. *Really!* That's what I reckon. Asian
   blokes do think that white women are easier to *get*, you know.

(PAD.3/*English*)

Here, despite her positive response to one aspect of the 'morning after' scene, Padma is far from being drawn into the discourses that ensue: nothing shows her disgreement with what she sees as the director's unsubtle moralising more clearly than her laughter and her derisive 'Yeah, *right!*'. Added to her sense of the director's false eulogising of Indian masculinity, Padma introduces a phenomenon that the young viewers in Bombay do not mention – some Asian men's belief that, while Asian women's virginity is so precious that it should be preserved at all costs, white women are easy 'to get', do not value their sexual purity, and hence can be used whenever desired. Padma's anecdotes, which follow her comment and are not included here, all describe the times and manner in which she has seen Asian men in Britain and in South Asia sexually harassing white women and, on occasion, being surprised by the angry response they receive.

The crude insertion of a discourse of nationalism and prudish morality into the 'morning after' confusion in the Swiss hotel scene in DDLJ clearly jarred even viewers in my sample who delight in the film, causing them to think through and articulate critiques of the very ideas Aditya Chopra, the director, was most keen to champion and *signalling that Hindi films may be at their least 'ideologically effective' when they are at their most didactic*. Jatin, a 24-year-old trainee professional from an unorthodox Hindu family, and one of the only British-Asian male viewers to question this scene in DDLJ, linked the emphasis on Indian male respect for Indian female chastity with an equal and, in his eyes, despicable tendency to disrespect and denigrate Western women:

Jatin: … there's one scene in the bedroom where she's drunk and she thinks she's had sex with him and he says, 'I know what respect is for Indian girls', and I just started cracking up! *I mean!* There's no way that [pause]. I mean [pause] *What does it mean?* Like girls in the West don't have any self-respect? I didn't like that either. Some of these films try to make out that the West is very permissive. There are films where guys are dancing with white girls in bikinis behind them – Salman Khan in [*Jab Pyar Kissi se Hota Hai*].

(JAT.2/*English*)

At various other points in the interview too, Jatin aired his suspicions of the ideologically loaded distinction made in Hindi films between the permissive West and chaste, self-respecting India.

In an unwitting exemplification of Padma and Jatin's suspicions about the effects of the representation of white women as sexually permissive while Asian women are depicted as 'chaste', 'virginal' or 'fallen', another British-Asian interviewee Kalpesh spoke of his one-time belief in the chastity of women of his 'own type':

Kalpesh: Well, I think watching the Blue movies, yeah, because it's the *white girls* [his emphasis] you accept it more. But when you see your own type, it's [pause] this is obviously going to sound really bad.
Shaku: Be honest.
Kalpesh: It's [sex is] more typical for [white women] because the white girls have more freedom in real life, haven't they?
Shaku: So, you think that because white girls seem to have more freedom, they'd be more likely to engage in sexual relationships with men than Asian girls would?
Kalpesh: Well [pause] I thought that. [pause] But when I grew up, I found that that's not true at all. I've found Asian women who are like that as well.

(KAL.2/English)

The subtle, but significant conflation of 'sex' with 'sex in front of a camera in pornographic movies' that takes place in Kalpesh's response is only one of many deliberately perpetuated misrepresentations of non-Asian women within South-Asian communities from which members of my sample hail. However – reminding one that in selecting 'bits' of interview transcripts for discourse analytical purposes in academic writing one often risks leaving out other bits that might alter or contradict something previously asserted – Kalpesh's somewhat shame-faced admission about thinking of white women as more likely to want or to engage in sexual intercourse than Asian women, in life or on-screen, is given a twist by his assertion that 'when [he] grew up, [he] found that that's not true at all'. Yet again, as in the cases of every other interviewee, but notably Farsana, Padma and Jatin, *experiences* that challenge the ideological standpoints of certain sequences in films can be seen to be crucial in undermining the claims to veracity and universality made by certain sequences, dialogues and representations in conventional Hindi films.

Although Kalpesh was uncomfortable with the thought of seeing Asian women becoming sexually involved with Asian men on screen, and also expressed open homophobia at the thought of two men having sex or being shown to have sex, he called Deepa Mehta's *Fire* (1996) – in which the heroines, Sita and Radha, who are unhappily married to brothers in a Hindu joint family, fall in love and have sex with each other – 'a brilliant film' and told me that he could quite easily accept the thought of lesbian sex. Of course, while at one level this may quite plausibly be an example of the not uncommon heterosexual male fantasy about watching women having sex, here I think it does indicate some openness to the thought of an alternative sexuality for South-Asian women. Nevertheless, despite the highly circumscribed, covert, simplistic, negative, or tangential depictions of non-heterosexual relationships in Hindi films (Gopinath 2000; Rao 2000; Ghosh 2002), there is now growing evidence that such relationships are central to understandings of Indian commercial cinema, and young people, both in Bombay and in London, wanted to talk about films that did try to represent same-sex relationships. Sometimes the issue was brought up in an aggressive and homophobic manner, as in the case of Nikhil, who said that an older man had tried to molest him when he was a boy and who also said that he found the depictions of gay sex in Kaisad Gustad's *Bombay Boys* (2000) – in which one of the three Non-Resident Indian heroes is represented as gay, and shown having an ambiguous relationship with an older Indian man – 'disgusting' and 'unnatural'. Ismail, however, asserted that he had enjoyed and accepted the depiction of mutual affection and sex between men in *Bombay Boys* and felt that the film was before its time:

> It was as if a film from 2012 has come down to Bombay early. [laughs] ... It was centred on the travails of men. It was about their masculinity (mardangi), about homosexual feeling [*Eng.*]. Now if that film had shown Hollywood actors doing those same things, then maybe the Indian public could have accepted it; but because it showed *Indian* men engaging in such feelings, most people I know simply dismissed it as dirty.
>
> (ISM.1/*Hindi*)

Ismail's articulation of the feeling that, had the film depicted *white men* engaged in homosexual sex, *rather than Indian men*, it would have received less opprobrium is borne out by the belief of more conservative interviewees[6] that the permissive ways of the 'West' make white women sexually active and white men engage in 'deviant' sexual acts, while also being responsible for what they firmly believe to be the higher statistics of rape and child pregnancy in 'the West'.

Off-tape, and with my agreement to total anonymity, two male interviewees in Bombay talked about the films *Bombay Boys* (Kaisad Gustad 2000) and *Naaraaz* (*Anger*, Mahesh Bhatt 1994) and the ways in which those films had 'led them' to 'reassess' homosexual encounters and feelings that they had had as teenagers. Although they asserted that they were 'mostly'

heterosexual, they also talked at length about scenes in Hindi films depicting affection and even love between male friends/brothers (from *Sholay*
and *Qurbani* (*Sacrifice*, Feroz Khan 1980) to HAHK and *Chal Mere Bhai*
(*Come On My Brother*, David Dhawan 2000)) and asserted that they often
enjoyed these scenes. Also off-tape, one young woman in Bombay described
her seduction, as a young teenager, by her closest female friend from her
shanty town. This young woman, a working-class Maharastrian Hindu,
who was too fearful to be interviewed, has been in a secret lesbian relationship with one of her older cousins for a number of years.[7]

The kind of requests for absolute secrecy which were felt necessary
in Bombay during discussions of and revelations about off-screen sexual
relationships were repeated in London, but not by everyone I interviewed.
On tape, but at the very end of my interview with her, Nisha described
her romantic 'first night' with her current boyfriend, ending with
her discovery that women do not always have to be passive to please
men: '*he* kissed *me* then [laughs], but now I realise that guys actually like
it when girls make a move.' More poignant and also on tape, was
Manish's description of his first highly complicated and possibly abusive
sexual relationship, aged 11, with a relative five years his senior which
left him, when it ended, heartbroken, confused, with memories of
ardent sex and no one to turn to. Manish's relationship with Hindi films
appears to be one of the only constant features of his youth; but there
too he found that the films did not always take the strict moral position
he would have liked them to. The following extract occurred at the
beginning of our interview during a discussion of the 1988 Mansour
Khan romance *Qayamat Se Qayamat Tak* and prior to his more painful
disclosures:

Shaku: You wouldn't recommend running away as Juhi and Aamir did?
Manish: No.
Shaku: Why is that?
Manish: Because there's no point. It's just bringing shame on the family.
   You can't run away from problems. You've got to just deal with them.
   [Serious voice.] You can run as much as you like but at the end of the
   day you have to come back. To the family ...
Shaku: How does that [pause] Am I right in thinking that you're gay?
Manish: No [pause, very embarrassed]. Well, actually, I'm Bi.
Shaku: Bisexual? Right. [pause] How do you deal with that in terms of
   your family?
Manish: At the moment I can't see myself telling anyone. Like I haven't
   told anyone.

Shaku: But your friends know?

Manish: Not my straight friends! No. But my gay friends ... and I've got a best mate that he's in the same situation as me. Like soon we want to go straight, you know, get married and have kids and that [pause] but at the moment I think we're just having fun. [coy smile] ...

Shaku: Let me see if this is what you're saying. At the moment you're bisexual and you're having gay sexual relationships, but you think you're going to put a stop to these gay relationships and 'go straight' and get married?

Manish: Well, that's what we think at the moment. Like we've both got it into our heads that we have to stop.

Shaku: Being gay? Bisexual? Really?

Manish: Yes.

Shaku: That's because?

Manish: Because of my family. [pause] I can't think how I can tell my family. It's like I come from a big family. [pause, low voice] I can't imagine my cousins and uncles and aunts finding out.

Shaku: Okay.

Manish: But especially my mum and dad. I can't imagine how they would feel.

(MAN.1/English)

Few more striking examples of self-contradiction within a viewer's account of life and films exist amongst my transcripts than this extract, which begins with Manish's disapproval of the lovers in *Qayamat Se Qayamat Tak* (QSQT), who risk their families' wrath by eloping together, leading to his self-righteous declarations about not running 'away from problems' and ends with his restrained and sensitive explanation about why he cannot reveal his sexuality to his family and must disguise or suppress it by 'going straight' and 'getting married'. Sadly, the psychological discourse about 'dealing with problems' initiated by Manish at the beginning of this exchange is not one to which he feels he can subscribe in practice, as the thought of 'bringing shame on the family', an entirely separate and *competing* discourse – which is, incidentally, challenged in parts of the film QSQT – leads him to decide upon a course of action which will mean both the deception of any woman he marries and/or the suppression of his own complex sexual desires. At the same time, Manish was also critical of what he saw as Hindi films' refusal to deal with sex on-screen and expressed a wish for explicit sex to be shown in order to challenge older members of Indian families into acknowledging the existence of sex within the community. And, like Ruksana who half joked that she learnt about 'sex' from *Eastenders* but about 'romance' from Hindi films, he also explained that he turned to British television programmes such as *Hollyoaks* for role models in matters to do with friendship, sex and relationships outside the family.

Other young non-heterosexual[8] Hindi film fans were, however, less interested in the aspects of Hindi film narrative that emphasised conformity and more interested in discussing multimodal aspects such as the music, stars and 'atmosphere' of Hindi films. Another Londoner, Ashok, for instance, who was unguarded about his sexuality and eager to discuss every aspect of relationships, desire and representation in Hindi films, had already faced the difficult and frightening task of 'coming out' to his Gujarati Hindu family. Like some of my Bombay interviewees, he too identified scenes in mainstream Hindi films as undermining what he saw as their own hetero-normativity via the types of bonds shown between male characters:

Ashok: [pause] You know sometimes you get scenes in Indian films that you wouldn't expect normal guys to do, you know, errr, erm, I think [pause]

Shaku: By 'normal' d'you mean 'heterosexual'?

Ashok: Yeah, [laughs, ironic; S: laughs] erm, I can't think of anything now, but seeing it, I've thought, 'Oh my God!' [surprised voice]

Shaku: Did you ever watch Hindi films and feel desire for the male characters?

Ashok: Yeah, when I was younger, yeah. Not now. I'm more confident now. When you're younger you just *think* [his emphasis, pause] ... I did fancy Aamir Khan a lot when I was younger, like in *Qayamat Se Qayamat Tak!* ... Bollywood films have been part of me from day one. Part of my life ... I'll always make time for it. Now I'm so confident and [other South-Asian gay] people say to me I'm so lucky and I try to say to them, 'Are you sure your parents wouldn't accept it? Have you tried them?' ... I think more people should come out, Asian people. You get *lonely*, and you *need* family. Now that I'm out, I can talk to them about anything. My sisters, my aunts.

(ASH.1/*English*)

Because of Ashok's 'confidence', our discussions of sexual attraction, romance, community values and films were fairly wide-ranging. I found interesting his assertion that, having grown up, come out and been accepted as gay with gay friends and a gay subculture in London to turn to, he no longer fantasises as much about Hindi film actors. Participating comfortably in the discourse of young crushes and romance that many avowedly heterosexual interviewees also chose to use, Ashok also views himself as having superseded the stage of merely needing to 'think' about sexually arousing images in Hindi films. Yet, despite his new milieu and the experiences open to him, these films continue to be a source of tremendous pleasure and passion. His assertion that 'Bollywood films have been a part of [him] from day one', an integral 'part of [his] life' and will continue to be so, leads him to speak about the ways in which his life has changed, the new support and openness that 'coming out' to 'sisters and aunts' has gained him. Ashok spoke very eloquently and interestingly about his love of song sequences, his sense of their boundless potential for tapping into emotions and memories, for making available moments of physical and romantic bonding suggesting both gay and lesbian desire. In this vein, he explained that his favourite actresses – Parveen Bhabi, Sarika and Zeenat Aman – could make viewers believe in the intensity of a film's pain and passion in ways that many more 'self-conscious' films fail to do. He commented: '[Even though there was a gay actor in it] I didn't really enjoy *Bend it Like Beckham*. Everything seemed so simple. It's funny, but I didn't really enjoy it.' His talk suggested, indeed, that it was not the case that he only watched Hindi films for the moments he saw as 'queer', transgressive and/or undermining of heterosexuality. On the contrary, he was equally eager to comment on films that dealt with some of the emotional complexities of heterosexual relationships, sometimes identifying himself openly with the female characters:

Ashok: And then, *Kuch Kuch Hota Hai* reminds me of situations in my own life.

Shaku: Yes? Tell me.

Ashok: Well, I'll tell you, this was before I realised I was gay. And I was at school then, and I had a really close friend, this girl, yeah, she was such a good person and a close friend and I started to feel that I wanted to be with her and she was with someone else and I told her and our friendship went a bit [pause] and every time I watch *Kuch Kuch Hota Hai* ... I think of that and when I heard that song it used to bring tears to my eyes ... Do you know *Chandni Bar*? [Madhur Bhandarkar 2001]

Shaku: I've heard of it.

Ashok: That was brilliant, really well made. It's not really got gay sex in it, but it has an incident where a guy gets raped. Those kinds of things do happen, you know.

Shaku: Yes.

Ashok: ... I don't think the older generation would be able to accept films like that.

Shaku: Tabu seems to be in several good films.

Ashok: Yeah, she is. *Astitva*! [Mahesh Manjrekar 2000] That was so brilliant! ... the way she handled it at the end. When she walked away at the end. You expect her to go back to this guy, but she doesn't!

(ASH.2/*English*)

In *Kuch Kuch Hota Hai*, the young Kajol who plays basketball and hangs out with boys is shown falling in love with her best friend, Shah Rukh. He, however, is oblivious to her passion – due, some viewers suggest, to her unmaidenly attire and the fact that she can beat the boys at basketball – and ends up marrying British-Asian lass, Rani Mukherjee, who is graceful, prays and has long hair. Ashok's sense of emotional involvement with the film, which springs in large measure from its early sequences and connects to his own experiences as an adolescent, is such that even today, as a confident and openly gay South-Asian in London, he feels close to tears on hearing the song that is played in the film as Kajol watches her beloved with another person. Saliently, Ashok expresses empathy in equal measure for Kajol, the heroine in Karan Johar's conventional family blockbuster *Kuch Kuch Hota Hai*, a character in *Chandni Bar* who experiences male rape, and Tabu, the housewife who walks away from her marriage in *Astitva* after being spurned by her husband and son for having sex with another man 25 years previously. This can be seen to reinforce the point, made throughout this book, that even films with themes and representations that may be classified as regressive, politically incorrect or ideologically authoritarian, may bear meanings that are none of these things for the young viewers who watch them.

6.4 Conclusion: films, experience and meaning

Many young viewers in Bombay and in London expressed the opinion that the Hindi films which they enjoyed watching were most able at representing romance that made sense to them and did not do justice to sex in any meaningful way. One argument used repeatedly both by young viewers in favour of greater openness about sex, and by those pessimistic about the possibility of this ever happening, was the *hypocrisy* of 'Indian' or 'South-Asian' communities who were, on the one hand, they asserted, condemning sexual representations on screen and preventing young people from doing so much as touching in public, and, on the other hand, delighting in pornography, lewd film dances and/or their own private sexual intrigues. I must emphasise, however, that these same young viewers were also sometimes highly complimentary about Hindi films that upheld such hypocritical discourses, albeit for reasons connected to aesthetics, romance, action sequences or affection between families or friends. Even the 'coyness' of Hindi films in depicting sex was sometimes exciting. Thus pleasure in the films was rarely hampered by ideological critique and/or discursive alienation over issues of dress and/or sexuality.

Encapsulating one of the central contentions of this book, Muraleedharan T. (2002: 183) argues there is no evidence that 'queer' moments in conventional Indian films may not carry as much psychological weight as the conservative heterosexual conclusions to these films. Feelings generated during a film's action, either by the visual, musical or narrative aspects of the film, need not be undermined by an ending that disavows these feelings. Supporting this theory, the gay and bisexual viewers I spoke to were confident that they did not feel excluded by Hindi films to any greater extent than they did, say, by Hollywood films, and told me that, usually, they were able to read Hindi films and respond to them emotionally regardless of the depictions of the sexuality of the protagonists. All the young bisexual or gay Hindi film viewers I spoke to were far more critical of off-screen social attitudes to sexuality than they were of those in Hindi films; furthermore, the experiences of alienation, depression, bullying and fear that they discussed were often alleviated rather than enhanced by some of the Hindi films they had viewed as adolescents. However, while the expression of romance in Hindi films was seen by some to be universal rather than heterosexual, some young gay viewers in my sample felt strongly that the conventional representations of 'Indian' family life reinforced the expectations that their families had about their (sexual) futures and their own sense of anxiety about breaking such patterns.

Clearly, many young viewers, regardless of the meanings they take away from the films, work with notions of ideological impact in their assessment of how 'other' viewers interact with Hindi films. For some young viewers, if the ideological positions that they attribute to films match their own nascent or deeply embedded moral values, then the 'effects' imputed are ideal or benevolent; for others, if they perceive the discourses in films to be rebellious, disrespectful, un-Indian and immoral *or* oppressive, hypocritical and motivated by self-interest on the part of a certain group, then the 'effects' arising from the scenes they refer to are coded as negative. More likely than the issue of sexuality to cause both heterosexual and gay viewers to take issue with, dislike or to lose interest in specific Hindi films, or to discuss the work necessary in order to identify with a particular character, were issues such as religion and/or modality during the depiction of violence, sexual violence or social unrest. And, often despite the sometimes positive *intersectionality* of religious, national, gender and sexual identities, several viewers in my sample demonstrated that quite aside from the prejudiced ideologies of race, gender and religion embedded in many contemporary Hindi films or the attempts of some films to shatter such bigotry, *prejudices circulating within communities* play a potent role in shaping viewer responses to screen representations as well as to off-screen sociopolitical events.

Many of the accounts of viewing given in this chapter confirm a complex interplay between gender/sexual politics and class, national and ethnic politics in the lives and opinions of viewers. Reviewers writing about the film *Fire* comment on the way in which it caused a furore not merely because it was about a lesbian relationship but because it was seen to be about a relationship between two *Hindu* women.[9] Middle-class 'Indian' male sexuality was coded in certain viewers' accounts, and clearly in some of the film sequences under consideration, as *heterosexual, controlled, respectful* and *dependent* on patriarchal authorisation, while 'Indian' female sexuality was portrayed as being *heterosexual, chaste* and a marker of clan *honour*. In contrast, the sexuality of groups that some viewers' despise, or who are characterised as the 'other' in Hindi films, was seen to be *potent, deviant, disrespectful, dangerous* and *uncontrollable*. Western (and sometimes Christian) women were commonly perceived by conservative interviewees as being willing to have sex with anyone, inside or outside a marriage, and also as being prostitutes, lesbians or acting in pornographic films. Western men, working-class South-Asian men and, on occasion, all Muslim men were perceived by these same viewers to be predatory and to have little reverence either for women or for the institution of marriage; thus it appeared less shocking if they were represented as having or wanting non-heterosexual relationships and sex than if middle-class Indian Hindu men were represented in that manner. Despite the apparent 'liberalisation' of the Indian media landscape and in tandem with the 'opening up' of the market, these are all views that have gained even greater purchase in India in recent years, especially in and due to the rhetoric of the Hindu Right and the failure of many on the Left to interrogate their own problematic relegation of sexuality to an *apolitical* realm.

The clear connections between gender politics and communal identity in supposedly 'apolitical' romantic films, and in viewers' accounts of these films, have far reaching implications for the ways in which films that are explicitly about gender, community and national identity will be understood. For instance, in the films *Bombay, Gadar, Maachis* and *Hey! Ram* there is a striking articulation of themes about gender and sexuality with those about politics. While these films all contain undeniable tropes of romance, even purporting to be, in the case of *Gadar*, about *nothing but love*, religious riots, communal gang-rape, kidnap, police brutality and terrorism all feature as significant aspects of these films' vision of national life. In the comments of academic film critics, too, there is clearly a connection being made between *gender politics* and *communal politics*. In fact, as Lynne Segal argues in relation to narratives of sex and the 'other': '[i]t is the dynamic interplay between power and desire, attraction and repulsion, acceptance and disavowal, which *eroticises* those already seen as inferior (and thereby gives them in fantasy a threatening power)' (2003: 102). To extricate the love-gender-sex subplots of these films from the aggression-ethnicity-nationalism subplots would be at best disingenuous and at worst dangerous. These are not, in fact, separate or separable realms. Therefore, in Chapter 7, via the accounts of social historians, academic critics and young viewers, Hindi film depictions of masculinity and femininity in the context of an alarmingly confident alliance between a right-wing Hindu state[10] and religious fascist organisations in India and the diaspora will be explored further.

7
Politics and Spectatorship 1: Viewing Love, Religion and Violence

Spectatorship is not just the relationship that occurs between the viewer and the screen, but also and especially how that relationship lives on once the spectator leaves the theatre.

(Judith Mayne 1993: 2–3)

There is a dark sexual obsession about allegedly ultra-virile Muslim male bodies and over-fertile Muslim female ones that inspires and sustains the figures of paranoia and revenge. [World Hindu Organisation] leaflets, openly circulating in Gujarat today, signed by the state general secretary promise: 'We will cut them and their blood will flow like rivers. We will kill Muslims the way we destroyed Babri mosque' ... At a mass grave that was dug on March 6 (2002) to provide burial to 96 bodies from Naroda Patiya [Gujarat, India], 46 women were buried. Bilkees Begum ... told a tale that seemed to confirm a recurrent pattern in most places, in most survivors' accounts. She was stripped, gang-raped, her baby was killed before her, she was then beaten up, then burnt and left for dead. There will be a massive effort by Hindu Rashtra to produce a will to forgetting, to make things that happened disappear from memory, to fill up memory with images of things that had not happened, to generate counterfeit collective memories, amnesias.

(Tanika Sarkar 2002)

7.1 Introduction

For me, the recent communal violence in India – specifically the organised, large-scale genocide of Muslims by Hindus belonging to or protected by the Indian state apparatus – is a subject that cannot easily be encompassed by words on a page. Yet in a book about the discursive universes of contemporary Hindi film viewers, it is necessary to reiterate the connections between right-wing discourses on gender, sexuality and religious intolerance in India that inflect both on- and off-screen beliefs and behaviours. The exhortation to Hindu men, in much right-wing Hindu literature circulated by the World Hindu Organisation (VHP) and the RSS, to purge India of Muslims (and now Christians)[1] has been shown to be inextricably bound up with Hindutva appeals to Hindus to 'recover' their 'masculinity' and to 'punish' Muslims via sexual humiliation and torture (see, amongst others Butalia 1995; Sarkar 2001 and 2002; Banerjee 2002; Mangalik 2002). Writers such as Purshottam Agarwal, Vasant Kannabiran and Kalpana Kannabiran urge a consideration of such fascist rhetoric side by side with each community's location of women, and 'femininity', as the site of a community's honour. In this context Agarwal argues that '[s]ocieties whose social values derive sanctity from and whose discourse of power is rooted in women's complete subjugation to men, tend to turn women into autonomous and inanimate symbols or carriers of social honour' and 'the rhetoric about the piety of the family and the dignity of "our" women only complement the aggressiveness such ideologies direct against the women of the "Other"' (1995: 30). Carrying this notion further, Kannabiran and Kannabiran maintain that

> The identity of a community is constructed on the bodies of women. This identity formation works in two ways – both of which are violent and are defined by and through the aggression on women of particular communities. First through the rape of women of minority or subordinated groups ... [Second] through the allegation by the dominant group of the rape of and aggression on their women by men of minority communities ...
>
> (1995: 122)

In tandem, the popularity of Hindi films purporting to depict national and religious 'conflict', the unsubtle and continuing 'Hinduisation' of representations of 'everyday life' in Hindi blockbusters and the recent reports and analyses of the systematic and spectacularised use of rape, sexual torture and mutilation against Muslims in India during pogroms (for instance, Mangalik 2002; Sarkar 2002; Narula 2002; Mishra 2002) raise several questions. To what extent might the discourses in popular Hindi films regarding the nexus between, for instance, *religion, violence* and *gender* or *class, violence* and *gender* be said to echo and/or challenge pre-existing prejudices and beliefs within communities of viewers? Is it possible for viewers to take away one set of meanings from a film's overt romantic (and supposedly feminine) discourses without being 'hailed by' and perhaps implicated in another (supposedly masculine) set? And finally, are the overtly gender-linked discourses pertaining to class, nation, religion and the state in Hindi films either reflective of the diversity of opinion amongst young viewers in London and Bombay or representative of a so-called 'majority voice'? In the light of such questions, Section 7.2 attempts to situate some of the concerns and beliefs of young Hindi film viewers within the broader context of Hindu chauvinist politics and gender ideology circulating in recent years across India.

7.2   Films, viewers and the politics of Hindutva fascism

In a crucial sequence during Anand Patwardhan's documentary *Father, Son and Holy War* (1994), the director interviews a group of right-wing cadre at a Hindu festival as they watch a giant installation depicting Mandakini, a popular Hindi film actress of the day. The men gape at the installation as the actress-figure pours water over her semi-clad form in repetitive, jerky movements and the conversation turns to the topic of rape. The sequence culminates in the admission – or boast – by one of the men, that while watching rape on screen is pleasurable, were it to happen to a woman in real life in front of them, they would probably participate in the rape rather than simply standing on the side-lines. In the light of recent detailed reports and accounts of gang-rape and mass-rape of Muslim girls and women during pogroms in Gujarat in 2002; (Anand and Setalvad 2002; Narula 2002), such boasts cannot be dismissed as mere posturing. Additionally, in the light of confirmations that in Gujarat Hindu women, too, watched and actively encouraged the rape of Muslim women (Banerjee 2002) and shielded the rapists from the police, the constantly changing identifications and subject positions of *women* too, as they watch sexual violence on screen, need to be borne in mind.

Amongst those I interviewed informally outside cinema theatres in Bombay over the summer of 2002, while there were expressions of concern about the Gujarat carnage, there were several Hindu men who openly asserted that 'rape' was too good for Muslim women and laughed at the idea that it was a *crime* that Muslims had been killed and/or forced to watch while their children were tortured and killed. A greater number, while reluctant to say that they would have participated in such violence, were in no way unhappy about its having taken place, viewing it as an important 'step forward' for the Hindu majority community. *In London*, outside Hindi cinema theatres, expressions of concern for those murdered in Gujarat were more frequent and the responses I received more diverse. Nevertheless, I did speak to some men and some middle-aged women who asserted that 'the Muslims asked for it' and 'started it' by burning a 'train full of Hindu women and children'.[2] Such comments, though not necessarily representative, do at least indicate one strand of community discourse. Another perspective expressed was that what occurred in Gujarat were 'riots' and that riots are simply uncontrolled fighting by 'unemployed youth'/'working-class'/'lumpen' elements in both communities. In some cases this was 'explained' away as government incompetence and in others it was *justified* by the notion of the government having pandered to the 'other' community and thus built up Hindu resentment.

The desire amongst many young viewers to ignore or forget the *systematic* nature of the sexual violence and murder as well as the sustained economic and social elimination of Muslims taking place in parts of India[3] and the organised political dimension to anti-Muslim prejudice[4] and to what they have come to term 'religious riots' is, meanwhile, sometimes subtly and sometimes openly endorsed by the Hindi films that they have seen depicting such 'riots'. Indeed, to differing degrees, films such as *Bombay*, *Hey! Ram* (Kamal Hasan 2000) and *Gadar* have been accused of a *deliberate* perpetuation of myths about Muslim 'otherness', the role of the Indian Muslim community during so-called 'riots' and the ways in which such 'riots' are instigated (Vasudevan 2000c and 2001a; Gopalan 2002). Many of my interviewees in London confirmed my sense that the scope and depth of anti-Muslim rhetoric in India has been reflected in diasporic Hindu communities. I was told on several occasions about fathers and elder brothers who, having eaten meat for years and socialised with Pakistani or Bangladeshi neighbours and colleagues, had in the past few years distanced themselves from their non-Hindu peers, become strict vegetarians, and involved themselves with 'temple associations', donating significant parts of the family budget to so-called 'cultural' or 'religious' Hindu groups. Although they did not dwell on such critiques, young British-Bangladeshi viewers mentioned 'stereotypical' or 'misleading' representations of Muslims in Hindi films as bearing little relation to their perceptions of themselves.

Exemplifying the anti-Muslim sentiments of several young viewers in Bombay, the following extract from my interview with Preeta, a 19-year-old

Sikh, serves both to confirm and to complicate analyses of communal stereotypes such as the ones offered by Kannabiran and Kannabiran:

Preeta: Because I am Sikh, I don't want my kid to marry a Muslim. Or a Christian. Any Hindu is fine, and our caste.
Shaku: Why is that?
Preeta: I don't like Muslims first of all. I do have Muslim friends but they're girls, not in boys at all. I don't like Muslim boys. [S: Why?] A few years back. One Muslim boy created a lot of problems in my house. ...
Shaku: So you've generalised this to all Muslim boys? They're all like this ...?
Preeta: Yes. All of them. I think so. It happens you know.
Shaku: And what about the Christian boys?
Preeta: No, I've got no reason for that. That's it. Just don't want to be an outcast.
Shaku: But you have friends from other religions who are girls?
Preeta: Yes. And they are very nice. My best friend's a Muslim and *even she* doesn't like Muslim boys. [S: Really?] Yeah, but she'll have to marry a Muslim [sympathy].

(PTA.3/English and Hindi)

What is noteworthy about Preeta's narrative (extensive parts of which I have edited out) is the way in which a single, sustained negative inter-action with a male from a different community to her own has resulted not only in her decision not to interact with Muslim men, but to her sense of all Muslim men as predatory and untrustworthy, unfitting mates for either herself, her children (as yet unborn) or her female Muslim friend. The innate trustworthiness of Hindu men is not, how-ever, brought into question for Preeta, a Sikh[5] woman, by the actions of a Muslim man. An experience that might, in other contexts, have made Preeta suspicious of *boys or men* in general acts, in the context of con-temporary India's political mobilisation of anti-Muslim sentiment, to make her suspicious of Muslims as a group. Significantly, Hindi films in the 1990s and early twenty-first century, having shied away from direct political critique of the climate and consequences of such prevalent anti-Muslim ideologies by confining themselves to individual depictions of the 'the good Muslim' or a personalised cross-religious romance, have not been so circumspect about utilising and incorporating the visual iconography and discursive landscape of the Hindu Right.[6] In coming sections I explore some responses I encountered amongst viewers as well as those of a number of Hindi film theorists and critics to depictions of 'religious' unrest, violence and cross-religious romance in a selection of key Hindi films.

7.3 'Counterfeit collective memories': riots, religion and subjectivity in contemporary Hindi films

The attacks on Muslims by the Shiv Sainiks were mounted with military precision, with lists of establishments and voters' list in hand ... (i) The immediate causes of the communal riots on 6th December 1992 were: (a) the demolition of Babri Masjid, (b) the aggravation of Muslim sentiments by the Hindus with their celebration rallies and (c) the insensitive and harsh approach of the police while handling the protesting mobs which initially were not violent.

(Volume 1,Chapter 2, in the *Srikrishna Commission Report on the Bombay Riots* of 1992–93)

7.3.1 *Bombay*

Few of the films named by interviewees called up such extended and explicitly political commentary as did *Bombay* (Mani Rathnam 1995). It could even be said that this film's choice of subject matter leads viewers to dwell on it in a manner similar to that of documentary footage or political propaganda rather than merely as fictional 'entertainment'. First screened in Tamil and later dubbed into Hindi, *Bombay* purports to tell the story of Shekhar Mishra, a modern, secular man from a Hindu family in a village in Southern India, and the woman he loves, Shailabano, a Muslim from the same village, who marry against their fathers' wishes. The film has the heroine leave her village in order to follow the hero to Bombay, where the couple are married in a registry office. Compared to the spectacular and obsessive representations of the Hindu wedding ceremony in Hindi films such as HAHK and diasporic ones such as *Monsoon Wedding*, this union is deliberately understated, accentuating the hero's distance from his parents' religion and his identification with the modern nation-state (cf. Vasudevan 2001a: 189–90). The development of their love after this point, though embedded in the tensions of daily life in an Indian city – a lack of private space in which to consummate their love, the need to work, the presence of disapproving 'voices' and 'looks' from members of the Hindu community that surround them and, in one salient instance, the passing of a parade of right-wing Hindus dressed in saffron on a march through the city – is depicted as both satisfyingly idyllic at a personal level and a confirmation, via their naming of their twin sons, of their commitment to secular Indian nationhood. What follows after the interval – namely the images showing the destruction of the Babri Mosque in Ayodhya, the faces of supposedly opposing Hindu and Muslim leaders exhorting their people to violence, the shadowy and menacing jump-cuts of Muslim men (wearing white skull caps) brandishing swords and filling bottles to make petrol bombs – culminates in personal tragedy for Shekhar and Shailabano. Their recently reconciled parents are annihilated when their house is burnt down by an invisible mob, and their twin sons – Kamal Bano and Kabir Narayan – go 'missing'.

The distressing scenes in which the two little boys, dressed apparently in versions of 'Hindu' and 'Muslim' garb, are almost burnt by a mob, pushed, stamped upon, violently forced to explain which religion they belong to, and at one point, separated from each other, are paralleled by sequences in which their distraught parents search for them in an ever-descending spiral of horror: on the streets, in their burnt-out neighbourhood and once laughter-filled home, in a hospital full of burnt and slashed victims and, finally, in a morgue. All this is accompanied by dramatic music and lyrics exhorting people to stop fighting each other in the name of religion, to find their common humanity and respect the nation. Inter-cut are sequences in which groups of indistinct men from each community – signified sometimes by their caps and sometimes by a flash of saffron – slash, burn and pillage throughout the city, and the police ineptly attempt to quell the violence. Vasudevan's analysis sensitively traces the connections between critical responses to the film and the manner in which modern historical events are deployed within the narrative and represented visually as spectacle. As he notes: '[*Bombay*'s] proximity to the events it depicts, and the invocation of documentary methods, the use of dates, newspaper headlines, and place names to situate the violence ... place the film in the arc of recent public memory and make it an intervention in the construction of that memory ... [or indeed,] a substitute for memory' (2001a: 194).

In an ending so abrupt as to be startling, Shailabano and Shekhar are reunited with their sons and various soft-focus figures join hands to form a human chain, reasserting normalcy and harmony in the city. Only minutes prior to this, the 'riots' die down as various members of each community take it upon themselves to reason with mobs, to place their own bodies in between mobs and their victims and to remind us of the interests of national unity above sectarian religious identifications. While much of the first half of *Bombay* concentrates on the protagonists' romance and the young Muslim heroine's acceptance of daily life in a

Hindu household, critics (cf. Vasudevan 2001a: 207) have argued that the film nevertheless reinforces right-wing Hindu conceptualisations of the Muslim 'other'. In the light of such contentions, it is worth exploring other – perhaps more widespread – perceptions of the film.

7.3.2 Viewing *Bombay*

In December 2001, not long before the beginning of the state-sponsored ethnic cleansing[7] which devastated her parents' home town, I interviewed Farsana, a 21-year-old Gujarati Muslim receptionist. An avid Hindi film fan with little avowed interest in national politics, Farsana seemed at ease discussing virtually every issue from sexuality to class, veiling and her job aspirations. Initially she spoke of *Bombay* in response to a question about the depiction of 'controversial issues' on screen. Within moments, however, the whole tone of the interview altered when her memories of the film narrative segued into her own personal narration of 'the Bombay riots', pushing me to shift the emphasis of the interview away from the film itself as she described her family's fear and pain. I present her memories of the film, which she had viewed some seven years previously, and of the 'riots', which took place some nine years before our interview, in order to give a sense of the interconnectedness of the screen events with history and politics in Farsana's mind:

Farsana: [I]n *Bombay*, they've shown about a love marriage. It's not a happy film. It's not encouraging to young people. And they've shown that riots are going on at that time … I was in a major bad area at that time. [She names a part of the city dominated by the Shiv Sena] … Our neighbours and us, we were the only Muslims there in that area. There were all Hindus around us. It was so bad. It was like, we'll be killed today or tomorrow. [Tears in eyes] So, when I saw *Bombay* in the theatre I was like, 'Oh I have come into the riots again'. [pause, very agitated] I couldn't breathe. It was unbearable. I saw it only once and I have not watched it again. [pause] You again feel that you have come back to that trauma. Some of the scenes that they have shown that is like reality what we have experienced. I was small at that time. [pause]

Shaku: Would you like to tell me about it?

Farsana: I was like 11 but I was very frightened … We had to keep our doors and windows literally boarded up … To make everyone think that we were away. Our Muslim neighbours, they hid with us. They had a shop downstairs and that … That time we felt if they came to kill them, they are also going to kill us. But the neighbours, the Hindus some of them were good to us. They told the mobs [pause] the Shiv Sena, every time they came, that 'they have gone away and there are all gas cylinders in the shop so don't burn it you will blow up the whole building.' So [the Shiv Sena mobs] burnt some stuff but they didn't enter our locked place.

Shaku: You were crying?

Farsana: *Crying? We could not think!* We could not eat food, dinner, lunch. For days and days. We were in such a state – it was beyond fear ... Those Muslim neighbours and us we used to live all in one room and we used to not sleep. It went on for two months. No communication. No talks with anyone. We stopped going to school ... So in *Bombay*, how could I watch that love story without thinking of the hitting and the killing, them picking up the children and running? That trauma which you've gone through is so bad that after that you will never wish that there should be any war, ever, any riots ever. [Tears in eyes] Even this war that is going on, I feel that they are just simply fighting and killing people and they are wasting time, money and energy. What do they want to prove, the Americans? That we are superior to you all, you Afghans? Tell me? Why are they doing it? What is the point? It is just men with no mind of their own, no career, no orientation, nothing, they are doing all that killing. Even in Bombay, *why* these riots started? All the men see, you might see a majority of useless men who have no work and want to fight.

(FAR.3/*English and Hindi*)

Farsana's consideration of *Bombay* leads her to ask questions about the nature of political violence in the contemporary arena; in answer to her own questions, she concludes that violence with which she cannot identify is carried out by 'a majority of useless men who have no work and want to fight', a view that is perfectly consonant with the more generalised depiction of riot mobs in Ratnam's film, but the incongruity of which may be acknowledged if not in relation to the Bombay 'riots', then at least in relation to her invocation of the American attack on Afghanistan. A displacement of the blame for, and political machinery or backdrop to, disproportionate violence on to an *irrational, unemployed, lumpen fringe* is perhaps, in some ways, less disempowering and devastating than the knowledge that even *narrowly elected and/or unpopular governments* may be responsible for the horrors she has witnessed and which she suspects are taking place in Afghanistan. Thus, while the movements inside Farsana's narrative – from displeasure with *Bombay* for what she sees as its *discouraging* representation of a love marriage to its apparent and, to her, *pointless* realism, and beyond that to descriptions of her family's traumatic period of hiding as anti-Muslim pogroms were carried out by the Shiv Sena in Bombay – are in some ways critical of Rathnam's vision in *Bombay*, her conclusion is not. The fact that she is so distraught by the screen violence in the film that she is unable to focus *either* on the sensual, alluring and spectacular aspects of the Hindu–Muslim love story *or* on its brief but repeated representations of the Muslim community as *initiators* of the violence in Bombay says more, I suggest, about spectatorship than it does about the accuracy or integrity of the narrative in *Bombay*.

So what does Farsana's response tell us about spectatorship other than that different viewers' experiences affect how they respond to films? First, I suggest, that spectatorship for those who perceive their lives as being similar to, or closely entwined with, the events taking place on-screen cuts off avenues for distancing open to other viewers: there may be risks involved in opening oneself up to film narratives at any time, but for those who have been victims of violence and who inhabit modalities that tie in closely with those of specific films, the risk is magnified many times. Farsana's experience of spectatorship is clearly coloured by recognition of aspects of *Bombay*'s modality.

Second, it is my contention that being *prepared* or *unprepared* for the kinds of visual depictions (whether of violence or other subjects) one is going to see in a film can alter the manner in which spectatorship takes place. While some of Farsana's dismay at finding herself watching what she perceives to be a realistic portrayal of a horrific event from recent history is caused by the fact that she has not discussed her family's experiences with anyone since the occurrence of the 1992–3 violence, her distress is enhanced by the fact that *Bombay*'s *mis-en-scène* and narrative take her by *surprise*. By her own account, 11 years old at the time of the violent events and 13 or 14 when she viewed the film, Farsana attests to her suddenly evoked memories of pain and loss via a simple question: 'So, in *Bombay*, how could I watch that love story without thinking of the hitting and the killing, them picking up their children and running?' This is a deceptively simple question: why would a director put violence into a film if he does not want spectators to *think* about it? Yet there is a sense in which *Bombay* both encourages its viewers to dwell on the violence in a manner dissimilar to the discontinuities of other conventional Hindi films, and then reverts to genre and discourages them from doing so by pulling back to allow the romantic thread of the narrative to progress. The space in the film occupied by two songs and a family reconciliation for the protagonists and their parents is inhabited, for Farsana, by memories of hiding and fearing for her life, an inability to sleep or to eat food, a curtailment of education, family space, public space, memories of being in a space 'beyond fear'. Farsana's question suggests that she understands that she might have been expected to respond to *Bombay* in a very different manner from the one she describes, that she senses the potential for *prepared, detached, optimistic* viewing and rejects it.

Third, the actual context of viewing – in a cinema hall with other, not necessarily like-minded audience members – turns her experience of the film into one of *losing control*. In viewing *Bombay* in a cinema hall, Farsana is *forced* to reimagine, to contemplate, a time of panic and powerlessness that she had tried to wipe from her mind. I will return in the next section to the notion that certain Hindi films may carry on the ideological work of the Hindu Right by isolating and confirming the 'abnormality' of viewers who (by watching them and feeling disturbed or by refusing to watch them) do not fully endorse their vision of the Indian nation-state.

Corroboration of both psychological and factual aspects of Farsana's account of the 'riots' comes from Kavita, a 20-year-old student also in Bombay, the younger daughter of a Christian father and a Hindu mother:

Kavita: I really liked [*Bombay*]. It was at the time when me and my sister were in school and in those days there were riots going on and it was so frightening; my sister fell from a bus and a man helped her up, it was in the middle of the rioting and people were throwing acid-filled bottles ... I was 10. I have shocking memories [pause] and that film really brought it all back in a big way ... It's just like real life. Really. I have seen it happening.

(KAV.2/*English and Hindi*)

Despite the use of words like 'shocking' and 'frightening', the emotional distance between these two accounts is clear: Kavita, a non-Muslim but a Bombayite like Farsana, and hence a spectator to the throwing of acid-filled bottles, speaks as a relative *outsider* to the emotional pain and disenfranchisement of the 'riot' situation in the film. Farsana's repeated assertion that she would not wish to see the film again, nor to see any such riots or violence ever again, testify both to her continuing sense of trauma and to her deep engagement with the film, while Kavita's insistence that the film is 'just like real life' does not preclude her willingness to remember it as fictional and hence likeable (in contrast to the actual 'riots'). During other interviews too, I found that emotional proximity to or distance from the *events* depicted in the film *as opposed to distance from the film itself,* acted to shape young viewers' desire to discuss aspects of the film other than the 'narrative'. Jatin, a 24-year-old Punjabi Hindu in London was a case in point, in that he moved through a series of increasingly 'distanced' responses in describing his reactions to the film but did not once mention the riots:

Jatin: By the late eighties I was more into English films, but then I saw *Bombay* and it blew me away! The direction was very slick and the dialogue wasn't over the top. And at the ending – there was a happy ending but nothing was resolved. There was still Hindu–Muslim tension and life goes on. So [pause] it wasn't a very realistic film, there was a lot of romanticism in there as well 'cause, like, a Hindu and Muslim they'd get more grief than that for marrying even before the riots. I haven't dated anyone who was Muslim. Maybe in the back of my mind there's something saying don't go there ... for my parents it would be the big thing.

(JAT.3/*English*)

Directing our attention precisely to viewers such as Jatin, Sumita Chakravarty takes issue with critiques of Mani Rathnam's films, *Roja*, *Bombay* and *Dil Se*, for focusing on 'exclusively "realist" criteria' and tending 'to ignore the more cinematic dimensions of these films, primarily their investment in the narrative and visual allure of the marginal' (2002: 232–3). Beginning with his colloquial assertion that the film 'blew [him] away' and moving through his explanation of this enjoyment as being attributable to the understated dialogue, 'slick' direction and momentarily happy but generally unresolved ending – all presumably contributions to a veneer of realism more prevalent in the 'English' films he was 'into' – Jatin is captivated by *Bombay* and nowhere speaks of being *disturbed* by the film. His emphasis on the happy, but unresolved ending testifies to his viewing of it as a fictional narrative at the same time as his use of the words 'direction' and 'dialogue' present him as a reflexive and literate user of the medium we are discussing.

In an effort to highlight the manner in which *emotional engagement* can sometimes be ignored or discounted when a viewer appears to use the 'vocabulary' of textual criticism with fluency, I return to Jatin's initial assertion that *Bombay* 'blew [him] away'. For me, this assertion serves as a reminder that to view spectatorship as an arena in which emotional and rational processes are discrete phenomena that sometimes coexist side by side and sometimes compete with each other is to fail to understand that the two are inextricably linked and often impossible to distinguish. The appositeness of Jatin's 'blown away' metaphor is precisely its powerful connotations of passionate engagement rather than detached assessment. Nevertheless, throughout my interview with him, Jatin displayed a consistently political, informed and active sense of the dangers of communal identity, critiquing what he saw as the erasure of Muslim identity from popular Hindi films and the promotion of a BJP right-wing Hindu agenda via narratives about marriage and women (cf. Chapter 4: JAT.1). In stark contrast, many of the other young people I interviewed in both cities, notably, but to varying degrees, Meeta, Bhiku, Preeta, Manish[8] and Harish, displayed a belief in the propaganda of the Hindu Right and a willingness to acknowledge and/or rationalise their distrust and dislike of Muslims.

I asked if there were any types of sequences in films that made Harish angry. His reply was unequivocal at first but became more and more incoherent as he began to doubt my agreement with his views:

Harish: [O]n a couple of occasions I've become really *very angry*. When I was watching *Hey! Ram*. When they [Muslims] rape Rani Mukherjee, that was a bad scene. Not because it was Rani Mukherjee – but they've shown *Muslims* doing that [pause] so that is *inviting them*, you know, and in Bhindi Bazaar they have started protesting about that [depiction] and [long pause]

Shaku: What are your religious views, actually? Are you a Hindu? Lots of Bombay people do have prejudices against Muslims ...

Harish: [long pause] I'm no different ... But I'm not that much. I don't *hate* them and I do have some Muslim friends [pause] but I think it's there, in their blood also [pause] Some Muslims, you know [pause] we call it as 'junoon' (madness).

Shaku: You don't think that this is the case with every religious group of humans?

Harish: [pause] Yeah, it's there, but with them the percentage is more [pause] it's like and the worst part of it is that everything that they think they do from here [he thumps his chest near his heart] not from here [hits his forehead] everything they do is 'right', they don't think of the results.

Shaku: Every Muslim?

Harish: No, not every one but those who are involved in this, the discrimination [against Hindus] that is happening here, I'm talking about them [pause]

Shaku: Did you see the film *Bombay*? How did you feel about that?
Harish: Yeah. It was bad actually. Real stuff … I've seen photographs of
  Dhagdi Chawl and [the director] has projected the same thing. Things
  were done on both sides, *both sides*, I won't take the side of the Hindus
  [pause] even I believe that I should take the Muslims' side because the
  police, this time they took the Hindus' side and in that case no one
  could help the Muslims, no one can help you [if the police are against
  you]. After that they are retaliating – that's pretty obvious.

(HAR.1/English)

In a discourse reminiscent of that used about women who are supposed
to be *irrational* and *emotional* rather than logical and considered, Harish
expresses and invokes several layers of sentiment towards and discourse
about 'Muslims'. Ironically, given the sentiments that he professes,
beginning with his 'anger' in line 1, which is, he asserts, provoked by
the notorious scene in *Hey! Ram*[9] (*Oh Ram!*, Kamal Hasan 2000) where
Muslims gang-rape the protagonist's wife during post-partition 'riots'
and ending with his assertion that the bombs that killed hundreds of
people in Bombay in 1993 were the work of Muslims in 'retaliation' for
the police bias during the 'riots', Harish expresses a view of the Muslim
community which posits them as *uncontrolled* and *prey to dangerous passions*. Even when he acknowledges that some Muslims might also qual-
ify as victims during riots, he does so with the dual purpose of shoring
up his view of himself as a rational and thoughtful individual and of cit-
ing evidence that he can then use to allow his assertion of collective
Muslim guilt for the Bombay bomb blasts to pass unchallenged.

While at some level there is no doubt that the mere fact of the rape of
a woman by men on-screen has made Harish angry, there is no question
that this is not the only reason he chooses to talk about this sequence
in *Hey! Ram*. First, he is infuriated by the possibility that the on-screen
rape that he witnesses, and which, implicitly, he takes to be a figurative
re-enactment of *real* historical events, may have the *effect* of causing
Muslims to think about raping Hindu women: his use of the words
'inviting them' is particularly striking in this context as it reminds us
of the ways in which the spectacularising of rape on-screen may be
suspected to be a pleasurable experience for 'others'. Delineating
the forcible articulation of discourses of sexuality and gender with those
of religion and nation in this particular sequence, Lalitha Gopalan
(2002: 191) argues that this film provides the space both for the implicitly masochistic enjoyment of the hero's suffering on watching his
wife being raped and for empathy with 'sadistic masculinity' when

he decides to enact his vengeance. Furthermore, she maintains that '[f]eeding into Hindu communal fantasies of Muslim men as predators and sexually violent, the segment depicts men marked as Muslim as a marauding crowd that preys on Hindu and Sikh women' (2002: 193). To a large extent, Harish's comments are consonant with Gopalan's analysis.

Second, Harish is angered by his belief that the gang-rape sequence gives Muslims (in general), whom he frequently refers to as 'them', what he sees as a pretext for coming on to the streets to 'protest'. Of course, this perception of Muslims, in particular, as a community easily roused to anger by any small cinematic depiction is not a prejudice that Harish holds in isolation. The Hindu Right has consistently tried to build consensus around the view that *Muslims* (in this instance in India) expect to be 'pampered' and positively represented.[10] This is not to say that Muslim fundamentalists in India do not protest about what they consider to be 'Un-Islamic' representations or negative representations of Muslims, denounce Muslims who do not share their views and demand the banning of certain controversial Hindi films.[11] Clearly, however, Harish makes little attempt to distinguish even superficially between 'Muslims' and 'fundamentalists'; nor, despite his repeated wish to discuss political issues and films and to present himself as well informed and knowledgeable, does he have a sense of the possible historical inaccuracies and political biases being played out in a film such as *Hey! Ram* (Vasudevan 2000c and 2000d). The fact that Harish continues to express his views, notwithstanding his awareness of my disagreement, testifies to the potency of his beliefs. In this instance, however, the film *Bombay* appears to act as a check to the notion that *nothing* was done to Muslims during the riots, that *only* Muslims were the aggressors, and that Hindus were *entirely* the victims until they began to defend themselves, a version of events that right-wing Hindus are keen to endorse.

Unlike Farsana, Kavita and Harish or Neetu and Kalpesh, some of my interviewees in Bombay, notably Sonali and Nikhil, both working-class Hindus, were not inclined to view *Bombay* either as a piece of 'documentary' evidence or as a love story. Their comments suggest that they watched it, and dismissed it, as another attempt by popular culture to intervene in a fraught political context that, both of them insist, has simply become more and more violent and cynical. In Nikhil's case I quote the extended piece of talk that led up to his brief and dismissive comments on *Bombay* because it delineates, far more clearly than his response to my later questions, his reasons for failing to be 'entertained' by or enthusiastic about Mani Ratnam's film. Prior to this extract, Nikhil had explained that Hindi films were the only form of entertainment that both he and his wife enjoyed:

Nikhil: In fact, last Sunday we went to see *Lagaan*. Took the baby along. It was the best film! We both enjoyed it very much, we cheered all the way, and every one of the three and three-quarter hours felt enjoyable and exciting. [... Pause] The villagers were illiterate, uneducated and poor. They had nothing. They didn't even know what cricket was. [... Laughs] The British had everything and they had the army. It was a film that made you feel that even the lowest can achieve something, can win. It was like that. There's an old man, there's a man who is dumb and cannot speak, there's an untouchable. Everyone gets together and does the deed. The Muslim and the Hindu stand side by side. That is what is inspiring. First the rest of the team oppose, that this man is an untouchable, he cannot play with us. Aamir says what's the difference? Today his blood comes out and it is red and yours too is red. No one has white blood, do they? It made my heart beat in a special way seeing all the religions, the Sikh man too [laughs] all coming together to fight in one cause. That is how it should be. There are enough adversities in life.

Shaku: You are in favour of all the communities living together side by side? You don't think Hindus are superior?

Nikhil: Of course I don't think Hindus are superior! No one is superior. We all have our good points and our bad points. Many people have disagreed with me in my life because of this that I have said. There was one boy from our shanty town, during the riots [*dange*] in 1992 I remember he had gone in secret in the night with the Shiv Sena men and he had thrown petrol on Muslim homes. He had also come to ask me to join him. He took me aside and said to me, 'Listen brother, what are you doing talking to Mohammed and Rafiq? Don't you know that they are Muslims?' I said to him, 'Look, why are you in school? Aren't you here to study and learn? Are you here to make differences between religions and castes? ('*Kya tum jaati bedh-bavh karne aaya hai?*') Those guys are my friends, Rafiq and Mohammed. And the guys you hang around with, they aren't even from our basti, they are strangers. You don't know them and I don't know them (*Na tum jaan-the unko, naa hum*). Why are you making a fight for no reason in our community? [Laughs] ...

Shaku: You're talking about the time of the riots in 1992–3?

Nikhil: Yes, the Shiv Sena riots. When they were killing and burning people. There was so much violence. In any Hindu areas the Muslim people's shops were looted and burned. And at that time, mostly it was just guys coming to take Muslim people's things. They didn't have the guts to earn a proper living so they're going to loot the belongings of the Muslim fellows who have worked hard for so many years! [Disgusted] These Shiv Sena fellows were just after goods. [Pause] And these are the same fellows, aren't they, who did 'Chalo Ayodhya'?

Shaku: Are they?

Nikhil: And who were the guys who did it? Ha? Tell me? They are ready to put bombs in mosques these guys, saying that Muslims *will* put bombs in temples! For God's sake, if you don't put bombs in their mosques, they would hardly go against your temples, *would they?* [Sweating profusely. Angry. Upset.]

Shaku: You feel very strongly about this.

Nikhil: Yes.

Shaku: Have you seen any of the films on this topic?

Nikhil: Yes. *Mission Kashmir* and I saw *Bombay*. But what good has come from those films? People are still carrying on in the same way. Aren't they? [Disgusted]

Shaku: Yes. [Long pause] You don't want to talk about those films? [He shakes his head and drinks water. Long pause]

(NKL.3/*Hindi*)

Perhaps coincidentally, none of my *middle-class* Hindu interviewees expressed such an open desire for, and involvement in, friendship between the communities as Nikhil did, none of them were as concerned with issues of caste and class as he was and few of them contradicted the right-wing Hindu discourse, openly put out across the country and covertly endorsed by films such as *Bombay*, that Muslims were always on the verge of violence. Instead, he names the right-wing Hindu cadre several times as being the initiators of violence. Reversing the commonly invoked discourse about Hindu self-defence against Muslim spilling of 'first blood' in India (whether this be present or past), he asks: 'For God's sake, if you don't put bombs in their mosques, they would hardly go against your temples, *would they?*' Although he is a Hindu, he distances himself from the community attacking Muslims, and his accusing question, while it maintains the confusion between ordinary Muslims and those who 'plant bombs' is nevertheless a challenge to the fiction about a Muslim *initiation* of aggression endorsed more or less overtly by films such as *Bombay*, *Hey! Ram* and *Gadar*.

In 2001 when I interviewed him, Nikhil had no way of knowing that only a year later Muslims in Gujarat would again be targeted by Hindu fascist cadres. Yet his questions, 'what good has come from those films? People are still carrying on in the same way. Aren't they?', imply a sense that at the level of personal interaction between the two communities, mediated interventions such as *Bombay* have failed to initiate any positive changes. However, in this context, Padma's response shows the ways in which even the abrupt ending of *Bombay* may hold a meaning for viewers that outweighs the other ideological discourses at work in the film: if Padma, whose mother openly tells her 'I don't want you to marry a Muslim or a Black person' can see her mother's racism for what it is and conclude from watching *Bombay* that everyone in India 'should unite across religions', then who am I to say that the film did not succeed in conveying a modernist national vision to *some* members of the audience? And who would deny that this vision and meaning is better than the (arguably) atavistic, fascist propaganda being peddled by many Hindi films[12] and, far more worryingly, by prominent members of the Indian and diasporic ruling elites (among many others,[13] see Bhatt 2001: 168–72)?

7.4 The pleasures and pitfalls of 'othering': inter-religious romance meets jingoistic nationalism

If you go by this movie, Pakistan should have never come into existence, Pakistanis are weird wacky Muslims, and that the state of India is all love and fun!'
('Pathetic racist trash', Internet Movie Database user comment on *Gadar*, 28 January 2002)

Gadar is a true story based on the partition of India. It is one of the biggest hits of bollywood and is a movie every Indian should see. Perhaps the only ones who wouldn't like this movie will be Pakistanis.
('A true patriotic Indian movie', Internet Movie Database user comment on *Gadar*, 28 August 2001)

Gadar: Ek Prem Katha (Anil Sharma 2001) did, as Kavita notes, cause political turbulence outside cinema halls[14] in India and a range of emotions in young viewers I spoke to, although these were far more pronounced in Bombay than in London, where few of my interviewees had bothered to watch it. The comments quoted above, all to be found on the Internet Movie Database website, though not reflective of all the positions taken up with regard to *Gadar*, are representative of two primary strands of audience response. It tells the tale of a Sikh truck-driver who, at the time of the 'partition' riots, saves the life of a wealthy Muslim girl whom he admires. Thinking her family has been massacred, she remains for a while in his home. The 'charm' of this 'cross-religious' romance is depicted in bright and glowing colours, with yearning, sad or joyful songs to match. The heroine settles down and has a son, only to discover through a chance newspaper article that her father is mayor of a major Pakistani city. Thus begins the second half of the film for, when she visits her father, he turns out to be a villainous and ideological hater of India, determined that his Muslim daughter should not return to her husband and child. Sunny Deol, the heroic star in the role of her husband, must fight off not only her father's henchmen but also half a battalion of what appears to be the Pakistani army in order to bring his beloved wife 'home'.

While the salience of *Gadar*'s discursive universe resides in its depiction of the 'Indian'/'Sikh' hero as willing to compromise with a 'Pakistani/ Muslim' and to respect Islam in order to regain his bride but absolutely resistant to speaking ill of his 'homeland' India, it is less Deol's patriotic refusal to shout 'Death to India' that resonates for this study than the film's representation of a uniform and distorted 'Pakistani Muslim' psyche, which cannot rest in peace, we are led to believe, if India prospers. Here I begin by examining the *pleasures* of the film from the viewpoint of some viewers in the Hindu majority in India or, slightly differently for Sikhs, via the history and body of the hero, Sunny Deol. I was first alerted to the complexity of these pleasures when I spoke with Bhiku, a lower-middle-class Gujarati in Bombay, whose posture of impartiality towards national politics wavered considerably during our interview:

Shaku: So in the theatre where you saw [*Gadar*], people liked those anti-Pakistan speeches?

Bhiku: Yes. Very much. Because people feel helpless to do anything against Pakistan but when this dialogue is delivered they are showing what is there inside … One thing I like in *Gadar* is that it has at least shown the pain that people face when leaving their roots, the trouble they would have faced in leaving that place. The cruelty which both the sides committed, they had tried to show the pain, but people would have seen the pain, would have seen the brutality, the violence, all people have a different angle to see, I couldn't even imagine the pain, that of people who lose their relatives at that time. Their Muslim priests are publishing [publicising] it more as [if it is] Muslims versus other communities, some of the acts of some Muslims that has made the majority [pause] and the government's acts also – the [Indian] government has tried to be neutral, to show themselves neutral, they have made injustices to the other – the Hindu community.

(BHK.1/*English and Gujarati*)

At one level, Bhiku's response to the film is perfectly consonant with the responses towards the film I received from many middle- and lower-middle-class Hindus in Bombay. His belief that the Muslim community in India has been appeased by the government in a manner unjust to Hindus showed that he took the film to be *redressing* this balance rather than critical of Pakistan. His awareness of the power of propaganda films (on both sides of the border) to stir up pleasurable feelings of self-worth and patriotism is not unique to this era, or to the divide between India and Pakistan. Few finer examples of jingoistic nationalism exist than the films produced by Hollywood in the wake of anti-communist government policy in the later 1940s and 1950s (Schindler 1979: 117–37). However, Bhiku's articulation of his pleasure in the film as one of needing to be *informed* about the brutal horrors of partition and of finding such information in the film, confirms a far more worrying replacement of 'real' with 'fictional' histories of partition in people's minds. As psychoanalytic theorist Sudhir Kakar notes, '[c]ultural psychology in India must necessarily include the study of the psychic representations of collective pasts, the ways the past is used as a receptacle for projections from the present' (Kakar 1996: 12–13). Read in the light of a trend towards the *erasure* of secular histories of India in the past decade and their *replacement* by fictions of Hindu fascist provenance (Butalia 1995: 58–81; Sarkar 2001: 268–88; Bhatt 2001: 92–4, 206–7), Bhiku's move from speaking of his enjoyment of the film *Gadar*, and that of others in the theatre where he viewed it, to the brutality and violence of partition and the inflammatory speeches of 'Muslim' priests (on both sides of the border) strikes me as extremely political and far from disinterested.

Indeed, the manner in which the film intertwines cleverly framed anti-Pakistani and pro-Indian audio-visual rhetoric with depictions of religion can in no way be deemed to be politically naive. Writing of (British, Australian and American) cinema, Graeme Turner argues that 'the idea of the nation can operate at the most basic levels of meaning and discourse. It becomes an overriding set of priorities, which define what is acceptable and what is not, what is normal and what is not ... all through defining what is [Indian] and what is not' (1999: 157). Thus, while one may not accept that films such as *Gadar* should be banned on the grounds that only *positive images* of any particular minority community are politically acceptable, it is clear that *Gadar* mobilises a set of discourses around the (Indian) nation that place certain religions as loyal but peripheral, others as central and yet others as constantly threatening the purity and essence of the (Indian) nation, either via the possibility of splitting or by that of dilution. Yet, and I stress this point, there were viewers who, in speaking of the film, were genuinely and entirely unaware of what I read as its barely concealed right-wing stance (in the predominant depiction of Pakistan as a place of fearful repression – an Indian Muslim recently arrived from across the border and suffering from the delusion that he is still in India is repeatedly refused permission to salute the Indian flag – religious fanaticism and hostility; and Pakistanis as almost uniformly violent, cowardly or hating towards every Indian). They interpreted its philosophy in the light of their own beliefs and values; 16-year-old Neetu, a working-class Sikh in Bombay, read it as a film about the overcoming of obstacles by personal loyalty and passion:

Neetu: And *Gadar*, even though that is an action movie it is very touching how she comes into his religion and all, like how she follows it and how she sacrifices and how Sunny Deol he is going to sacrifice and even he is ready to take over the Islam religion. That is a good thing that even he is willing to take on her religion. I think such relationships can work across religions. That was very touching to me.
Shaku: Oh Yes?
Neetu: Yes. Because nowadays there are many Hindus marrying Muslims and Muslims marrying to Christians and all. It can work. [Very vehement] I agree with those things. I believe in those things because I believe in love. Even we have to sacrifice and even they have to sacrifice.

(NTU.1/*English*)

Neetu's genuine enjoyment of the film and her reading of it as an endorsement of cross-religious romance is clear in this extract. Her beliefs and attitudes towards religion and romance struggle for articulation in her endorsement of sacrifices and potential sacrifices on the part of both protagonists in *Gadar* and bursts out in her statement, 'I believe in love'.

At no point in our interview did Neetu allude to the near gang-rape of the Muslim heroine at the opening of *Gadar* when she is fleeing a mob of Sikh men bent, according to the film dialogues, on avenging their own raped mothers and sisters; nor did she mention that, unlike the hero who makes a conscious decision to accept Islam in order to keep his wife and child, the heroine does not *choose* how she 'comes into' the hero's religion. Unable to convince the mob of fellow Sikhs to spare her life as a *Muslim woman*, he resorts to on-the-spot conversion, symbolically claiming her by marking her forehead with his blood and making her into a 'Sikhni'. The fact that this 'redefining' of the heroine by the hero as a Sikh rather than a Muslim deters the men who were seconds before hell bent on sexual assault and murder forms part of the film's latent gender imaginary, but does not in any way affect Neetu's understanding of the film narrative as recommending that couples should *convert* for each other with equal willingness.

Neetu's firm and unambiguous positing of religious affiliation as *secondary* to personal attachments is, it should be noted, quite unusual within my sample. Even viewers opposed to communal politics wished to insist upon the importance of their own natal religious affiliations. However, lest it be thought that all Hindu viewers were unaware of the dangers of such fictions of history as those configured in the wake of the misrepresentations of nations and communities in Hindi popular films, I quote Jatin, who discusses his discomfort with *Gadar* in no uncertain terms as being linked to its political subtext:

Jatin: ... I actually got irritated with *Gadar*. That Sunny Deol Film.
Shaku: Why was that?

Figure 7.1 Young viewers contemplate the intended gang-rape of the heroine in *Gadar*

Jatin: Well, he's Sikh, but he calls himself a Hindu all the time. And I thought – 'He says, 'We Hindus, we don't buckle down to you Muslim people', and it's just basically him destroying Pakistan on his own. [laughs] And it's like a Sikh marrying a Muslim, but it's like she becomes virtually a Hindu! So you can see the BJP funda[mentalist] values coming out there. [laughs]

(JAT.4/*English*)

Saliently, the *feelings* of individual and/or collective frustration, impotence, victimhood, anger or righteousness to which such films speak and which they generate are as much a part of the spectatorial process as the actual dialogues, props, actors and songs. What, for Jatin, is a cause for concern and 'irritation', namely the manner in which the film appears to posit some essential 'Hinduness' about being Indian and represents Pakistani identity as fanatically Muslim and anti-Indian, is, for other viewers, a representation of something *they believe to be the case and that they gain enjoyment from believing*. Thus the destruction of imagined enemies and the annihilation of the technology, humanity and self-respect of the imaginary oppressive 'other' forms one of the key pleasures for spectators of this film with no emotional ties to 'the other'.

One viewer in Bombay, Ravi, a 23-year-old musician and journalist, who was carving out a career for himself against the wishes of his strict middle-class Hindu family, explained the pleasure of the propaganda film as akin to that of the backbiting that one finds between groups in a college or workplace: 'Like gossip in talk, here cinema is the form, and you are just showing that here Pakistan is a *very sad* country and we finally win and they are *so* evil they are perpetrators, like in *Gadar* ... a movie to make Indians feel more patriotic about their own country.' When I asked him what *he* felt when watching such films, he mentioned a split between how he felt in the cinema hall and his assessment of the film when he came out of the theatre:

Ravi: Well, it's very entertaining to watch, it's very nice to see for three hours. [S: Um Hum] But I don't think that it's very much the case in reality. Countries don't just fight for religious differences. They don't wage war for 50 years for religious differences. There has to be something more to it! And I don't think the way it is shown in our movies is right, that *our* army is so *good* and efficient and is winning with the least number of casualties like in *Border* [sarcastic; pause]. Okay, but that's just a movie. But a lot of people believe it, they get carried away by it and it does build up national feelings.

(RAV.1/*English*)

For me the idea that one might watch the film for the sake of entertainment and pleasure without necessarily retaining, outside the theatre, any vestiges of the ideology or sentiments at play while watching the film was perfectly plausible. After all, I myself have both read and watched, with great enjoyment and involvement, narratives that conflict with my beliefs and values as well as with my politics in the 'real' world. However, Ravi himself finds the possibility that *everyone* might share the same viewing pleasures and strategies as himself unconvincing, and he quickly begins both to question the representation of history in films such as *Gadar* and *Border* and to articulate his own version of an effects theory. I found Ravi's testimony particularly pertinent because he was clearly not averse on aesthetic or moral grounds to the chest-thumping, openly xenophobic aspects of films such as *Gadar* and *Border*. On the contrary, he evidently found them entertaining partly because they allowed him to participate in a collective fantasy of national pride and supremacy, and to articulate various degrees of scorn or compassion for the 'other'. Unmasking the 'enemy' – generally Pakistanis – as cold, brutal, chauvinistic but also cowardly and defeatable, – while at the same time playing with one's own national identity as compassionate, brave and patriotic, as Ravi emphasises, both *Gadar* and *Border* offer a whole range of narcissistic pleasures to some Indian or 'India-identified' viewers. Although *Gadar*, and films like it, do contain a limited number of potentially conflicting viewing positions via their incantations on love and their positing of a tolerant and inclusive 'Indian' masculinity, it is significant that viewers such as Ravi do not appeal to these other viewing positions to justify their enjoyment of the film. Their pleasure is as much, if not more to do with *the manner in which the film addresses them*, as it is to do with costumes, songs and actors. The fact that, on emerging from the three-hour fantasy, Ravi questions the representations he has witnessed in the light of his political knowledge and expresses his awareness of the manipulation of national images indicates that *not all viewers* who enjoy watching such xenophobic fantasies pursue correspondingly xenophobic or right-wing politics outside the cinema-hall.

It appears, then, that in addition to its overtly political aspects, *Gadar* does contain references to romantic love and sacrifice that might bind young viewers, who would otherwise be opposed to its politics, to aspects of its vision. However, it would be a mistake to suggest that there is a *wide* range of contradictory positions from which to enjoy the film or that all these positions are *equally* available to *all* viewers. Excluded, via their ambiguous religious status *vis-à-vis* the newly Hinduised 'Indian' nation, from comfortable participation in many filmic fantasies of 'national' success, my interviews suggest that many Muslim viewers either choose not to watch such films or try to dwell on their individual narratives, remaining on the periphery of the humiliation and defeat of the film 'others'. Some non-Muslim viewers, too, remain sceptical and unconvinced by the rhetoric of these films, some to the point where they reject the films entirely and do not enjoy major sequences. Thus, perhaps unintentionally, such 'propagandist' Hindi films could be said to play a role in provoking thought about, and engagement with, the politics they embody where, otherwise, there would be no popular arena for such engagement. This, of course, links back to a point made in Chapter 6 regarding the 'Swiss hotel' sequence: it is possible to see how Hindi films might be at their least 'ideologically effective' for a number of viewers when they are at their most didactic.

7.5   Conclusion

7.5.1   Hindi film politics

Given the growth of right-wing Hindutva beliefs and organisations both inside and outside India in the past decade and a half, *and* given the defence and justification of such politics by considerable sections of the urban Indian population, there is no way in which Hindi films such as *Bombay, Hey! Ram, Gadar, Border, Mission Kashmir* and *Maachis* can be seen as anything but *political interventions*. However, these are popular films, intended for a mass audience both inside and outside the Indian borders, and part of the condition for their popularity lies in their ability to leave open the possibility of a number of – potentially contradictory – viewing positions. For instance, issues of *masculinity* and *religious identity* are complicated by the inclusion of sequences (that might be considered rhetoric by some critics) about the kind-heartedness, justness and protectiveness of specifically Hindu or Sikh men towards (Muslim or Pakistani) others, when these 'others' are considered to be 'innocent'. But, from the point of view of this research, the fact that many Hindi films, unlike the rhetoric of the Hindu Right reviewed ear-lier, do depict, in however naive and patronising a manner, some Muslims as 'good', some Muslims as patriotic Indians and/or worth

saving, and some Pakistanis as brave/loyal friends has two potential repercussions. On the one hand, viewers have a certain degree of choice in
terms of their overall political interpretations of these film discourses.
On the other hand, the films' apparently 'balanced' and 'liberal' representations of individuals can make the invitations of their overall politics more difficult to negotiate. Thus these films maintain their appeal
for a diverse public that includes Harish and Bhiku, Padma and Ruksana,
Nikhil and Ismail. Nevertheless, I maintain, *in some of these films*, the primary and most easily achieved viewing position, for those whose ethnic
and religious identity allows this, is cast in a fascist mould, with imagery
and discourses implicitly endorsing a violent, sexist, ethnically monolithic and rigidly authoritarian idea of the nation. And, given that several
of these films deal with events in recent history, it would seem that Anton
Kaes (1989) is right to assert that these films come to constitute a 'techno-
logical memory bank', accessible to all and, in many cases, a *replacement*
for history. Alternatively, as Tanika Sarkar (2002) poignantly expresses it,
these films may become allies in the Hindu Right's 'will to forgetting' as
they *assist* in making 'things that happened disappear from memory', in
filling up 'memory with images of things that had not happened', and
in generating 'counterfeit collective memories, amnesias'.

7.5.2 Politics beyond the texts

My discussions with young viewers of sequences in films such as *Gadar*,
Bombay and *Border*, like the discussions of romantic and sexual sequences
in preceding chapters, appear to confirm Judith Mayne's contention that
spectatorship inheres not merely in the act of viewing a film on screen,
but lives on in the relationship between film and viewer once the viewer
leaves the theatre (1992: 2–3). The manner in which this relationship
exhibited itself, however, was very diverse within my sample. Certain
films were invoked both as reasons for and evidence of the justness of
certain political beliefs; repeatedly, they were referred to as having provided frameworks for understanding contemporary political conflicts,
human suffering or the history of a preceding generation.

In some cases, however, young viewers articulated an awareness of the
pleasures or discomforts on offer for them in films utilising a national-
ist/ patriotic (and exclusionary) mode of address and chose to view or to
refrain from viewing these films on this premise. Such articulated
choices were echoed by a wish to distance the viewers' own politics and
beliefs about national identity, religion and community in everyday life
from those they believed to be purveyed by the films in question.
However, saliently, it would be foolish not to acknowledge that some of

the young viewers I interviewed as part of my sample displayed what can only be called a *predisposition for aspects of fascist politics*. Their ease with the 'racial' nomenclature and rhetoric of the ultra-nationalist Hindu Right, regarding *both* Indian border disputes *and* Muslims, was evident, and their belief in the righteousness of what they were saying was on a par with, if not greater than, many viewers' acceptance of the justness and inevitability of sexist gender roles. In some cases discussed in this chapter, ambivalence about Muslims (or Pakistanis) on the part of some viewers, or even outright dislike, could be linked in the course of an interview to sequences, representations and events in specific Hindi films. Notwithstanding this connection between off-screen understandings of films and viewers' politics, I did find that when questioned at more than a superficial level, *young viewers rarely chose* to respond to these Hindi films as *organic* and *unitary* texts or, throughout an interview, with *consistency* and *uniformity* (as the statements 'It was a good film' or 'I didn't like it' might seem to imply).

Young viewers I spoke to were more inclined to respond differently to different segments of Hindi films and to view many films as fragments rather than entire texts, and many fragments of films as being part of a larger, more coherent set of meta-discourses, narratives or practices. The nature of my interviewees' testimony on this issue appears to point to a fundamental aspect of Hindi film spectatorship: its refusal of critical positions on *particular* film texts arguing for inherent, singular and cohesive textual effects. The sets, colours, costumes, music, lyrics, dialogue, choreography and physical attractiveness of the central protagonists may thus operate to give young viewers in my sample grounds for engagement with and delight in sequences of a Hindi film for *one* or *even two* out of three hours, where the primary focus of the narrative would have lost their attention or their liking within minutes. However, I suggest, it is equally the case that where young viewers in my sample took the *style* of the films for granted, were sceptical of the allure of visual beauty and annoyed by the frequency and placing of the musical interludes, their attention was held by the film's dominant narrative and/or its primary discursive framework, and it was to aspects of the *narratives* of these films that they would turn, as if for confirmation, during discussions of social and political issues, showing that their watching of these films unquestionably played a role in their interpretation of the world, just as their beliefs and values gleaned from lived experience, families, peers or communities shaped their interpretations of the films.

7.5.3 Class and religion

Speaking of lived experience, I found that, within my Bombay sample, intersections of geography and religion with *social class*, more than those with gender, began to emerge as factors inflecting the depth and scope of young viewers' attitudes to those Hindi films overtly raising issues of communal and national consciousness. Although this study does not purport to be *representative* of Hindi film viewers' beliefs and opinions *en masse*, it is worth mentioning that in Bombay, Hindu viewers such as Sonali and Nikhil from staunchly working-class families were more concerned to foster intercommunal harmony, more critical of nationalist and communal discourses in Hindi films and more aware of the politics and tactics of the Hindu Right than their middle-class Hindu and Jain peers. Also, clearly with the exception of Preeta, most viewers from Sikh, Christian and Muslim backgrounds such as Neetu, Kavita, Ismail, Farsana, Jasmine and Azhar were either anxious to explore or knowledgeable about the manner in which discourses of religion, culture and nationalism in certain films might tie in with these discourses in public life. In the light of the amorphous belief, expressed repeatedly by viewers such as Farsana, that 'riots' are primarily caused by the actions of *thoughtless, spontaneous* mobs composed of a lumpen underclass or of unemployed *working-class male* thugs, Nikhil's account of the highly organised and systematic nature of Shiv Sena manipulation and co-option of young Hindu men before and during the 1992–3 Bombay pogroms cannot but be read as highly significant. Arguably, if one wishes to combat communal hatred, then along with myriad other sectarian and fascistic rhetoric, this nebulous belief about 'riots' – in my view, sustained rather than undermined by aspects of films such as *Bombay* – would have to be systematically challenged by academic, literary, journalistic and filmic representations of religious riots.

In London, the responses of young viewers to overt representations of Indian nationalism, religious tension and/or terrorism (as will be seen in Chapter 8) did not fall neatly either along class, gender or religious lines, but appeared to be connected rather to levels of general/historical knowledge, political engagement and identification with India/South Asia as a homeland. Thus Padma and Jatin, two Hindu viewers evincing most interest in politics, history and issues of identity, were both clearly the most alert to connections in Hindi films between discourses of nation and to subtle representations of Hindutva consciousness. Hamidul, Ruksana and Hena, young Muslim viewers in London who sensed these connections, did not (or were not confident enough to[15]) articulate them as such. Other Hindu viewers in London were either uninterested in these discourses and hence did not dwell at length on films utilising them or, like Manish, were themselves implicated in the communal consciousness of particular films. Significantly, given the growing tendency to see Hindi films as being aimed at a so-called 'NRI market', I did not find in any way whatsoever that the young viewers in my London sample showed a greater attraction towards, or predisposition for belief in, the quasi-nationalist and sectarian discourses of Hindi films than did their peers in Bombay.

7.5.4 Spectatorship: experience, rationality, emotion

At a different level, within my sample, a clear distinction arose – amongst those with firsthand experience of 'religious riot' situations or pogroms – between those who, like Farsana, Ismail and Azhar, had suffered during 1992–3 and those who had simply witnessed events from the 'outside'. Thus the consideration of films such as *Bombay* and *Gadar* amongst viewers in my sample tended to differ, based both on religion and class: the more distanced viewers were in an emotional and physical sense from the violent events and ideologies with which these films purported to deal, the more their spectatorship left room for a range of pleasures and interpretations. This does not mean, however, that viewers with greater emotional investments in the events under consideration had somehow allowed some 'pure' or authentic form of critical spectatorship to be 'compromised' or 'distorted'. To imply that emotion somehow *detracts from* or *undermines* the status of (critical) judgments made about Hindi films mistakenly assumes that rationality and emotion exist as two distinct states of mind and in hierarchical relationship with each other. Such an evaluation also presupposes, equally erroneously, that emotion and rationality have a pure or authentic form outside of the discursive contexts that shape their expression. The notion of spectatorship emerging from my discussions of films dealing with religion and politics is one that sees viewers as being always, to some extent or another, making judgements about films that are both rational and emotional, regardless of the pleasure or the criticism involved. As such, the 'critical' evaluations of these films by theorists must be read within this context merely as exemplifying a set of *potential alternative readings* (from within a limited number of possible readings) to those offered by Ismail, Farsana, Jatin, Harish and the others, rather than as embodying *the definitive meanings* of the texts.

My interviews in both countries suggest that alongside amusement and approval, *ironic* and *critical* readings of these films do exist in the minds of young viewers. Discriminations are frequently made by view-ers between different Hindi films' politics and narratives in a manner not usually acknowledged in theoretical accounts focusing on the films (among others, see Valicha 1988; Chatterji 1998; and Prasad 1998). Perhaps shying away from the complex contradictions inherent in view-ers' responses – that display an enjoyment of film discourses that they may also be logically, morally and/or politically wary of – such textual accounts delineate or predict cohesive and singular responses. Yet view-ers do not simply accept film makers' positionings of their films. Contra-dicting a view of the cinema-going public as basically apolitical and interested in 'mindless entertainment', frequently *Gadar*, and other films on terrorism or national security such as *Mission Kashmir*, *Roja* and *Border*, would be introduced by young viewers *in the context of* discus-sions of modern politics. While exploring such responses, in Chapter 8, the themes of repression, terrorism and political unrest in films come cen-tre stage, along with notions of supposedly 'patriotic' and 'anti-national' responses to Hindi cinema.

8
Politics and Spectatorship 2: Young Men Viewing Terrorism and State Violence

By and large female viewers in my sample, while frequently wishing to speak of violence and prejudice, were less likely to mention the topic of *terrorism* in relation to films than their male counterparts. Ismail, a working-class, 19-year-old in Bombay, 16-year-old British-Bengali Jomir, and 24-year-old Harish, whose comments regarding *Hey! Ram* were quoted in Chapter 7, represent a cross-section of the young men in my sample and it is to their comments that this chapter is primarily devoted. The films spoken of by these three young men – *Maachis* (Sampooran Singh Gulzar 1996), *Fiza* (Khaled Mohammad 2000) and *Mission Kashmir* (Vidhu Vinod Chopra 2000) – form a springboard for the young men to speak of aspects of their politics and beliefs. In all three films, and despite their very confused sympathies and very different ideological standpoints, sympathy for the hero – who is provoked or impelled to seek *personal* justice or revenge by entering a terrorist organisation – is the one factor that unites these three very different viewers.

8.1 Countenancing cinematic terrorism: young men take on the state

Maachis, Gulzar's tale of a young Punjabi man who joins a terrorist group when an innocent friend of his commits suicide after being interrogated and tortured by the Indian police, has been called the 'anguish of the middle class', an 'embalming of middle-class melancholia' and a transformation of the civil family into one of 'weaponised masculinity' (Gupta 1999). The manner in which the hero's concerns at an individual level, his subjectivity and that of his fiancée – his friend's sister, who also ends up becoming a terrorist once she has lost him – shape one's perceptions of terrorism and terrorists is used, according to Gupta, to

160

blot out the *social and political realities* of insurgency, non-violent civil responses to it, as well as to state repression, and to shift the discourse around terrorism and state repression into a register where a greater degree of violence is normalised for the *middle-classes*. This reading is, I believe, both challenged by the accounts given by some young viewers (see ISM.2), and borne out by certain viewers who experience in *Maachis* a sense of the fragility of their *middle-class* rights, their security and comfort, in the face of a corrupt and violent state. Harish, for instance, moved from speaking about the violence of the police during the Bombay 'riots' to speaking of political corruption, terrorist responses to it and the violence in *Maachis*:

Harish: I like the movie *Maachis*. I felt sympathy for the terrorists [pause] and in Punjab the Jat caste itself is normally very hot-tempered, very aggressive and if something like this happened to them, you can't think of stopping them.

Shaku: What would you do if you found yourself in a situation like the man in *Maachis*?

Harish: Hypothetically, I would first like to resolve this issue by taking it to some top authorities. But I won't stay back, I won't wait for the decision for years [pause] after my trying officially, legally for a year, I'll go the same way he did.

Shaku: You really think so?

Harish: He didn't go for justice from the big-shots. He went directly for terrorism. I wouldn't do that. I *would try*, but after that, definitely, because it would have happened to me [pause] after a week or a month, it could happen to anyone. It *does* happen to anyone. I'll do the same thing he [Chandrachur, in *Maachis*] did ... The police are corrupt ...

(HAR.2/*English*)

Here Harish introduces the notion of police corruption and the idea that 'it could happen to anyone' as justification for his sense that he too would take to *terrorism* if something happened to him similar to what happened to the hero in *Maachis*. In a sense he is asking: 'if the state can turn against *anyone*, including the Indian middle-classes, then why should one be loyal to that state?' This feeling clearly does not affect Harish's sense of himself as an *authentic Indian* in any way, for his patriotism as expressed at the beginning of the interview is far more clearly linked to an amorphous notion of Indian 'culture' and values than it is to the state. I was singularly struck by Harish's use of the words 'top authorities' and 'big-shots' when he was explaining how he would proceed if a friend of his had been brutalised by the police. The notion of any form of protest that is not either *with the help of* the state or violently *directed against the state* does not exist in the moral and political universe that Harish sees himself as sharing with the film *Maachis*. His confidence in asserting that he would go to the top in order to seek justice before resorting to terrorism turns entirely on his belief in himself as a member of the Indian middle classes. Similarly, his confidence that he might have to turn to terrorism to redress his wrongs is also built into this same sense of himself as a member of the class most frequently asked for bribes in order to achieve anything. Confirming my growing sense of the way in which Hindi film viewers often dwell on parts of the films *other than the endings* in their coding of the film's discourses, at no point does Harish dwell either on the way in which the hero and heroine's terrorism is shown to bind them to a futile and destructive vision, or on the manner of their annihilation.

Dealing with the violence released in the Muslim hero by trauma suffered during the Bombay 'riots', his sister's efforts to find him and his efforts to dissociate and protect himself from the terrorist group he had joined, *Fiza* (2000) shares aspects of *Maachis'* pessimistic vision while *Mission Kashmir* (Vidhu Vinod Chopra 2000), more overtly than the other two films, owes its allegiance to the discourses of patriotism, conventional romance and heroic violence in other mainstream Hindi films. All three films rely heavily on the charisma of their main characters, on beautiful cinematography and lyric song sequences to appeal to members of the audience not directly interested in the complicated/political plots. In some ways particularly pertinent to this analysis is the case Sumita Chakravarty builds in relation to the narratives of Mani Ratnam's films *Roja, Bombay* and *Dil Se*:

> If terrorism in different guises is a looming presence in these characters' lives, it is also a means of interrogation of national ideals gone awry, and of evoking the faces and voices of the estranged who must be brought back into the mainstream. In focusing, however obliquely, on the communal or terrorist Other, the films suggest that the nation is problematic if not compromised and needs to be rethought. For the films do not explore the polarities between friends and enemies (nations and their terrorists) but rather the linkages through the theatrics of violence, between dominant and subordinate, friend and foe, the nation and its would-be fragments. The latter entities end up mirroring each other, for terrorist violence is spawned by state violence and oppression.

> (2002: 232)

Harish was a viewer who clearly understood the film *Maachis* as an 'explanation' of the terrorist psyche, and framed for himself a link between his own urban middle-class life and that of the protagonist via a notion of state corruption, inadequacy and betrayal. Ismail too suggests that the 'nation is problematic and needs to be rethought', also exploring, for different reasons, the connections between the other and the nation. He explained his reasons for liking *Maachis*, which he had watched aged 14, as being about *realism* and the depiction of *social injustice*:

Ismail: I liked *Maachis* because I felt that there was a certain kind of *reality* (*asliyat*) about how it is shown. And because that kind of thing is *really* what has happened to the people of that region. They did nothing wrong and the police came to brutalise them. The guy Jimmy – no, the friend, his dog is called Jimmy and he had done nothing and the police were so bad, they ill treated him with such violence. And it is to be taken for granted that if such terrible treatment is meted out to a person close to you, you wouldn't be able to bear it and you would want to retaliate. You wouldn't sit silent. And when that kind of thing goes on again and again, it would be absurd to expect people to sit silent again and again. And that film, which fit into a certain group of films, which you could call those that are against injustice, which is about the struggle against a particular ill treatment, I feel strongly about that .... [I]f the law gives no succour, as in that situation, then I would also have done what he did.

Shaku: And you have seen other films on this topic?

Ismail: I guess you could say that *Fiza* too is about this. In that too [pause] Hrithik too has this kind of treatment and then he has to start a whole new life and when he comes out and his friends call on him one by one in a threatening manner, and when he goes to ask the police for protection because they are going to kill him, the police tell him, 'Go to Pakistan, there is no place for you here.' They refuse to protect him! This is not right. Even 52 years after independence, you people [tum log] are still keeping this thing in your hearts that 'You are not an Indian if you are a Muslim'! If you travel on public trains in Bombay, to and from work, then people can tell as we talk to each other that we are Muslims. Just from the Urdu language we use, just as we can tell they are non-Muslims by the kind of Hindi they speak. Sometimes the Hindus who are listening, they treat us like this, they feel confident to say 'This is not your country, why are you here?' It is painful. [long pause]

Shaku: Yes, 50 years is a long time to feel this way. Why do you think people feel that way about Muslims then?

Ismail: [unclear sentence] You know the disturbing things, like that the Shiv Sena Chief, Bal Thakaray, [S.: Yes?] So many of his statements are against Muslims. But the government can do nothing to him. Why can't they? He should be in jail. This is what you have to ask. He has had case after case made against him, but nothing touches him. And with such anti-Muslim sentiments around, how do people expect the Muslims in this country to feel that India is our country?

(ISM.2/*Hindi-Urdu*)

Ismail's commentaries on *Maachis* and *Fiza* raise different issues to do with notions of being a terrorist, in line with each film's emphasis. Ismail's major points about *Maachis* are, first, that it appears to him to be a *realistic historical* narrative about those caught up in the aftermath of the Indira Gandhi assassination, the Indian government 'offensive' against 'insurgents' and the terrorist backlash and, second, that it appears to him to be a *realistic psychological* account of how those who have been brutalised not once but many times by the state, despite their manifest innocence, turn to terrorism.

Both Harish and Ismail feel that their sense of self is in some way challenged by *Maachis*' depiction of the hero's choice, which appears to be between remaining a passive observer of the brutality that destroyed his friend and taking violent action. To this extent these two young men's psychological responses proceed side by side. However, it is my opinion that Ismail, perhaps by virtue of his *working-class* status, views the landscape of the film differently to Harish and sees *Maachis* as being part of a body of films that detail fights against 'injustice' rather than being about 'corruption'. With regard to *Fiza*, Ismail dwells primarily on the manner in which a young Muslim man, who has become a terrorist, is unable to turn back or to halt his path because the state will not accept his reformation and offer him the protection that he requires to alter his 'terrorist' status. At this point in the extract, it is significant that when Ismail paraphrases what the police in the film say to the hero, 'Go to Pakistan, there is no place for you here!', his thoughts immediately lead him into an extended digression about *the interconnected communal and national consciousness* of the Indian state and populace (whom he indeterminately names as 'you people', 'they' and 'the Hindus'). His sense of the attitudes of communal Hindus towards Muslims embodied in the phrase, 'You are not an Indian if you are a Muslim', evokes notions of an 'authentic' national character in which religion and language play a central role. Showing a subtle awareness of the ways in which national *belonging* is a matter of sentiment and emotion far more than it is a matter of essential or 'authentic' characteristics, Ismail contends that feeling India to be *one's country* is a matter of reciprocity, of dialogic commitment.

Unlike Ismail, who did not regard these films in the nature of *guides* to *moral action*, Jomir, a GCSE student in London, looked very favourably on what he interpreted as the moral subtext of *Mission Kashmir*, the convoluted story of a young (Muslim) man in Kashmir who joins a terrorist organisation after discovering that his adoptive father is none other than the policeman responsible for the deaths of his blood-family in an 'anti-terrorist' raid some years before:

Jomir: I quite liked [*Mission Kashmir*] because it shows what's really happening in Kashmir. They show Muslims and things fighting. I really liked it because in a way they show the people who are going off their culture and everything 'look, this is what's happening in Kashmir'. We could get rid of those fighting and the people who are modernising in this country think they [the Kashmiris] are nothing to do with us, we're living in England. But they're your people. People here are not going to think you're British-Asian. They're going to look at your skin and say you're Asian. That's it. [pause] In *Mission Kashmir* when his family gets killed and he just shouts and reacts, it just shows that there is family and I liked it when he finds out that Sanjay killed his family and he becomes [pause]
Shaku: You sympathise with Hrithik becoming a terrorist?
Jomir: No! Never! ... I would never become a terrorist myself. Then I would become known as a terrorist and that gives a bad name to me. [long pause].

(JOM.3/*English*)

As I listened to Jomir speak, I was reminded more forcefully than ever that trying to pin a single cut and dried interpretation on to an entire film is not a fruitful activity. Jomir found in *Mission Kashmir* a utopian vision of worldwide South-Asian solidarity that I had not considered an avenue for exploration. His sense that the people he most despises in his own environment – those Asians whom he deems to wish to become more Western (modern) and to forget their roots in South Asia – will be enlightened about the trials and tribulations of their brothers and sisters in Kashmir, as well as inspired by the loyalty to family depicted by this film, entirely overrides any problematic issues of *representation* that trouble other Muslim viewers such as Ruksana and Azhar. Nevertheless, Jomir's comments entirely obscure the real context of the conflict in Kashmir and between India and Pakistan over Kashmir, just as critics claim the film aims to do.

8.2 Conclusion

Significantly, for all three young male viewers quoted in this chapter, Hindi films provide scenarios that allow them to explore their relationships (in one case class-based, in another religion-based and in the third, based on regional ethnic identity) to situations of political crisis. For all three, unspoken, but critical, is a 'message' about ways of being active (violently) rather than passive in response to injustice. Also, regardless of the films' aesthetic choices and of their own identity positions, these young male viewers are able to read into them explanations for 'terrorism' and to view them as *realist* commentaries on recent political events in the subcontinent. However, whereas for middle-class Hindu Harish much of the discussion of 'injustice' is theoretical or identified as 'corruption', for working-class Muslim Bombayite Ismail, and for working-class British-Bengali Jomir, the realities of ethnic (religious/racial) discrimination form a bitter backdrop to their viewing and lead them to identify themselves not simply with the active/aggressive heroes of these films but also as *vulnerable* members of the societies they inhabit. This is crucial for, again, linking back to earlier discussions of the heroic subjectivity in *Bombay* (see Vasudevan 2001a) and to Carol Clover's arguments about male horror fans' victim-identified responses to films (1992), this suggests that all Hindi films do not speak only to a single aspect of masculinity that is about power and strength, but also invite male viewers to take up more supposedly feminine or *masochistic* subject positions. Consolidating the observations in foregoing chapters further, Chapter 9 looks back at the findings of this research and forward to what they might signal for Hindi film criticism in particular and for studies of cultural politics, media representation and spectatorship in general.

9

Conclusion: The Tricky Politics of Viewing Pleasure

9.1 Looking back at texts and audiences

In this chapter I turn first to the most wide-ranging conclusions of this study that relate, in this instance, to Hindi films and the ways in which viewers in general appear to interact with them. As such, the theoretical positions delineated here should be seen as informing and inflecting many of the other findings on gender, sexuality, ethnicity, class, context and spectatorship that follow.

9.1.1 Spectatorship and identity

While this book rejects the notion of identity as unbounded, amorphous, entirely unpredictable and totally free, the identities of film viewers are flexible enough to complicate the task of anyone hoping to second-guess their responses to and interpretations of entire films. In fact, I found that Hindi films are not necessarily remembered and interpreted in their entirety, but viewers appear to develop their own 'pathways' through Hindi films, focusing their attention on details and sequences that have particular relevance for their lives and appeal to their imaginations. Crucially, my study shows, it is in this sense that *the intersectionality* of identity becomes pivotal, as viewers do not watch entire films or all films, or even the same film twice, from an identical identity position. The politics of representation and the politics of viewers' experiences collide at various points in films making *different aspects of identity come to the fore or become active at different times.*

9.1.2 Realism, pleasure and ideology

The diversity of identity positions that viewers may adopt when watching Hindi films is mirrored by the diversity of pleasures on offer in the texts themselves. According to most viewers in the sample, the delights of Hindi film viewing are multiple: melodrama, music, lyrics, spectacular dances, colourful costumes, fashion, slapstick comedy, exotic settings and charismatic heroes and heroines. Judgements about 'realism' – that refer to this concept at times in its most positivist sense – are, nevertheless, central to the readings of Hindi films offered by most viewers in my sample. While it would be foolish to deny the existence and significance for spectators of modalities grounded in emotion, a notion of realism that is *entirely disconnected* from the material might not only be a commercial mistake when making a 'popular' Hindi film but also show a deep misunderstanding of the connections between fantasy and material existence, pleasure and ideology amongst sections of the audience. Certain Hindi films provoke anger in sections of the audience by too easy an assumption of their acquiescence in the films' moral and ideological universe. Crucially, it appears that *emotional and material realism are often mutually interdependent*: for most viewers in my sample, *a suspension of disbelief has to be earned and is not automatically granted* to a Hindi film text.

9.1.3 Alternatives, not escapes

This study has found that *Hindi films by and large are far from ideologically vapid*. They contain a *circumscribed, but significant range of discourses* on gender, sexuality, family, class, religion, violence and a plethora of other themes. Furthermore, these themes *are deployed or excluded in a limited number of ways*. Contingently, the charge of 'escapism' made against all commercial Hindi films and frequently applied even by viewers to their own viewing, appears to be seriously mistaken or else a semantic misnomer. The fact that Hindi films encourage 'fantasy' (rather than, say, 'revolution' or revolt against social injustice) is *per se* neither a positive nor a negative ethical attribute. *Fantasy is not an end-point but a process.* The films open up for viewers a limited range of alternative discursive positions, give them glimpses into alternative lifestyles, and endorse a narrow range of moral options that might, nevertheless, be different from those already available to them. Always these 'fantasy' lifestyles and moral choices intersect at the level of politics with the choices and discourses already available to viewers. The positions and attitudes adopted via Hindi film fantasies coincide with particular historical moments and political developments and can be either empowering and liberatory or, as frequently, authoritarian and fascistic. Likewise, if viewers have experienced some or all aspects of the emotional and material content of the film in their own lives, then the taking up of 'detached' viewing positions – such as ironic amusement, excitement about multimodal features such as music, costumes and setting or enthusiasm for a perceived ideological discourse in the film – becomes almost impossible.

9.1.4 Ending not closure

Really popular commercial Hindi films are, frequently, not viewed just once, but actually revisited on a number of occasions. Amongst my viewers were those who had been to the cinema to see their favourite films over 20 times. Young viewers knew the songs and many of the 'dialogues' by heart, and frequently interjected or recited them during interviews. They tended to look out for and watch films with storylines extremely similar to the ones they liked and containing the same or similar combinations of actors. They also listened to the songs from films at home and, if they enjoyed them, watched these songs on television repeatedly, thus gaining even more time with their favourite films. In this sense the *narratives* of Hindi films could be said to be cyclic and continuous, rather than linear; the experience of Hindi film *viewing* appears to be cut to this pattern. In general, the endings of Hindi films – which tend to erase differences, reconcile contradictions, silence criticism and, via melodramatic triumphs of individual will, disavow the need for collective resistance to authoritarian behaviour – do not appear to carry *any greater psychic and interpretive weight* for the young viewers in my sample than those at the beginning or in the middle. In fact, my interviews indicate that sequences in the middle of popular blockbusters may frequently have more lasting impacts in terms of viewers' interpretations and memories of the film, and their behaviour afterwards, than the films' concluding scenes. *In many instances, textual closure does not equal psychic closure*. Whether or not this is a 'good' thing from a pedagogical and political point of view, it has implications for textual analyses of Hindi films, suggesting that it might be fruitful to rebalance attention from the apparent closure at the ends of films to other moments in them that might come to the fore for certain viewers or after repeated viewings.

To recapitulate, then, *although Hindi films encourage and allow a diversity of experience, they do not have an infinite number of meanings*. Nor do they 'tell' viewers what to think and how to act such that there are no options left open for viewers. However, my research does show that, as argued by Fareed Kazmi (1999), Hindi films *do make specific claims on viewers' emotions by appealing to them to think of certain issues in specific ways*. I also found that moments of didacticism in some Hindi films backfire precisely by provoking ideological critique because, for many viewers, they do not ring true with either the films' material or psychic landscapes. Contrary again to implications about ideological interpellation and textual effects, Hindi film *form* and *representational techniques/stereotypes do not predetermine the meanings made*. Aesthetic enjoyment and political outrage can and do coexist in many accounts of viewing experiences, just as aesthetic critiques are frequently made alongside an acceptance of a film's moral presuppositions.

9.2   Looking back at gender, sexuality and spectatorship

9.2.1   Gendered visions?

A significant strand of broadly feminist writing with regard to gender and media is theoretically wedded to the belief that the media purvey stereotypical sex roles that implicitly become part of viewers' own gender identities. In such accounts, the effect of media stereotypes on human identity is immediate, monolithic and almost unbounded. To a large extent, this book rejects the premises of fixed, rational and essential identities in favour of the more nuanced explications of gender identity and media in the work of Christine Gledhill (1987, 1995); Robert Connell (1995); Shohini Ghosh (1999); and Purnima Mankekar (2000). These theorists, while mindful of the importance of fantasy and the unconscious in shaping human identity, move away from the notion of 'roles' and the 'unconscious' adoption of these roles to a notion of subjectivity that allows greater agency (however problematic) and flexibility (albeit limited by specific experiences and material contexts) in viewers' interactions with the media. In tandem, such theories acknowledge that media representations might have a greater range and manner of effects than previously allowed. In line with this theoretical framework, the opinions, beliefs and actions of viewers, as described by them during interviews, were frequently at odds with their purported judgments about courtship, romance and marriage in Hindi films. For instance, several unmarried female viewers in both countries who expressed deep enjoyment of film narratives about the importance of chastity and the sacrifice of daughters' personal desires in the face of parental authority or out of love/respect for fathers, were themselves engaged in clandestine sexual relationships and desirous of acceptance of these relationships by their parents. Several young male viewers, having championed the rights of film heroines and real-life women to self-determination, described complacently how they acquiesced in the subordination of their own girlfriends'/wives' autonomy to their wishes or their families' supposed 'traditions' and values. Regardless of young viewers' gender, age, religion or location, they deployed *available discourses* for talking about both on- and off-screen gender. While some of these were stereotypical (assuming the fixed and essential nature of gender identity) and some were quite clearly counter-stereotypical (assuming that men and women can become and be different from how they behave or appear at particular times), they frequently coexisted in accounts of viewing.

In terms of viewing *preferences*, although several female viewers asserted that when they were 'in the mood' they really enjoyed action films and, overall, both male and female interviewees showed significant affective investments in the love-courtship-family narratives of Hindi films, at cinema halls showing action films there were generally twice as many men as women. With regard to the representation of women on screen, I found that young viewers wanted to talk about much more than just the depictions of nudity and/or vulgar/scanty outfits in dance scenes or on vamps. The pleasures to be received from filmic displays of colours, styles and fashions, the vicarious enjoyment to be had from watching others wear outfits that one is not allowed to wear or prevented by lack of money from purchasing, the sexual excitement of watching both heroes and heroines cavort, and display their bodies, both in and through their screen garments, were often described *alongside* ideological critiques of the discourses evoked through other aspects of film costume. Saliently, I found that when discussing and responding to Hindi films, young viewers did not deploy 'ideological' positions around gender in ways that were always consistent, cohesive or linked to their everyday choices and behaviours. *Thus, the meanings they made from and assigned to depictions of masculinity and femininity in Hindi films were neither coherent nor always constant, but varied quite dramatically from sequence to sequence, film to film, and viewing to viewing.*

9.2.2 Sexual tales?

Several viewers in my sample expressed the feeling that the Hindi films which they enjoy watching are most talented at representing romance that makes sense to them, but do not depict sex in a respectful or meaningful way. While some viewers deplored what little kissing is already shown in Hindi films and felt that any greater licence in the form of explicit depictions of the body or of sex would be a danger to the 'traditions' of 'India' and to the morals of the South-Asian/diasporic populace, several other young people spoke with ambivalence about this subject because, while they yearned for clearer, more romantic depictions of sex in Hindi films, they were also embarrassed to watch such scenes with their families. Many, however, though aware of these potential embarrassments were eager to express their wish for greater openness in the depiction of sex and sexuality on the Hindi film screen.

In line with Judith Mayne's contention that 'desire and pleasure in the cinema may function to problematize the categories of heterosexual and homosexual' (1993: 97), I found little evidence to suggest that young viewers who did not question heterosexuality off-screen were unable to enjoy moments of homosociality and homoeroticism on-screen or that young gay viewers disliked or could not identify with the narratives of most Hindi films because these were heterosexist. Although they clearly had to work harder than their heterosexual counterparts to find moments of narrative pleasure – frequently choosing song and dance sequences, unhappy love-affairs and thwarted romance as their moments of key affective involvement – the other pleasures of viewing remained and, in several cases, enjoyment was in no way precluded. However, I also spoke to gay viewers who felt that almost all Hindi films reinforced notions of what it meant to be an 'ideal' Indian man or woman, and what it meant to be a 'good' son or daughter; these, they felt, contributed to the community and family contexts of heterosexism and homophobia within which they had to exist. In this sense, they suggested, having openly positive depictions of non-heterosexual partnerships in Hindi films could be both exciting and constructive.

It must be noted that *the self-contradictions identified during discussions* about on- and off-screen attire, *and the tendency to fall into such contradictions, appear to be inherent features of talk about personal and social relations, norms and values in relation to life and Hindi films.* Therefore, I argue not against ideological readings of clothing and bodies in films *per se*, but in favour of sensitive discussions of these issues that take on board the complicated matrix of meanings possible from even ideologically coded and loaded visual discourses in Hindi films and countenance the possibility that even, or perhaps precisely, repressive discourses may have untold pleasures for viewers who encounter them. As Preeta said of flirting (just before telling me she'd watched pornographic films with her friends), 'I prefer it – *under cover*'!

Discussions around issues of dress and 'eve-teasing' or sexual harassment and sexual violence show the greatest degree of variation in my sample between experiences of viewers in India and of those in Britain. However, in line with Shohini Ghosh's (2002) insistence on the *inconsistent, heterogeneous and unpredictable impact of mediated images of gender and sexuality*, while a great deal of anger and criticism was generated by young women's sense of *female objectification* in films, young viewers' own desires and pleasures in clothing were frequently linked, often explicitly but sometimes in an obscure or covert manner, to screen representations of both male and female bodies, clothing and physical intimacy.

Finally, and not unexpectedly, I found that *salient moments of sexuality or unpredictable and counter-stereotypical gender behaviour on-screen tended to hold more significance (either positive or derogatory) in the accounts of the young viewers I spoke to than they do for academic critics writing about these film texts*. Thus, in terms of discourses of gender and sexuality on-screen, this book finds that it is vital initially to map, textually, the invitations of meaning, or most plausible interpretations, of individual sequences, but then to reassess these in light of the ways in which audiences respond to such invitations.

9.3 Politics and spectatorship

Throughout this book the narratives of Hindi films were shown either crudely or subtly to interleave discourses about masculinity, femininity, sex and sexuality with those about ethnicity and nation. Understandings of the politics of nation and ethnicity were also shown to be intimately linked to interpretations of gender politics in contemporary Hindi films and are not merely extrinsic impositions upon an otherwise unconnected topic. Correspondingly, one of the presuppositions of this book was that *wider political events contribute significantly to the meanings that viewers make from Hindi film representations*, rendering textual features such as narrative less fixed than might be thought. Confirming this assumption, issues of masculinity, violence and religion in Hindi films were used by viewers as ways in to speaking about the events of 11 September 2001; the bombing of Afghanistan and anti-Muslim pogroms in India.

Several of the films discussed may be seen to be *attempts at intervention in contemporary politics around issues such as terrorism, nation, religion, community and gender*. The supposedly 'historical' settings of some of these films, that directors may attempt to represent merely as *backdrops* to 'love-stories', are frequently read as *being important contributions to historical knowledge* and are, in some instances, *confused with history itself*. In these circumstances, the discourses about gender contained in such films can be seen to reflect the directors' views about women, for instance, as 'representatives' of communal honour, along with men from certain communities (Muslim) and classes (the unemployed), as likely molesters and/or prone to terrorism while others (Hindus/middle-class men) are represented as loyal, patriotic and protectors of women's (and hence community/national) honour.

Thus, certain Hindi films that purport to be about Indian 'history' may be seen to mobilise a set of discourses around the (Indian) nation that place certain religions as loyal but peripheral, others as central and yet others as constantly threatening the purity and essence of the nation, either via the possibility of splitting or by that of dilution. Several of the viewers I met are either (a) quite openly engaged by and in agreement with the politics of these films, or else (b) utterly critical and suspicious of them. Other viewers take up a range of 'ironic' positions, playfully defending their viewing of what they themselves categorise as 'jingoistic' or 'absurdly patriotic' narratives and arguing that their attitudes in 'real' life are not symbolised by their pleasure in these films or that there's nothing wrong with denigrating Pakistan when one assumes the 'other' is also doing this across the border. Yet other young people appear to be genuinely unaware of what I (and many other 'academic' reviewers) read as their barely concealed authoritarian stances and interpret such films in the light of their own beliefs and values about love, families and coexistence. Here again it is possible to see that *ideological discourses in films operate differentially within specific contexts of family and community; they interact with viewers' own existential frameworks and beliefs before being interpreted, rather than being 'taken up' whole and absorbed, or critiqued and rejected entirely, by all who encounter them.*

Perhaps worth exploring further was my finding that in London, the only Hindu viewers who explicitly and consistently critiqued what they saw as the communalisation of Hindi film discourses – Padma and Jatin – were both doing social science degrees and were overtly interested in the history and politics of South Asia. In Bombay, ironically, while film narratives about so-called 'riots' were apparently interpreted as a confirmation of certain viewers' belief that religious violence is caused by gangs of lazy, 'lower-class' (unemployed or working-class) men, of the two male and three female viewers who most clearly rejected communal narratives in films and commented on the ideological work they felt was being carried out by the Hindu Right, *three* – Ismail, Sonali and Nikhil – were *working-class* and lived in shanty towns. While other young Hindu viewers who expressed 'dislike' for Muslim men or working-class men, and tacit support for the Hindu Right in India, cited parental advice, communal stereotypes and 'examples' from films to support their beliefs, Sonali and Nikhil explained their dislike of Hindu fascist organisations and cadres as springing from *direct contact.*

What is suggested here, tentatively, is that *ideological discourses in Hindi films work most powerfully to confirm conservative politics when there is already in existence either great ignorance or prejudice on the issues dealt with and when the issues are seen to be mediated in an apparently 'balanced' and 'liberal' manner.* Such prejudices are not separable from the contexts in which the films are produced, but they are, most certainly, *already a part of viewers' belief-systems before* they come into contact with the Hindi films that encourage them. Nevertheless, the fact that gender and sexuality are tied to ethnic and national identities, and the diversity of young viewers' responses on these topics, confirms my belief in the need for *more discussion and a wider access* to – mediated or direct – experiences of 'others' and historical events, rather than censorship of Hindi films that purport to represent them.

9.4 India and the United Kingdom

Chapter 2 raised a series of theoretical questions about diasporic identity and film viewing that needed confronting. Of central significance amongst these were two questions. First, is there a uniquely 'hybrid' diasporic or 'diasporically hybrid' subject position from which young British-Asian viewers watch Hindi films? And, second, if Hindi films have tried to represent a unified, homogenous, apparently 'authentic' version of 'Indian tradition' to the diaspora, then how is this apparently 'authentic ethnicity' interpreted by young diasporic viewers? Looking across both Indian and British-Asian samples to answer these questions, I discovered several ironic patterns.

9.4.1 Class and modality

First and foremost, *class* appeared clearly as a factor in discussions of lifestyles in recent Hindi films. All the working-class British-Asian viewers I spoke to complained or commented that family 'back-home' watch Hindi films about the lavish lifestyles and material pleasures of life abroad and want to get their children married off to British-Asians on the basis of the 'false' idea that anyone living in the United Kingdom must be minting money. Even middle-class British-Asian viewers were aware and critical of such misleading stereotypes. While they were pleased that some aspects of life 'abroad' are being considered by Hindi films, most British-Asian viewers in my sample also commented on the 'unrealistic' behaviour and dress of diasporic characters in Hindi films. In India, several viewers decried a trend they had noticed in recent Hindi films to set entire films 'abroad' and to exclude the depiction of what they considered to be 'normal' lifestyles. This objection was repeated in various forms about the expensive clothes, cars, houses and holiday destinations shown, suggesting that to both sets of viewers these material tropes of 'upper-classness' were not intrinsically appealing: however, while British-Asian viewers did not object to representations of wealth so much as to the *perceived effects* of these representations on others, many viewers in India felt positively *excluded* by the ostentatious displays of wealth on the part of supposedly empathetic characters.

9.4.2 The social experience of film viewing

This study found that the immediate context of the social act of viewing Hindi films in a group, along with members of an audience, in a quasi-public space such as a cinema hall or a crowded living room, *can have a profound impact on the nature of spectatorship, inflecting and even colouring entirely the experience of film viewing and the interpretation of particular sequences in films.* The verbal and non-verbal responses of young viewers and the 'looks' of older ones inside cinema halls in Bombay, though sometimes humorous, ironic and undermining of hegemonic discourses on class and gender, were certainly not uniformly liberal or liberatory. As Janet Staiger (2000) cautioned, certain audience groupings do evince immediate responses to certain sequences in films that cannot but be construed as oppressive of other groups within the cinema hall and supportive of authoritarian and/or misogynist attitudes. The politics of on-screen and off-screen were thus not always clearly separable within cinema halls.

9.4.3 Cultural 'authenticity'

Recent critiques of the concept of diasporic 'hybridity' urge a consideration both of people and cultural products as leading situated historical and political existences, which are deeply implicated in the politics and discourses of nation, race, religion, gender, class and sexuality of their milieus. *I found that young viewers in London did not use Hindi films to reconcile or understand notions of 'tradition' and 'modernity' to a much greater extent than their counterparts in Bombay.* Certainly each set of viewers appeared to be attempting to cope with the transitions between adolescence and adulthood, the need to *be* a certain way within communities, with parents, peers and partners, inside religious and class groups and as part of an apparently secular society. Indeed, viewers in London do have aspects of their Hindi film viewing and identity complicated by the fact that their parents are bi- or multinational but still recognisably 'Indian', 'Pakistani', 'Bangladeshi' or 'Nepali', while they are somehow, amorphously, 'British-Asian'; however, those in Bombay are faced with parents who are first-generation 'migrants' from villages or other regions, with all the specific rituals, prohibitions and nostalgia that such ties bring. In both countries, most young viewers I spoke to in-depth regard themselves as, to a certain extent, products of differing traditions and intersecting sets of cultural values but many, for want of a commonly accepted vocabulary with which to talk about culture and tradition, would fall back upon the words 'Indian tradition'.

As expected, although no one spoke as poignantly about feeling like an 'outsider' and having their culture 'rejected' as Ismail, a young working-class Muslim man in Bombay, most young viewers in London (Ruksana, Hena, Hamidul, Jatin, Ashok, Nisha) had a sharper perception and understanding of racism in a national context. Similarly, in the United Kingdom, I found that viewers were more likely to have access to alternative academic and/or media texts dealing with sex and sexuality. Both sets of viewers were generally keen to *talk* about gender, sexuality, politics and films. However, whilst in London it was *the whole experience of Hindi film viewing* that motivated the talk, and that viewers felt they did not often get the opportunity to discuss or think about outside their quite set milieux; in Bombay, there appeared to be a desire for some forum wherein all the issues, but especially those *of sex and sexuality*, could be candidly explored.

For many young South Asians in the United Kingdom viewing Hindi films was about *much more* than experiencing supposedly 'Indian' traditions or experiencing representations of the South-Asian diaspora. In fact, exemplifying Avtar Brah's notion of diasporas as 'contested cultural and political terrains', some young South Asians in the United Kingdom, who think of Hindi films as being specifically about Indian tradition, consciously choose not to watch them, while some who do watch them regularly are appreciative of their aesthetics and their narratives far more than they are of their symbolic functions as markers of a 'homeland' consciousness. Ultimately, this suggests not only the segmentation of British-Asian Hindi film audiences but also the *futility of trying to fix and essentialise aspects of diasporic cultural life* such as Hindi film viewing.

9.5 A note of caution

Problematising the whole project of drawing from one's findings a book that is logical, coherent and uniform or that employs cohesive frames of reference, in terms of my judgements of Hindi film texts, I am conscious at points of my own – perhaps post-structuralist – urge to report glowingly on the mischievous and/or ironic manner in which certain sexist or heterosexist representations or the exclusion of certain classes or sexualities, for instance, may be engaged by viewers in my sample, while at the same time – perhaps reverting to 'mass audience' panic mode – reacting with straightforward moral disapprobation to repressive ideological discourses about religion and nation. Apparently, confident of my position as a feminist and aware of feminism as a force in social critique, I am able to countenance a variety of positions taken up by viewers that may, in actuality, have negative consequences for women. After all, even the literature quoted in this book suggests that the sufferings caused by the heterosexist, authoritarian and patriarchal attitudes so frequently recognisable in sequences of Hindi films are daily realities for many women, boys, girls and young men in India and the diaspora. Yet, outraged by the sudden increase in misogynistic ethnic hate propaganda, vicious communal violence and state-sanctioned rape and murder of Muslims in India as I conducted my interviews, I was less willing to allow that films overtly on these topics, which were not explicitly critical of such practices, could give rise to a range of readings or have benign meanings for certain viewers. How to reconcile the feelings that lead to these contrasting modes of analysis – based on the tensions between politics and pleasure and between textual studies and audience research – and whether to pursue them to their apparently logical conclusions are questions that continue to trouble me.

9.6 Implications for the future

It must be noted that the urge to consider spectators, texts and contexts as interlinked in a broad sociopolitical field does itself present certain difficulties of space and emphasis. The need to explore, with adequate respect, different aspects of viewer experience and response has to be balanced against the practicability of including information on, for instance, *class* and *national consciousness* or the *history of political religion* as well as against the possibility of generating *original critical evaluations* of Hindi films. There are, however, several interesting lines of research that would deepen the analysis of these aspects of film viewing, compare other aspects of viewing in London and Bombay and, perhaps, include other locations, significantly rural ones, in the study.

It would be interesting to explore the connections between social class and film meanings in greater detail and the connections between education and film viewing in separate studies. Also, given the predilection of many of the male viewers I spoke to for films about relationships, romance and family, a comparative study with South-Asian/British-Asian viewers of Hindi films and African-Caribbean and white British viewers of Hollywood films might yield interesting insights about culture, masculinity and spectatorship. Additionally, while Lalitha Gopalan's recent study of the action genre in Indian cinema (2002) provides textual analysis, audience research into the ways in which different classes and genders respond specifically to the narratives and iconography of these films would provide a much-needed glimpse into an underdocumented realm. Recent textual work on Indian English films and diasporic cinema (Desai 2004; Gopinath 2005) is breaking new ground in an area of burgeoning interest. To complement such studies, research into the differences between the kinds of audiences targeted by different types of diasporic media production (television satire such as *Goodness Gracious Me*; films such as *Bend it Like Beckham*; and stage shows such as *Bombay Dreams*) might be fascinating. In tandem, I suspect that mixed quantitative and qualitative studies of audiences, as well as thorough ethnographies, that would be both much more specific and wider ranging than mine, and would include both rural and urban viewers, and perhaps diasporic viewers in different locations, as well as a range of different audio-visual media (television and the Internet as well as films), would be immensely instructive with regard to issues such as nationalism, politics and religion in Hindi films.

The fact that most viewers are able to get at least some pleasure from Hindi films as they are *at present* is not an endorsement or celebration of the films or, necessarily, of that pleasure. All the same, at the level of film production, script-writing and direction, it would be worth exploring ways to initiate the changes in Hindi films that would mean that certain viewers (such as, perhaps, some men, women, Muslims and gay people) would not have to work so hard to gain equal pleasures from these texts. In this context, my study has shown that there is a dearth of forums within which young South Asians both 'back-home' and in the United Kingdom can discuss issues related to the media, sex and sexuality. While new television programmes on satellite channels, as well as internet chat rooms are providing spaces for some young people to air their thoughts on such issues, regular sex education lessons and/or discussion groups in schools, colleges and youth groups would be welcomed by young viewers in both countries. Also, in India, as there is a growing need for spaces where young people can learn and speak about politics and media in conjunction, the gap in the school curriculum where media and film studies should be looks vast at present.

Given the plurality of meanings that young viewers are able to take away from the same sequence in a film, the ways in which interpretations and experiences of viewing alter perceptions of filmic content and the fact that viewers' identities are made up of *intricate intersections* of factors such as age, class, gender, ethnicity and sexuality, any pedagogy that seeks to *tell people what a text is about* is misconceived. My study suggests that fears about the ways in which the Hindi films *manipulate* audiences by *making them think in specific ways* are not justified. Nor is it the case that the act of viewing is always either distanced and rational or emotional and uncritical. *Responses to Hindi films, like the politics from which these responses spring and to which they sometimes contribute, are both rational and emotional at the same time.* Thus it would be pointless having lessons that aimed to arm young people against the 'seductions' of the media by teaching one 'mode' of viewing in place of another. However, questions about *why* viewers are drawn to certain imaginaries rather than to others and *why* certain (Hindi film) narratives position certain members of society as peripheral or certain versions of cultural activity as 'traditional'/'legitimate' are fundamental and must be asked. Similarly, an acknowledgement of the multiple and contradictory pleasures of Hindi film viewing discovered here, while demystifying audience responses, does not validate teaching about popular media in a uniformly celebratory way. Instead, locating film discourses on, for instance, childhood, sex, sexuality, class, ethnicity, religion, nation, masculinity and femininity within a given history and society, understanding their roots, seeing them within the context of other social phenomena and alongside other mediated discourses, for instance those on *the news*, and recognising their pleasurable potential, would be empowering activities for young people if carried out in an atmosphere free of didacticism and censorship. Certainly, the need for political action and involvement on the part of young people in India and the diaspora to combat fascistic and authoritarian values and trends is as great as ever. Hopefully, historically aware, media-educated viewers would be empowered to challenge authoritarian politics both in private and public spheres: one aspect of this empowerment might be to demand that the films they enjoy watching include a far wider range of discursive positions and values; another would be to defend their right to engage with and judge the *entire range of popular media products* for themselves rather than being told what they should and should not be watching. Antonio Gramsci once wrote that '[t]he intellectual's error consists in believing that one can know without understanding and, even worse, without feeling and being impassioned' (1975: 1505). I conclude with the hope that this book will contribute to a kind of 'knowing' that is both understanding and impassioned.

Notes

Preface

1 The words 'discourse' and 'discourses' as used in this book refer not to units of speech or writing, however small or large, but rather to structured and sedimented ways of defining and understanding the world.

Chapter 1 Hindi films: theoretical debates and textual studies

1 Famous film critic and theorist from Calcutta, author of *Talking About Films* (New Delhi: Orient Longman, 1981) and *The Painted Face: Studies in India's Popular Cinema* (New Delhi: Roli Books, 1991), Dasgupta has been a consistent proponent of the idea that mass films and spectators of these films are mired in a premodern frame of mind which is leading India, via an irrational attachment to certain (politico-religious) ideologies and myths, towards imminent political collapse.

2 Nandy (1998: 2–5) delineates a notion of commercial Hindi cinema as a means of expression for the frustrations, views and idioms of 'slum' life, a vehicle for the fears, desires and angst of those members of the population dispossessed by the state or lingering on the margins of cities.

3 For an interesting discussion of 'escapism' and soap opera see Modleski's argument in 'The Search for Tomorrow in Today's Soap Operas' (1982).

4 For instance, see Theodore Adorno's (1991) argument that the 'mass' production and distribution of cultural artefacts, rather than democratising culture, are leading to a standardised and totalitarian mentality that is being imposed upon the masses.

5 Some of the films *Chori Chori Chupke Chupke* 'copies' or borrows' from are *Pretty Woman* (USA, Garry Marshall 1990) *Doosri Dulhan* (*A Second Bride*, Lekh Tandon 1983) and *Bewafa se Wafa* (*From Infidelity to Fidelity*, Sawan Kumar 1992).

Chapter 2 Audiences and Hindi films: contemporary studies

1 Primarily due to the extensive analysis and theorisation of this subject elsewhere: Bhabha 1990; Young 1995; Brah 1996; Modood and Werbner 1997; Sreberny 2000; Radhakrishnan 2000; Maira 2002; and Matthews 2002, to name but a few.

2 Following the *initial* referencing of director and date, Hindi films will be referred to by name only; otherwise, look in the Filmography.

3 The politics of 'Hindutva' can be categorised as fascist in the broad sense, in that it inculcates a deep belief in the superiority of the 'Hindus' over all

others and is grasping at political power through state-sanctioned violence. See Sarkar (1993) and Hensman (1995).
4 Senior members of the BJP, like L. K. Advani, regularly attend functions held by the RSS leader K. S. Sudharshan who has, among other things, been responsible for inciting violence against so-called 'Christian missionaries' and other social activists like Graham Staines who was murdered along with his children by an RSS cadre in 1999. Although currently the opposition party, the BJP swept to power on the back of the horrific and brutal killing of Muslims that ensued after the demolition by Sangh Parivar activists of the Babri Masjid on the 2 December 1992 in Ayodhya.
5 One of Mankekar's interviewees acknowledges how she was molested by her father-in-law with her husband's knowledge.

Chapter 3   Contemporary Hindi film-going and the viewing context in two countries

1 July 2001, 'Cinemax' Goregaon, Bombay.
2 See also Barker and Brookes (1998); Austin (2002); and Kuhn (2002).
3 Ronald Inden (1999: 50) notes that 'New expensive facilities with a smaller seating capacity (300–600), but with state-of-the-art projection and sound systems, have appeared in Mumbai and New Delhi.'
4 'Apart from [59 viewers] killed, over 150 people were injured when a fire broke out at the Uphaar cinema hall in New Delhi on June 13, 1997' (Singh 2001).
5 See Chapter 7 and Filmography.
6 The *Guardian* Wednesday 26 July 2000.

Chapter 4   'A man who smokes should never marry a village girl': comments on courtship and marriage 'Hindi film-style'

1 Many eighties' Hindi films which purported to show the avenging of sexual violence or the 'reality' of sexual violence in Indian society included extended rape sequences. *Brasthachar (Rape*, 1989) and *Aaj Ki Awaz (The Voice of Today*, B. R. Chopra 1984) are only two of more than two dozen well-known and over a hundred B- and C-grade films to utilise violent rape sequences. Shoma A. Chatterji (1998: 160) is unequivocal in her revulsion at what she takes to be titillation and an encouragement to rapists.
2 The meaning of talk, like the meaning of films themselves, is contingent on context.
3 Barbara Lobodzinska (1979) explores the significance accorded to the notion of 'love' in the decision to marry amongst Polish youth. Her findings are not dissimilar to those gathered amongst British-Asians (Gillespie 1995; Ghuman 1999).
4 A study carried out in 1973 by V.V. Prakasa and V. Nandini Rao amongst college students in India found that 'a majority of the students indicated that they wanted to know their future spouse for some time before marriage' and a significant number wanted to select their own marriage partner and obtain parental agreement after doing so (1979: 28–30).

5 David Morley (2000: 220–1) writes of the 'self-enclosure' of various ethnic groups and their belief that they cannot be aided or understood by those 'outside' the group.

6 Breakwell describes 'compartmentalisation' as the simultaneous holding of 'mutually exclusive self-definitions' (1986: 95).

7 Among the films in which such heroes play a leading part is Subhash Ghai's famous *Khalnayak*.

8 I met a friend of Kavita's several months later and learnt that Kavita's sister had been overtly distressed during her arranged-marriage ceremony, in the words of the friend: 'her face was so swollen from crying and it could be also his [the father's] slaps that I did not feel like attending the wedding.'

9 See 'Listen to Your Heart and You Die' by Sakina Yusuf Khan, *The Sunday Times of India*, New Delhi, 2 September 2001; 'Panchayat nod for Murder?', Lucknow, *The Hindu*, 22 August 2001; 'Courting Death' by Vijaya Pushkarna, *The Week*, 9 September 2001; 'When Will We Learn?: How many more dead brides will it take before we address the issue of forced marriages?' by S. Gill, *Eastern Eye*, London, Friday, 17 January 2003; and 'Daughter Killed over Secret Boyfriend' BBC News (Online), Wednesday 6 February 2002.

10 Lest it be thought that *all* Hindi films follow similar discursive pathways with regard to marriage, elopement and 'tradition', I draw attention to, *Pyar Ka Toofan* (*Cyclone of Love*, S. M. Iqbal 1990) in which the working-class hero urges the upper-caste and upper-class heroine to elope and *she* refuses.

11 Lalitha Gopalan, however, sees in these close-ups of the lead pair singing 'Hum Aapke Hain Koun ...!'/'Who am I to You ...!' an invitation to us *as viewers* to 'reflect on our relationship to cinema' and suggests that via this ironic device we are drawn 'into a triangular economy of desire, making us an integral part of [the] love story' (2002: 3).

12 Only a relatively small number of interviewees (three out of 30) suggested that they may never marry.

Chapter 5 Short skirts, long veils and dancing men: responses to dress and the body

1 See Amithaba Bagchi, (1996) 'Women in Indian Cinema'; and Deepa Gahlot (2003) 'Sexy Anytime, Anywhere'.

2 The view that depictions of women as 'sex objects' on-screen and the responses these representations provoke in men being directly linked to the harassment of women on the streets is commonly held by lay people and critics alike in India.

3 The question which springs foremost to mind is whether all sexual desire is not to some extent inevitably 'objectifying' and, if it is, then what does objectification actually mean in each of its contexts of use? For instance, can any look be construed as 'sexual' and hence objectifying? Or, are certain types of look designated thus in order to pathologise the 'looking' done by 'others'?

4 Kathy Myers argues that 'There is a sense in which sight and perception necessarily entail objectification in order to conceptualise and give meaning to the object of our gaze' (1995: 267). Furthermore, she insists: 'we have to clarify

whether it is the process of necessary objectification entailed in perception which we object to ... or the meaning it carries for women under specific patriarchal formations ....'
5 See Shohini Ghosh (1999) on censorship and the feminist movement; see also Mary E. John and Tejaswini Niranjana (1999).

Chapter 6 More or less spicy kisses: responses to sex, love and sexuality

1 See Gopinath 2000 and 2005; Ghosh 2002; and Waugh 2002 for excellent discussions of the way in which both mainstream and art cinema or 'third' cinema in India and the diaspora, depict non-heterosexual characters and relationships.
2 See Christine Brosius's account of a young viewer's similar experience at a Hindi film in Germany (2005).
3 A fear that would be shared by many women from other cultures and countries.
4 Sonali mentioned the same feature of films such as *Hum Dil De Chuke Sanam* by Sanjay Leela Bhansali and *Kuch Kuch Hota Hai* by Karan Johar.
5 To my disappointment, Asima said she had only recently 'got into' Hindi films and Kalpana was unable to be interviewed for my project as she was about to leave London for an extended period. I did discover, however, that both women were Gurinder Chaddha fans and asked them about *Bend it Like Bekham*. Kalpana was unequivocal: 'I love that film, I do, but I still feel pissed off about it, a bit disappointed inside – maybe because everyone thought it was just such a joke, such a funny hahaha misunderstanding that Jules's mum thinks she and Jess are lesbians. So predictable, na? I kept waiting for them to kiss.'
6 Bhiku, Neha and Meeta all either imply or state explicitly that sexual violence and child pregnancy are phenomena that occur in the West or because of Westernisation.
7 Daniel Lak (1998) discusses the positive ways in which Indian lesbians responded to the impending release of Deepa Mehta's *Fire* in India. In this article he quotes Indian lesbians who are in relationships, but have to maintain their anonymity.
8 Wherever possible, when describing viewers, I have tried to respect viewers' self-definitions. However, in relation both to gender and sexuality, these categories are not entirely bounded and fixed and certainly cannot be linked to essential traits or fixed identifications and ways of responding to Hindi films.
9 A demand was made by cadre from the Hindu Right for the names of the two central characters to be altered from Hindu to Muslim. Theatres that screened the film were threatened with arson by the Shiv Sena in Maharashtra and in New Delhi cinema halls were attacked (Cf. Gopinath 2005: Chapter 5).
10 Now no longer in government, but still a significant threat as the opposition.

Chapter 7 Politics and spectatorship 1: viewing love, religion and violence

1 For an example of the on-line dissemination of such fascist propaganda, see www.HinduUnity.org (the website of the Bhajrang Dal, the grass-roots cadre

of the fascist Hindutva movement). Other anti-Muslim and anti-Christian speeches are quoted in the film *Men in the Tree* (Vachani 2002) and in Tanika Sarkar's *Hindu Wife, Hindu Nation*, where she notes that one of the highest ranking female Hindutva ideologues, Sadhavi Rithambara, has repeatedly exhorted Hindu women to 'produce sons who will kill Muslims' (Sarkar 2001: 284).

2 For discussions of this atrocity and the organised pogroms that followed, see Dugger (2002); Popham (2002); and Swami (2002).

3 While this book concerns itself with *Indian* communal politics and *Hindi* films, massacres of Hindus and Christians have occurred both in India and in Pakistan and Bangladesh. See *Amnesty International* report on atrocities against the Hindu minority in Bangladesh at http://web.amnesty.org/ai.nsf/ Recent/ASA130062001!Open (accessed January 2004).

4 For an interesting discussion of anti-Muslim Hindutva politics as employed by the BJP in India (especially Gujarat), see 'A Hindu's Protest' by Sudhir Chandra (2002).

5 Preeta is too young to have experienced the discrimination towards her community in the 1984 anti-Sikh pogroms. Other Sikh women, however, would not regard Hindu men as such desirable matches as interviews by Mankekar in New Delhi in the early 1990s suggest (Mankekar 2000).

6 Manisha Sethi (2002) notes that 'Traditionally, mainstream Bollywood has reserved normalcy for the Hindu Hero while encoding minorities with signs of cultural exaggeration ... But a perceptible shift has occurred in films from the late 1980s through the turbulent 1990s and beyond – that of deploying aggression as one of the defining characteristics of the minority community ... [Nevertheless, ironically] [t]he casting of Muslims as terrorists is often balanced by the presence of a "nationalist Muslim" whose blood must be expiated as proof of his patriotism.'

7 Cf. *BBC News*/South Asia, on-line edition, Thursday, 25 April 2002, 'UK Report Censures Gujarat Rulers'; 'More Dead in Religious Violence', *Guardian Unlimited*, 1 March 2002; and S. Narula (2002). *Human Rights Watch* Report, 'We have no orders to save you': State Participation and Complicity in Communal Violence in Gujarat'.

8 Deepika Bahri (2001: 227–8) reminds us that 'superidentification with a reified and exclusionary Hindu identity, produced under the stress of migration, led a number of expatriate Hindus to play a pivotal if unwitting role in precipitating the disastrous events in Ayodhya' in December 1992 and in the pogroms against Muslims that followed.

9 See R. Vasudevan (2000c), 'Another History Rises to the Surface: melodrama theory and digital simulation in *Hey! Ram*'.

10 See Internet Movie Database user comments Index for *Hey! Ram* and *Gadar: Ek Prem Katha*; see also 'Sena terms Muslim protestors of Gadar anti-national', on www.rediff.com 25 June 2001.

11 See 'Storm over partition love story', BBC news on-line, 27 June 2001.

12 See Gahlot (2001) '*Lagaan* is not about Cricket, *Gadar* is not about Love'; and Vasudevan, (2000d) '*Hey Ram* rams home wrong message'.

13 Cf. *Men in the Tree*, director Lalith Vachani 2002, and *Evil Stalks the Land*, director Gauhar Raza 2002 (in Filmography); also Praveen Swami 'Saffron Terror', *Frontline*, Vol. 19, Issue 6, 19–26 March 2002, and Sukumar Muralidharan,

'Appeasing the Hindu Right', *Frontline*, Vol. 19, Issue 6, 19–26 March 2002; Chetan Bhatt (2001: 168–72).

14   See 'Sena terms Muslim protestors outside cinema halls anti-national' on the rediff website 25 June 2001, and 'Storm over partition love story', BBC news on-line on 27 June 2001.

15   All three were 16 or 17 years old and had little access to the 'cultural capital' of books, libraries, lectures and discussions possessed by Jatin and Padma.

Bibliography

Abraham, L. (2002) 'Bhai-Behen, True Love, Time Pass: Friendships and Sexual Partnerships Among Youth in an Indian Metropolis', in *Culture Health and Sexuality*, Vol. 4, No. 3: 337–53

Abraham, L. and Kumar, A. K. (1999) 'Sexual Experiences and Their Correlates Among College Students in Mumbai City, India', in *International Family Planning Perspectives*, No. 25: 139–46

Adorno, T. (1991) *The Culture Industry: Selected Essays on Mass Culture*, New York: Routledge

Agarwal, P. (1995) 'Surat, Savarkar and Draupadi: Legitimising Rape as a Political Weapon', in T. Sarkar and U. Butalia (eds) *Women and the Hindu Right: A Collection of Essays*, New Delhi: Kali for Women

Alexander, C. E. (2000) *The Asian Gang*, Oxford and New York: Berg

Ang, I. (1985) *Watching Dallas: Soap Opera and the Melodramatic Imagination*, London: Methuen

Anand, J. and Setalwad, T. (eds) (2002) *Genocide: Gujarat 2002, Communalism Combat*, Special Issue, March–April 2002, Year 8, No. 77–8, Bombay: Sabrang Communications and Publishing

Austin, T. (2002) *Hollywood, Hype and Audiences: Selling and Watching Popular Films in the 1990s*, Manchester: Manchester University Press

Bachmann, M. (2002) 'After the Fire', in R. Vanita (ed.) *Queering India: Same-Sex Love and Eroticism in Indian Culture and Society*, New York and London: Routledge

Bagchi A. (1996) 'Women in Indian Cinema', last accessed 18 March 2004 at: http://www.cs.jhu.edu/~bagchi/women.html

Bahadur, S. (1978) 'The Context of Indian Film Culture', in *Film Appreciation Study Material*, Series No. 2, India: National Film Archives of India

Bahri, D. (2001) 'The Digital Diaspora: South Asians in the New *Pax Electronica*', in M. Paranjape (ed.) *Indiaspora: Theories, Histories, Texts*, New Delhi: Indialog Publications

Banaji, S. (2002) 'Private Lives and Public Spaces: The Precarious Pleasures of Gender Discourse in *Raja Hindustani*', in *Women: A Cultural Review*, Vol. 13, No. 2: 179–94

Banaji, S. (2005) 'Intimate Deceptions: Young British-Asian Viewers Discuss Sex and Sexuality on and off the Hindi Film Screen', in *Journal of South Asian Popular Culture*, Vol. 3, No. 2, October 2005: 177–92

Banerjee, P. (2003) 'In the Belly of the Beast: The Hindu Supremacist RSS and BJP of India: An Insider's Story' last accessed 24 October 2005 at: http://www.geocities. com/indianfascism/fascism/an_insider_story.htm

Banerjee, S. (2002) 'Natural Born Killers', in *Asian Woman*, Summer 2002: 98–102

'Bangladesh: Attacks on Members of the Hindu Minority' (2001), *Amnesty International Index* 13/006, last accessed 24 October 2005 at: http://web.amnesty.org/ library/index/engASA130062001!Open

Barker, C. and Galasiński, D. (2001) *Cultural Studies and Discourse Analysis*, London/ Thousand Oaks/New Delhi: Sage

Barker, M. and Brooks, K. (1998) *Knowing Audiences: Judge Dredd, its Friends, Fans and Foes*, Luton: University of Luton Press

Barnouw, E. and Krishnaswamy, S. (1980) *Indian Film*, New York/Oxford/New Delhi: Oxford University Press

Bhabha, H. (ed.) (1990) *Nation and Narration*, London: Routledge

Bhalaki. (1951) 'Vijayawada Jaihind Talkies', in 'Andhra Pradeshlo Theatrelu', *Roopavani*, September: 37

Bharucha, R. (1995) 'Utopia in Bollywood: *Hum Aapke Hain Koun ...!*', in *Economic and Political Weekly*, 15 April, Vol. 30, Issue 15: 801–4

Bharucha, R. (1998) *In the Name of the Secular: Contemporary Cultural Activism in India*, New Delhi: Oxford University Press

Bhatt, C. (2001) *Hindu Nationalism: Origins, Ideologies and Modern Myths*, Oxford and New York: Berg

Bhattacharya, N. (2004) 'A Basement Cinephilia: Indian Diaspora Women Watch Bollywood', *South Asian Popular Culture*, Vol. 2. No. 2: 161–83

'BJP Slams Report on Gujarat Massacres' (2002) by the Special Correspondent, *The Hindu*, New Delhi, 23 November

Brah, A. (1996) *Cartographies of Diaspora*, London: Routledge

Breakwell, G. (1986) *Coping With Threatened Identities*, London: Methuen

Brosius, C. (2005) 'The Scattered Homelands of the Migrant: Bollyworld through the Diasporic Lens', in R. Kaur and A. Sinha (eds) *Bollyworld: Popular Indian Cinema Through a Transnational Lens*, New Delhi: Sage

Bruzzi, S. (1997) *Undressing Cinema: Clothing and Identity in the Movies*, London and New York: Routledge

Buckingham, D. (ed.) (1993) *Reading Audiences: Young People and the Media*, Manchester and London: Manchester University Press

Buckingham, D. (1996) *Moving Images: Understanding Children's Emotional Responses to Television*, Manchester: Manchester University Press

Buckingham, D. and Bragg, S. (2004) *Young People, Sex and the Media: the Facts of Life*, Basingstoke: Palgrave Macmillan

Butalia, U. (1995) 'Muslims and Hindus, Men and Women: Communal Stereotypes and the Partition of India', in T. Sarkar and U. Butalia (eds) *Women and the Hindu Right: A Collection of Essays*, New Delhi: Kali for Women

Butcher, M. (1999) 'Parallel Texts: the Body and Television in India', in C. Brosius and M. Butcher (eds) *Image Journeys: Audio-Visual Media and Cultural Change in India*, New Delhi/Thousand Oaks/London: Sage

Chakravarty, S. (1998) *National Identity in Indian Popular Cinema: 1947–1987*, New Delhi: Oxford University Press

Chakravarty, S. (2002) 'Fragmenting the Nation: Images of Terrorism in Indian Popular Cinema', in M. Hjort and S. Mackenzie (eds) *Cinema & Nation*, London and New York: Routledge

Chandra, S. (2002) 'A Hindu's Protest', in *Seminar*, No. 513: 49–52

Chatterji, S. A. (1998) *Subject Cinema, Object Woman: A Study of the Portrayal of Women in Indian Cinema*, Calcutta: Parumita Publications

Chaudhary, P. (1998) 'Enforcing Cultural Codes: Gender and Violence in North India', in J. Nair and M. E. John (eds) *A Question of Silence: the Sexual Economies of Modern India*, New Delhi: Kali for Women

Clover, C. J. (1992) *Men, Women, and Chain Saws: Gender in the Modern Horror Film*, Princeton, NJ: Princeton University Press

Connell, R. W. (1995) *Masculinities*, Cambridge: Polity Press

Dasgupta, C. (1981) *Talking About Films*, New Delhi: Orient Longman

Dasgupta, C. (1991) *The Painted Face: Studies in India's Popular Cinema*, New Delhi: Roli Books

'Daughter Killed over Secret Boyfriend' (2002) *BBC News On-line*, 6 February, last accessed 24 October 2005 at: http://news.bbc.co.uk/1/hi/england/1804707.stm

Davison, W. P. (1983) 'The Third-Person Effect in Communication', *Pubic Opinion Quarterly*, 47: 1–15

Derné, S. (2000) *Movies, Masculinity and Modernity: An Ethnography of Men's Film-Going in India*, Westport, CT, and London: Greenwood Press

Desai, J. (2004) *Beyond Bollywood: The Cultural Politics of South Asian Diasporic Film*, London and New York: Routledge

Desai, N. and Krishnaraj, M. (1987) 'Violence', in N. Desai and M. Krishnaraj (eds) *Women and Society in India*, New Delhi: Ajanta Books

Dickey, S. (1993) *Cinema and the Urban Poor in South India*, Cambridge, MA: Cambridge University Press

Dines, G. and Humez, J. M. (eds) (1995) *Gender, Race and Class in Media*, Thousand Oaks/London/New Delhi: Sage

Dirks, N. (2001) 'The Home and the Nation: Consuming Culture and Politics in *Roja*', in R. Dwyer and C. Pinney (eds) *Pleasure and the Nation*, New Delhi and London: Oxford University Press

Doane, M. A. (1996) 'The Economy of Desire: The Commodity Form in/of the Cinema', in John Belton (ed.) *Movies and Mass Culture*, New Brunswick, NJ: Rutgers University Press

Docherty, D., Morrison, D. and Tracey, M. (1987) *The Last Picture Show? – Britain's Changing Film Audiences*, London: BFI Publishing

Donald, J. (ed.) (1998) *Fantasy and the Cinema*, London: BFI Publications

Doraiswamy, R. (1995) 'Hindi Commercial Cinema: Changing Narrative Strategies', in A. Vasudev (ed.) *Frames of Mind: Reflections on Indian Cinema*, New Delhi: UBSPD

Dudrah, R. K. (2002) 'Vilayati Bollywood: Popular Hindi Cinema-Going and Diasporic South-Asian Identity in Birmingham (UK)', in *Javnost – The Public: Journal of the European Institute for Communication and Culture*, Vol. 9, No. 1: 19–36

Dudrah, R. K. and Rai, A. (2004) 'Moving Pictures: Bollywood Cinema-Going and the Social Spaces of Immigrant Identity in Jackson Heights and Times Square, New York', paper presented at the Twenty-Ninth Conference on Literature and Film, Florida State University, February 2004

Dugger, C. (2002) 'After Deadly Firestorm, India Officials Ask Why', in *New York Times*, 6 March, Section A: 3

Durham, M. G. (2004) 'Constructing the "New Ethnicities": Media, Sexuality, and Diaspora Identity in the Lives of South Asian Immigrant Girls', in *Critical Studies in Media Communication*, Vol. 21, No. 2: 140–61

Dwyer, R. (2000) *All You Want is Money, All You Need is Love*, London and New York: Cassell

Eagleton, T. (1991a) *Ideology*, London: Verso

Eagleton, T. (1991b) *The Ideology of the Aesthetic*, Cambridge, MA, and Oxford: Blackwell

Fazila-Yacoobali, V. (2002) 'Yeh mulk hamara ghar: the "national order of things" and Muslim identity in John Mathew Mattan's Sarfaroosh', *Contemporary South Asia*, Vol. 11, No. 2: 183–98

Foucault, M. (1976) *The History of Sexuality*, Vol. 1, Harmondsworth: Penguin

Gahlot, D. (2001) '*Lagaan* is not about Cricket, *Gadar* is not about Love', 22 June, last accessed 24 October 2005 at: http://www.rediff.com/entertai/2001/jun/22deepa.htm

Gahlot, D. (2003) 'Sexy Anytime, Anywhere', 28 June, last accessed 24 October 2005 at: http://www.rediff.com/movies/2003/jun/28deepa.htm

Geraghty, C. (2000) 'Cinema as a Social Space: Understanding Cinema-Going in Britain 1947–1963', in *Frameworks: 42*, last accessed 24 October 2005 at: http://www.frameworkonline.com/42cg.htm

Ghosh, S. (1999) 'The Troubled Existence of Sex and Sexuality: Feminists Engage with Censorship', in C. Brosius and M. Butcher (eds) *Image Journeys: Audio-Visual Media and Cultural Change in India*, New Delhi/Thousand Oaks/London: Sage

Ghosh, S. (2002) 'Queer Pleasures for Queer People: Film, Television, and Queer Sexuality in India', in R. Vanita (ed.) *Queering India: Same-Sex Love and Eroticism in Indian Culture and Society*, London and New York: Routledge

Ghuman, P. A. Singh (1994) *Coping with Two Cultures: A Study of British-Asian and Indo-Canadian Adolescents*, Clevedon: Multilingual Matters

Ghuman, P. A. Singh (1999) *Asian Adolescents in the West*, Leicester: BPS Books

Gill, S. (2003) 'When Will We Learn?: How Many More Dead Brides Will it Take Before We Address the Issue of Forced Marriages?', *Eastern Eye*, Friday, 17 January

Gillespie, M. (1995) *Television, Ethnicity and Cultural Change*, London and New York: Routledge

Gledhill, C. (ed.) (1987) *Home Is Where the Heart Is: Studies in Melodrama and the Woman's Film*, London: BFI Books

Gledhill, C. (ed.) (1991) *Stardom: Industry of Desire*, London: Routledge

Gledhill, C. (1995) 'Women Reading Men', in P. Kirkham and J. Thumim (eds) *Me Jane: Masculinity, Movies and Women*, New York: St Martin's Press

Gledhill, C. (1999) 'Pleasurable Negotiations', in S. Thornham (ed.) *Feminist Film Theory: A Reader*, Edinburgh: Edinburgh University Press

Gokulsing, K. and Dissanayake, W. (1998) *Indian Popular Cinema: A Narrative of Cultural Change*, London: Trentham Books

Gomery, D. (1992) *Shared Pleasures: a History of Movie Presentation in the United States*, London: BFI Publishing

Gopalan, L. (1998) 'Coitus Interruptus and Love Story in Indian Cinema', in V. Dehejia (ed.) *Representing the Body: Gender Issues in Indian Art*, New Delhi: Kali for Women

Gopalan, L. (2002) *Cinema of Interruptions: Action Genres in Contemporary Indian Cinema*, London: BFI Publishing

Gopinath, G. (2000) 'Queering Bollywood: Alternative Sexualities in Popular Indian Cinema', in *Journal of Homosexuality*, Vol. 39, No. 3/4: 283–97

Gopinath, G. (2005) *Impossible Desires: Queer Diasporas and South Asian Public Cultures*, Durham, NC, and London: Duke University Press

Goward, P. (2002) *Everyday Intersectionality*, paper delivered at *Beyond Tolerance: National Conference on Racism*, Sydney Opera House, 12 and 13 March at: Last accessed 14 March 2004 http://www.humanrights.gov.au/racial_discrimination/beyond_tolerance/speeches/goward.htm

Gramsci, A. (1975) *Quaderni Dal Carcere*, Torino: Einaudi

Gupta, R. (1999) 'Cinema and Terrorism in India: 1990s', last accessed 18 January 2006 at: http://members.tripod.com/~ascjnu/cinema.html

Hall, S. (1980) 'Encoding/Decoding', in S. Hall et al. (eds) *Culture, Media, Language,* Birmingham: CCCS
Hall, S. (1990) 'Cultural Identity and Diaspora', in J. Rutherford (ed.) *Identity, Community, Culture, Difference,* London: Lawrence & Wishart
Harvey, D. (1989) *The Condition of Postmodernity: An Enquiry into the Origins of Cultural Change,* Cambridge, MA: Basil Blackwell
Henriques, J., Holloway, W., Urwin, C., Venn, C. and Walkerdine, V. (1984) *Changing the Subject: Psychology, Social Regulation and Subjectivity,* London: Methuen
Hensman, R. (1995) 'Fascism, Democratic Rights and the State', *Economic and Political Weekly,* 27 May 1995: 1262
Herzog, C. (1990) ' "Powder Puff" Promotion: The Fashion Show-in-the-Film', in C. Herzog and J. Gaines (eds) *Fabrications: Costume and the Human Body,* New York and London: Routledge
Hodge, B. and Tripp, D. (1986) *Children and Television,* Cambridge: Polity Press
Holloway, W. (1984) 'Gender Difference and the Production of Subjectivity', in Henriques et al. (eds) *Changing the Subject,* London and New York: Routledge
Holloway, W. (1989) *Subjectivity and Method in Psychology: Gender, Meaning and Science,* London/Beverley Hills/New Delhi: Sage
Holstein, J. A. and Gubrium J. F. (1998) 'Active Interviewing', in D. Silverman (ed.) *Qualitative Research – Theory, Method and Practice,* London/Thousand Oaks/ New Delhi: Sage
Inden, R. (1999) 'Transnational Class, Erotic Arcadia and Commercial Utopia in Hindi Films', in C. Brosius and M. Butcher (eds) *Image Journeys: Audio-Visual Media and Cultural Change in India,* New Delhi/Thousand Oaks/London: Sage
Jenkins, H. (2000) 'Reception Theory and Audience Research: The Mystery of the Vampire's Kiss', in C. Gledhill and L. Williams (eds) *Reinventing Film Studies,* London: Arnold
John, M. E. (1998) 'Globalisation, Sexuality and the Visual Field', in J. Nair and M. E. John (eds) *A Question of Silence: The Sexual Economies of Modern India,* New Delhi: Kali for Women
John, M. E. and Niranjana, T. (1999) 'Mirror Politics: "Fire", Hindutva and Indian Culture', in *Economic and Political Weekly,* 6–13 March: 531
Juluri, V. (1999) 'Global Weds Local: The Reception of *Hum Aapke Hain Kaun ...!*', in *European Journal of Cultural Studies,* 2 May 1999: 231–48
Kaes, A. (1989) *From Hitler to Heimat: The Return of History as Film,* Cambridge, MA: Harvard University Press
Kakar, S. (1990) *Intimate Relations: Exploring Indian Sexuality,* New Delhi: Penguin
Kakar, S. (1996) *The Colours of Violence: Cultural Identities, Religion and Conflict,* Chicago and London: The University of Chicago Press
Kannabiran, V. and Kannabiran, K. (1995) 'The Frying Pan or the Fire?: Endangered Identities, Gendered Institutions and Women's Survival', in T. Sarkar and U. Butalia (eds) *Women and the Hindu Right: A Collection of Essays,* New Delhi: Kali for Women
Kapur, R. (1998) '*Fire* Goes up in Smoke', *The Hindu,* 13 December: 26
Kapur, R. (1999) 'Cultural Politics of Fire', in The *Economic and Political Weekly,* 22 May: 1297
Karlekar, M. (1995) 'Search for Women's Voices: Reflections on Fieldwork, 1968–93', in *Economic and Political Weekly,* Vol. xxx, No. 17, 29 April

Kasbekar, A. (2001) 'Hidden Pleasures: Negotiating the Myth of the Female Ideal in Popular Hindi Cinema', in R. Dwyer and C. Pinney (eds) *Pleasure and the Nation*, New Delhi and London: Oxford University Press

Kawale, R. (2003) 'A Kiss is Just a Kiss ... Or Is It? South Asian Lesbian and Bisexual Women and the Construction of Space', in N. Puwar and P. Raghuram (eds) *South Asian Women in the Diaspora*, Oxford: Berg

Kazmi, N. (1998) *The Dream Merchants of Bollywood*, New Delhi: UBSPD

Kazmi, F. (1999) *The Politics of India's Commercial Cinema: Imaging a Universe, Subverting a Multiverse*, New Delhi: Sage

Khan, S. Y. (2001) 'Listen to Your Heart and You Die', in *The Sunday Times of India*, New Delhi, 2 September

Kishwar, M. (1999) 'The Naïve Outpourings of a Self-Hating Indian: Deepa Mehta's *Fire*', in *Manushi*, No. 109: 6

Kuhn, A. (1982) *Women's Pictures*, Pandora Press

Kuhn, A. (2002) *An Everyday Magic: Cinema and Cultural Memory*, London and New York: I. B. Tauris

Kvale, S. (1996) *Interviews: An Introduction to Qualitative Research Interviewing*, Thousand Oaks, CA, and London: Sage

Lak, D. (1998) 'Lesbian Film sets India on Fire' *BBC on-line*, 13 November, last accessed 24 October 2005 at: http://news.bbc.co.uk/1/hi/world/south_asia/213417.stm

Larkin, B. (1997) 'Bollywood Comes to Nigeria', in *Samar* 8, Winter/Spring 1997, last accessed 9 March 2004 at: http://www.samarmagazine.org/archive/article.php?id=21

Leonard, K. (2000) 'Identity in the Diaspora: Surprising Voices', in M. F. Manalansan IV (ed.) *Ethnographic Explorations of Asian America*, Philadelphia: Temple University Press

Lobodzinska, B. (1979) 'Love as a Factor in Marital Decision in Contemporary Poland', in G. Kurian (ed.) *Cross Cultural Perspectives of Mate Selection and Marriage*, Westport, CT, and London: Greenwood Press

Maira, S. M. (2002) *Desis in the House: Indian American Youth Culture in New York City*, Philadelphia: Temple University Press

Mangalik, M (2002) 'From the Heart of Darkness', in *The Hindustan Times*, 26 July

Mani, B. (2003) 'Undressing the Diaspora', in N. Puwar and P. Raghuram (eds) *South Asian Women in the Diaspora*, Oxford: Berg

Mankekar, P. (2000) *Screening Culture, Viewing Politics: Television, Womanhood and Nation in Modern India*, New Delhi and Bombay: Oxford University Press

Mathur, V. (2002) 'Women in Indian Cinema: Fictional Constructs', in J. Jain and S. Rai (eds) *Films and Feminism: Essays in Indian Cinema*, Jaipur and New Delhi: Rawat Publications

Matthews, J. (2002) 'Deconstructing the Visual: The Diasporic Hybridity of Asian and Eurasian Female Images', in *Intersections: Gender, History and Culture in the Asian Context*, Issue 8, October 2002 on-line journal, last accessed 19 March 2004 at: http://www.sshe.murdoch.edu.au/intersections/issue8/matthews.html

Mayne, J. (1993) *Cinema and Spectatorship*, London and New York: Routledge

Mazumdar, R. (2000) 'From Subjectification to Schizophrenia: The "Angry Man" and the "Psychotic Hero" of Bombay Cinema', in R. S. Vasudevan (ed.) *Making Meaning in Indian Cinema*, New Delhi: Oxford University Press

McCracken, E. (1992) *Decoding Women's Magazines, From "Mademoiselle" to "Ms"*, London: Macmillan

McGivering, J. (2002) 'UK Report Censures Gujarat Rulers', *BBC News On-line*, Thursday 25 April, last accessed 15 March 2004 at: http://news.bbc.co.uk/1/hi/world/south_asia/1951471.stm

Mercer, C. (1986) 'Complicit Pleasures', in T. Bennet, C. Mercer and J. Woollacott (eds) *Popular Culture and Social Relations*, Milton Keynes and Philadelphia: Open University Press

Miller J. and Glassner, B. (1998) 'The "Inside" and the "Outside": Finding Realities in Interviews', in D. Silverman (ed.) *Qualitative Research*, New York/London/New Delhi: Sage

Miller, J. (2002) (news segment) 'Funding Gujarat Extremists', Channel 4, broadcast on 12 December, last accessed 16th March 2004 at: http://www.awaazsaw.org/c4script.htm

Mishra, V. (1985) 'Towards a Theoretical Critique of Bombay Cinema', in *Screen*, Vol. 26, No. 3–4

Mishra, V. (2002) *Bollywood Cinema: Temples of Desire*, New York and London: Routledge

Modleski, T. (1990) 'The Search for Tomorrow in Today's Soap Operas', in T. Bennett (ed.) *Popular Fiction: Technology, Ideology, Production, Reading*, New York and London: Routledge

Modood, T. and Werbner, P. (eds) (1997) *Debating Cultural Hybridity: Multi-Cultural Identities and the Politics of Anti-Racism*, London and New Jersey: Zed Books

Moorti, S. (2000) 'Fire, the Woman Question and the Policing of Cultural Borders', in Genders, No. 32, last accessed 19 March 2004 at: http://www.genders.org/g32/g32_moorti.html

'More Dead in Religious Violence' (2002) *Guardian Unlimited*, 1 March

Morley, D. (2000) *Home Territories: Media, Mobility and Identity*, New York and London: Routledge

Mulvey, L. (1989) *Visual and Other Pleasures*, Basingstoke: Macmillan Press

Mulvey, L. (1999) 'Visual Pleasure and Narrative Cinema', in S. Thornham (ed.) *Feminist Film Theory: A Reader*, Edinburgh: Edinburgh University Press

Muraleedharan, T. (2002) 'Queer Bonds: Male Friendship in Contemporary Malayalam Cinema', in R. Vanita (ed.) *Queering India: Same-sex Love and Eroticism in Indian Culture and Society*, London and New York: Routledge

Muralidharan, S. (2002) 'Appeasing the Hindu Right', in *Frontline*, Vol. 19, Issue 6: 19–26

Murdock, G. (1997) 'Thin Descriptions: Questions of Method in Cultural Analysis', in J. McGuigan (ed.) *Cultural Methodologies*, London: Sage

Myers, K. (1995) 'Towards a Feminist Erotica', in G. Dines and J. M. Humez (eds) *Gender, Race and Class in Media*, Thousand Oaks/London/New Delhi: Sage

Nair, B. (2002) 'Female Bodies and the Male Gaze: Laura Mulvey and Hindi Cinema', in J. Jain and S. Rai (eds) *Films and Feminism: Essays in Indian Cinema*, Jaipur and New Delhi: Rawat Publications

Nandy, A. (1995) *The Savage Freud and Other Essays on Possible and Retrievable Selves*, Oxford/New York/New Delhi: Oxford University Press

Nandy, A. (1998) 'Introduction', in A. Nandy (ed.) *The Secret Politics of Our Desires: Innocence, Culpability and Indian Popular Cinema*, New Delhi: Oxford University Press

Narula, S. (2002) ' "We have no orders to save you": State Participation and Complicity in Communal Violence in Gujarat', *Human Rights Watch Report*, New York, April 2002, on-line last accessed 20 March 2004 at: http://www.hrw.org/reports/2002/india/gujarat.pdf

Oakley, A. (1981) 'Interviewing Women: A Contradiction in Terms', in H. Roberts (ed.) *Doing Feminist Research*, London: Routledge

'Panchayat nod for Murder?' (2001), in *The Hindu*, Lucknow, 22 August

Pendakur, M. (2003) *Indian Popular Cinema: Industry, Ideology, Consciousness*, New Jersey: Hampton Press

Petley, J. (1979) *Capital and Culture: German Cinema 1933–45*, London and Colchester: BFI Publishing

Pfleiderer, B. and Lutze, L. (eds) (1985) *The Hindi Film: Agent and Re-Agent of Cultural Change*, New Delhi: Manohar

Popham, P. (2002) 'The Hate Train', The *Independent*, 20 March

Potter, J. and Wetherell, M. (1987) *Discourse and Social Psychology: Beyond Attitudes and Behaviour*, London: Sage

Prabhu, M (2001) *Roles: Reel and Real: Image of Woman In Hindi Cinema*, New Delhi: Ajanta Books

Prakasa, V. V. and Rao, V. N. (1979) 'Arranged Marriages: An Assessment of the Attitudes of the College Students in India', in G. Kurian (ed.) *Cross Cultural Perspectives of Mate Selection and Marriage*, Wesport, CT, and London: Greenwood Press

Prasad, M. M. (1998) *Ideology of the Hindi Film: A Historical Construction*, New Delhi/Thousand Oaks/London: Oxford University Press

Pushkarna, V. (2001) 'Courting Death', in *The Week*, 9 September

Radhakrishnan, R. (2000) 'Adjudicating Hybridity, Co-ordinating Betweenness', in *Jouvert: A Journal of Postcolonial Studies*, Vol. 5, Issue 1, last accessed 20 March 2004 at: http://social. chass.ncsu.edu/jouvert/v5i1/radha.htm

Rai, A. S. (2002) 'First Day, First Show: The Pleasures and Politics of Hindi Film Culture', in *Samar* 15, Summer/Fall 2002, last accessed 17 March 2004 at: http://www.samarmagazine.org/archive/article.php?id=120

Ralston, H. (1999) 'Identity and Lived Experience of Daughters of South Asian Immigrant Women in Halifax and Vancouver Canada: An Exploratory Study', paper *International Migration and Ethnic Relations Conference* 'Youth in the Plural City: Individualized and Collectivized Identities', at Norwegian Institute, Rome, 25–28 May

Rajagopal, A. (2001) *Politics After Television: Hindu Nationalism and the Reshaping of the Public in India*, Cambridge: Cambridge University Press

Rangoonwala, F. (1975) *75 Years of Indian Cinema*, New Delhi: Indian Book Company

Rao, M. (1995) 'To Be a Woman', in A. Vasudev (ed.) *Frames of Mind: Reflections on Indian Cinema*, New Delhi: UBSPD

Rao, R. Raj (2000) 'Memories Pierce the Heart: Homoeroticism, Bollywood Style', *Journal of Homosexuality*, Vol. 39, No. 3/4: 299–306

Rubin, G. S. (1999) 'Thinking Sex: Notes for a Radical Theory of the Politics of Sexuality', in R. Parker and P. Aggleston (eds) *Culture, Society and Sexuality: A Reader*, London: UCL Press

Sarkar, S. (1993) 'The Fascism of the Sangh Parivar', in *Economic and Political Weekly*, 30 January: 163–8

Sarkar, T. (2001) *Hindu Wife, Hindu Nation: Community, Religion and Cultural Nationalism*, New Delhi: Permanent Black

Sarkar, T. (2002) 'Semiotics of Terror', *Economic and Political Weekly*, Vol. 37, No. 28, 13–19 July: 2872–6

Sarkar, T. and Butalia, U. (eds) (1995) *Women and the Hindu Right: A Collection of Essays*, New Delhi: Kali For Women

Schindler, C. (1979) *Hollywood Goes to War: Films and American Society, 1939–1952*, Boston, MA: Routledge and Kegan Paul

Schoenbach, K. (2001) 'Myths of Media and Audiences', in *European Journal of Communication*, Vol. 16 (3): 361–76, London/Thousand Oaks/New Delhi: Sage

Segal, L. (1999) *Why Feminism?*, Cambridge: Polity Press

Segal, L. (2003) 'Only the Literal: The Contradictions of Anti-Pornography Feminism', in J. Weeks, J. Holland and M. Waites (eds) *Sexualities and Society: A Reader*, Cambridge: Polity Press

Seiter, E. (1999) *Television and New Media Audiences*, Oxford: Oxford University Press

'Sena Terms Muslim Protestors of Gadar Anti-National' (2001) on www.rediff.com, 25 June, last accessed 16 March 2004 at: http://www.rediff.com/entertai/2001/jun/25gad4.htm

Sethi, M. (2002) 'Cine-Patriotism', in *Samar*, 15, Summer/Fall. Last accessed 18 March 2004 at: http://www.samarmagazine.org/archive/article.php?id=115

Shah, A. M. (1998) *The Family in India: Critical Essays*, New Delhi: Orient Longman

Singh, O. (2001) 'Uphaar Tragedy Judgement Deferred till 27 Feb', *Rediff on the Net*: 22 February 2001, last accessed 12 March 2003

Smith, S. (1999) 'The Image of Women in Film: Some Suggestions for Future Research', in S. Thornham (ed.) *Feminist Film Theory*, Edinburgh: Edinburgh University Press

Sodhi, G. and Verma, M. (2000) 'Sexual Coercion Among Unmarried Adolescents of an Urban Slum in India', paper presented at 'The International Conference on Adolescent Reproductive Health: Evidence and Programme Implications for South Asia', Bombay, November 2000

Sreberny, A. (2000) 'Media and Diasporic Consciousness: An Exploration among Iranians in London', in S. Cottle (ed.) *Ethnic Minorities and the Media*, Buckingham: Open University Press

Srikrishna, Dr Justice (1999) *The Complete Srikrishna Commission Report on the Riots in Bombay: December 1992 and January 1993*, last accessed 20 March 2004 at: http://www.sabrang.com/ srikrish/sri%20main.htm

Srinivas, S. V. (2000) 'Is there a Public in the Cinema Halls?', in *Framework*: 42, last accessed 18 March 2004 at: http://www.frameworkonline.com/42svs.htm

Staiger, J. (2000) *Perverse Spectators: The Practices of Film Reception*, New York and London: New York University Press

Stempel, T. (2001) *American Audiences on Movies and Moviegoing*, Kentucky: University of Kentucky Press

'Storm Over Partition Love Story' (2001) BBC *News On-line*, 27 June, last accessed 20 March 2004 at: http://news.bbc.co.uk/1/hi/world/south_asia/1410142.stm

Swami, P. (2002) 'Saffron Terror', in *Frontline*, Vol. 19, Issue 6, 16–29 March 2002

Thapan, M. (1997) 'Femininity and Its Discontents: Woman's Body in Intimate Relationships', in M. Thapan (ed.) *Embodiment: Essays on Gender and Identity*, Delhi: Oxford University Press

196   Bibliography

Thomas, L. (2002) *Fans, Feminisms and Quality Media*, London and New York: Routledge
Thomas, R. (1985) 'Indian Cinema: Pleasures and Popularity', in *Screen*, Vol. 26, Issue 3–4: 116–31
Turner, G. (1999) *Film as Social Practice*, London and New York: Routledge
Uberoi, P. (1997) 'Dharma and Desire, Freedom and Destiny: Describing the Man–Woman Relationship in Popular Hindi Cinema', in M. Thapan (ed.) *Embodiment: Essays on Gender and Identity*, New Delhi: Oxford University Press
Uberoi, P. (1998) 'The Diaspora Comes Home: Disciplining Desire in *DDLJ*' in V. Das, D. Gupta, and P. Uberoi (eds) *Tradition, Pluralism and Identity – In Honour of TN Madan*, New Delhi/Thousand Oaks/London: Sage
Uberoi, P. (2001) 'Imagining the Family: an Ethnography of Viewing *Hum Aapke Hain Koun*', in R. Dwyer and C. Pinney (eds) *Pleasure and the Nation: The History and Politics of Indian Popular Culture*, New Delhi: Oxford University Press
Vachani, L. (1999) 'Bachchan-Alias: The Many Faces of a Film Icon', in C. Brosius and M. Butcher (eds) *Image Journeys: Audio-Visual Media and Cultural Change in India*, New Delhi/Thousand Oaks/London: Sage
Valicha, K. (1988) *The Moving Image*, Bombay: Orient Longman
Vasudevan, R.S. (1990) 'Review of "The Hindi Film: Agent and Re-Agent of Social Change" ' by L. Lutze, and B. Pfleiderer, in *Screen*, Vol. 31. No. 4
Vasudevan, R.S. (ed.) (2000a) 'Introduction', in *Making Meaning in Indian Cinema*, New Delhi: Oxford University Press
Vasudevan, R.S. (2000b) 'Shifting Codes, Dissolving Identities: The Hindi Social Film of the 1950s as Popular Culture', in R. S. Vasudevan (ed.) *Making Meaning in Indian Cinema*, New Delhi: Oxford University Press
Vasudevan, R.S. (2000c) 'Another History Rises to the Surface: Melodrama Theory and Digital Simulation in *Hey! Ram*', *Media City/FilmCity* 2000
Vasudevan, R.S. (2000d) '*Hey Ram* Rams Home Wrong Message', *Asia Times On-line*, 17 March
Vasudevan, R.S. (2001a) '*Bombay* and Its Public', in R. Dwyer and C. Pinney (eds) *Pleasure and the Nation*, New Delhi and London: Oxford University Press
Vasudevan, R.S. (2001b) 'An Imperfect Public: Cinema and Citizenship in the Third World', in *The Public Domain: Sarai Reader 01*, New Delhi: CSDS
Vasudevan, R.S. (2002) 'The Exhilaration of Dread: Genre, Narrative and Film Style in Contemporary Urban Action Films', in *The Cities of Everyday Life: Sarai Reader 02*, New Delhi: CSDS
Viario, M. (1993) *A Certain Reason: Making Use of Pasolini's Film Theory and Practice*, Berkeley/Los Angeles/London: University of California Press
Virdi, J. (2003) *The Cinematic Imagination*, New Brunswick/New Jersey/London: Rutgers University Press
Vishwanath, G. (2002) 'Saffronizing the Silver Screen: The Right-Winged Nineties Film', in J. Jain and S. Rai (eds) *Films and Feminism: Essays in Indian Cinema*, Jaipur and New Delhi: Rawat Publications
Vitali, V. (2000) 'The Families of Hindi Cinema: A Socio-Historical Approach to Film Studies', in *Framework: The Journal of Cinema and Media*, No. 42, last accessed 18 March 2004 at: http://www.framework.com/42vv.htm
Waugh, T. (2002) ' "I sleep behind you": Male Homosociality and Homoeroticism in Indian Parallel Cinema', in Ruth Vanita (ed.) *Queering India: Same-Sex Love and Eroticism in Indian Culture and Society*, New York and London: Routledge

Weeks, J. (1986) *Sexuality*, London: Tavistock

Williams, L. (2000) 'Discipline and Fun: Psycho and Postmodern Cinema', in C. Gledhill and L. Williams (eds) *Reinventing Film Studies*, London: Arnold

Young, R. J. C. (1995) *Colonial Desire: Hybridity in Theory, Culture and Race*, London: Routledge

Younge, G. (2000) 'The Big Picture', in The *Guardian*, Wednesday 26 July

Filmography

Aaina (*Mirror*) Deepak Sareen, 1993
Aks (*Reflection*) Rakesh Omprakash Mehra, 2001
Astitva (*Existence*) Mahesh Manjrekar, 2000
Baazigar (*Soldier*) Abbas Alibhai Burmawalla, Mastan Alibhai Burmawalla (Abbas-Mastan), 1993
Bombay (*Bombay*) Mani Rathnam, 1994
Bombay Boys (*Bombay Boys*) Kaisad Gustad, 2000
Border J. P. Dutta, 1997
Chal Mere Bhai (*Come On My Brother*) David Dhawan, 2000
Chandni Bar (*Chandni Bar*) Madhur Bhandarkar, 2001
Chori Chori Chupke Chupke (*By Theft, Softly, Softly*) Abbas-Mastan, 2001
Darr (*Fear*) Yash Chopra, 1994
Deewar (*Wall*) Yash Chopra, 1975
Devdas (*Devdas*) Sanjay Leela Bhansali, 2002
Dil Chahta Hai (*The Heart Yearns*) Farhan Akthar, 2001
Dilwale Dulhaniya Le Jayenge (*The One with the Heart Takes the Bride*) Aditya Chopra, 1995
Dil Se (*From the Heart*) Mani Rathnam, 1998
Dil To Pagal Hain (*The Heart is Crazy*) Yash Chopra, 1999
Dhadkan (*Heartbeat*) Dharmesh Darshan, 2000
Evil Stalks the Land (documentary) Gauhar Raza, 2002
Father, Son and Holy War (documentary) Anand Patwardhan, 1994
Fire (*Fire*) Deepa Mehta, 1997
Fiza (*Fiza*) Khaled Mohammad, 2000
Gadar: Ek Prem Katha (*Hurricane: a Tale of Love*) Anil Sharma, 2001
Haan Maine Bhi Pyaar Kiya (*Yes, I too am in Love*) Dharmesh Darshan, 2002
Hey! Ram (*Oh Ram!*) Kamal Hasan, 2000
Hum Aapke Hain Koun ...! (*Who Am I to You?*) Sooraj Barjatya, 1994
Hum Dil De Chuke Sanam (*I Have Given my Heart, My Love*) Sanjay Leela Bhansali, 1999
Hum Saath Saath Hain (*We Are All Together*) Sooraj Barjatya, 1999
Kabhie Kushie Kabhie Gham (*Sometimes Happiness, Sometimes Sorrow*) Karan Johar, 2001
Kaho Na ... Pyar Hai (*Oh, Say It's Love*) Rakesh Roshan, 2000
Khalnayak (*The Anti-Hero*) Subhash Ghai, 1993
Koi Mere Dil Se Pooche (*Someone's Asking My Heart*) Vinay Shukla, 2002
Kuch Kuch Hota Hai (*Something's Happening*) Karan Johar, 1997
Kya Kehna? (*What is to be Said?*) Kundan Shah, 2000
Lagaan (*Tax*) Ashutosh Gowarikar, 2001
Lajja (*Shame*) Raj Kumar Santoshi, 2001
Love Ke Liye Kuch Bhi Karega (*I'll do Anything for Love*) Fardeen Aktar and E. Niwas, 2001
Maachis (*Matches*) Sampooran Singh Gulzar, 1996

Maine Pyar Kiya (I've Fallen in Love) Sooraj Bharjatya, 1989
Mangal Pandey: The Rising (The Rising: Ballad of Mangal Pandey) Ketan Mehta, 2005
Men in the Tree (documentary) Lalith Vachani, 2002
Mission Kashmir (Mission Kashmir) Vidhu Vinod Chopra, 2000
Mohabbatein (Loves) Aditya Chopra, 2000
Naaraaz (Anger) Mahesh Bhatt, 1994
Naseeb (Destiny) Manmohan Desai, 1981
Padosan (The Neighbour) Kesto Mukherjee and Jyoti Swaroop, 1968
Pardes (Abroad) Subhash Ghai, 2000
Pyaasa (Thirsty) Guru Dutt, 1957
Pyar Ka Toofan (Cyclone of Love) S. M. Iqbal, 1990
Qayamat Se Qayamat Tak (From Judgement Day to Judgement Day) Mansour Khan, 1988
Qurbani (Sacrifice) Feroz Khan, 1980
Rahul (Rahul) Prakash Jha, 2001
Raja Hindustani (Indian King) Dharmesh Darshan, 1996
Roja (Rose) Mani Rathnam, 1992
Shalimar (Shalimar) Krishna Shah, 1978
Shareef Badmash (The Honest Scoundrel) Raj Khosla, 1973
Sholay (Embers) Ramesh Sippy, 1975
Swades (Our Land) Ashutosh Gowarikar, 2004
Trishul (Trident) Yash Chopra, 1978
Veer-Zaara (Veer-Zaara) Yash Chopra, 2005
Virrudh (Against) Mahesh Manjrekar, 2005
Yaadein (Memories) Subhash Ghai, 2001
Yes Boss (Yes Boss) Aziz Mirza, 1997
Zanzeer (Chain) Prakash Mehra, 1973

Index